Chaucer as
Children's Literature

The First Day

At the Tabard ; the Beginning of the Pilgrimage.

LONG ago, when Richard II. was King, the highways of England must have been a far gayer and stranger sight than they are nowadays. The roads themselves were bad ones, little better than rough, muddy lanes, and often very dangerous by reason of the robbers who lurked in the woods which were so widely spread over the land. But on these roads, bad as they were, travelled wayfarers

Chaucer as Children's Literature

Retellings from the Victorian and Edwardian Eras

Velma Bourgeois Richmond

Montante Family Library
D'Youville College

McFarland & Company, Inc., Publishers
Jefferson, North Carolina, and London

First page of F.J. Harvey Darton's *Tales of the Canterbury Pilgrims* (1906), drawings by Hugh Thompson. Chaucer is pictured telling stories to children.

LIBRARY OF CONGRESS CATALOGUING-IN-PUBLICATION DATA

Richmond, Velma Bourgeois.
    Chaucer as children's literature : retellings from the Victorian and Edwardian eras / Velma Bourgeois Richmond.
        p.   cm.
    Includes bibliographical references and index.

    ISBN 0-7864-1740-4 (softcover : 50# alkaline paper)

    1. Chaucer, Geoffrey, d. 1400—Adaptations—History and criticism. 2. Chaucer, Geoffrey, d. 1400—Appreciation—English-speaking countries. 3. Children—Books and reading—English-speaking countries—History—19th century. 4. Children—Books and reading—English-speaking countries—History—20th century. 5. Children's literature, English—History and criticism. I. Title.
PR1872.R53   2004
821'.1—dc22
                                      2003028282

British Library cataloguing data are available

Cover illustration: "Mine Host Assembling the Canterbury Pilgrims," frontispiece to *Chaucer for Children*, written and illustrated by Mrs. Haweis (1876).

Manufactured in the United States of America

McFarland & Company, Inc., Publishers
  Box 611, Jefferson, North Carolina 28640
    www.mcfarlandpub.com

For the students of the MA Program in English,
Holy Names College, Oakland, California
1958–2001

Contents

Preface

This book is an extension of my interest in Chaucer to a wider audience, earlier expressed in an introductory book, *Geoffrey Chaucer* (Continuum, 1992), and an educational videotape, *A Prologue to Chaucer* (1986), distributed by Films for the Humanities. It describes and affirms attitudes toward Chaucer at the end of the nineteenth and start of the twentieth century, when Victorians and Edwardians who wrote and lectured about Chaucer addressed a general audience that included a few academic and many amateur scholars, working men's clubs, women, university students, and schoolchildren. This study considers Chaucer's stories that have been simply retold for children and shows both their underlying intentions and achievement. I explain and sustain their dedication to the great storyteller and to the English language.

A study like this involves not only literature, history, and art but also developments in publishing and education, the relation of academic and popular culture, and women writers and artists. Much of the material is neither widely known nor readily accessible, since academic studies of Chaucer are not usually about children's literature and writing about children's literature is generally not about retellings of canonical authors. Thus the connections made have been little recognized.

My research about the retelling of medieval stories—romances, sagas, epics, and histories, as well as historical novels with medieval settings—as children's literature reveals a vast and complex subject. The function of Chaucer's works as children's literature at the turn of the twentieth century has such significance, albeit largely neglected, that it warrants separate treatment. I believe that it offers a context for greater understanding

1

of how knowledge and love of literature are formed over a lifetime. I bring together the concept of Chaucer as the Father of English Poetry and how this role was developed at the end of the nineteenth and start of the twentieth century as part of an articulation of national and racial identity. This involves the expansion of general education and the creation of English studies at the university, as promulgated in the Newbolt Report on *The Teaching of English in England* (1921), and parallel American interests and efforts, including the establishment of libraries for youth. Also significant are developments in publishing. My interest is not only in Chaucer and children's literature but also in pedagogy and the history of the book and illustration. I present evidence of the emphasis upon traditional stories, concurrent with the much celebrated fiction that many consider the "Golden Age" of the genre, and the significance of these forgotten children's books to the study of English and a broader appreciation of Chaucer.

Thus I examine in detail Chaucer books for children, both the stories and the pictures that enhanced them. The illustrations created for these books are varied and often quite beautiful, many by distinguished artists (W. Heath Robinson, Hugh Thomson, Gordon Browne, and Anne Anderson). There is also frequent use of medieval images, especially the Ellesmere pilgrims, and later paintings (Ford Madox Brown), so that Chaucer becomes a splendid example of the relation between verbal and visual storytelling that was salient in children's literature during a period of unusually beautiful book production. The popular chapbooks of the seventeenth and eighteenth centuries, which were antecedents of books published for a child audience, provided a model for the combination of words and pictures. But the illustration that was axiomatic for Victorian and Edwardian readers and publishers lost favor, so that novels ceased to contain illustrations except in children's books. Interestingly, a return to the value of presenting visual images, as a way of telling the story, has become increasingly typical of scholarly books in recent years.

Through considerations of which tales were favored, the adjustments in retellings for children, and the subjects illustrated, I show that Chaucer for children at the turn of the twentieth century is a distinctive record of "social life." This phrase defines the role of children's literature identified by F.J. Harvey Darton, author of both the seminal literary history of children's literature and one of the finest Edwardian retellings of *The Canterbury Tales*. Darton thus anticipates today's definition of "cultural studies." How retellers of Chaucer for children altered the medieval texts gives insight into historical, political, educational, and social contexts, especially gender. These writers and editors, many unknown, are among the early Chaucerians who expanded English studies, and they should be acknowledged, not least because of current distress about the future of the discipline. Ongoing challenges about the place of canonical works and the recognition of children's literature as part of English studies suggest that a study of Chaucer for children is cogent.

I am a medievalist, with special interest in Chaucer and romance, but I have long been devoted to children's literature—which I first taught in 1979 and which forms part of my comprehensive study of *The Legend of Guy of Warwick* (Garland, 1996)—and to medievalism, my current area of concentration. My research has been kindly supported by staffs at several libraries where I have often worked: the British Library, the National Library of Scotland, Edinburgh University Library, the Hunterian Library in Glasgow, the Harry Ransome Center at Austin, the Huntington Library, and Doe Library at the University of California at Berkeley. In pursuing my interests in popular literature I have also been helped by the courtesy and knowledge of many antiquarian booksellers in both the United Kingdom and the United States. Similarly useful were comments and encouragement from academic colleagues about papers that I presented at the International Chaucer Conferences in London in July 2000 and in Boulder, Colorado, in July 2002 and at the 2001 meeting of the Medieval Academy/Medieval Association of the Pacific in Tucson, Arizona, where "children" was a favored topic. Finally, I express my gratitude to my husband, whose personal support and professional advice, generously given for this and many other projects, have contributed to my joy in the work.

1

Contexts and Criticisms

Geoffrey Chaucer is the major author for Middle English studies, but he usually receives at most a casual glance in studies of children's literature.[1] For centuries he has been regarded as the Father of English Poetry, but his influential role in Edwardian children's literature, which contributed to the development of the study of English, has been excluded, although there have always been fascinating affinities between Chaucer and children. Four fifteenth-century manuscripts give the title "Brede and milke for children" to Chaucer's *Treatise on the Astrolabe,* and H.E. Marshall's history, *English Literature for Boys and Girls* (1909) employs this title for her biographical chapter, "Chaucer—Bread and Milk for Children."[2] Yet David Matthews, who puts Chaucer at the center of development, has no reference to children's versions in his comprehensive tracing of the process by which Middle English texts were presented.[3] Similarly, Stephanie Trigg does not include children among the "congenial souls" who have read Chaucer; however, her study of his reception offers possible explanations. She argues that in contrast to the open declarations of earlier readers, editors, and critics, today's Chaucerians have been taught to repress "the love of Chaucer and his poetry that barely dares to speak its name in contemporary criticism." Trigg concludes that, in spite of this, the older view of Chaucer reenters through more accessible "satellite publications," even though "Chaucer studies has done its best to expel the popular Chaucer from consideration."[4]

Steve Ellis's recent consideration of modern efforts to popularize Chaucer—varied and numerous but inadequate and limited in effect— includes a brief survey of "Children's Chaucer," but he stresses that

5

Victorian and Edwardian retellings were in some ways a disservice to Chaucer, a process of accommodation and suppression, that "may have something to do with unfavorable childhood experience of some of these texts." The judgment is that such retellings were "sentimental infantalization," only slightly bettered by some efforts made since the 1980s with the inclusion of, indeed emphasis upon, the *fabliaux* and the introduction of subversive elements to support current academic views of Chaucer.[5] Greater recognition of the special nature of children's literature suggests a different evaluation.

There is an extraordinary affinity between Edwardian "adjustments" for children and the earliest recognized designation of Chaucer as an author for children. The *Book of Curtesye*, a didactic poem printed by Caxton in 1477, urges students

> Redith his werkis / ful of plesaunce
> Clere in sentence / in langage excellent ...
> Redeth my chylde / redeth his bookes alle
> Refuseth none / they ben expedyente
> Sentence or langage / or both fynde ye shalle
> Ful delectable / for that good fader mente
> Of al his purpose / and his hole entente
> How to plese in euery audyence
> And in our tunge / was welle of eloquence
> [337–38, 344–50].[6]

Chaucer is thus recommended for both his meaning or themes and for his language. Attention to meaning seems to explain why Henry Scogan included Chaucer's lyric *Gentilesse* as part of his moral ballad for the sons of King Henry IV, for whom he was tutor; Edwardian books for children continue this pedagogy by favoring the *Wife of Bath's Tale*, with its passage on "gentilesse," and occasionally include the lyric.[7]

How a viable text was formed for the fifteenth-century child is indicated by the evidence in two manuscripts, richly analyzed by Seth Lerer. The Helmington manuscript, he suggests, was a "family book," complete with childish scribbling and notable battering; he notes its ranking by modern editors as a "bad text" and consequent lack of scholarly attention. This failure to recognize the manuscript's value as a record of "social life"—F.J. Harvey Darton's claim for the significance of children's literature when he wrote the first history of the subject—shows a continuity of neglect of Chaucer for children evident across more than five centuries. The second manuscript, in the Huntington Library, is an anthology of stories directed at young apprentices; it includes a simplified and more explicitly didactic *Clerk's Tale*, with adjustments similar to those made in Victorian and Edwardian versions for children.[8] Its inclusion in every collection signs the popularity of Griselda, as will be indicated.

These children's versions were part of the endeavor to expand Chaucer's role, a need illustrated by a notable example of his exclusion in the mid-nineteenth century. The Royal Commission of Fine Arts decided in 1836 that murals should decorate the newly rebuilt Houses of Parliament and set the subjects for the first competition to be from British history or to illustrate Spenser, Shakespeare, or Milton—not Chaucer. The entries were exhibited in July 1843. The exclusion is pointed, since Chaucer's *Canterbury Tales*, unlike much of medieval literature, was never unavailable—in editions by William Caxton (1478), William Thynne (1532, etc.), Thomas Speght (1598), John Urry (1721), and Thomas Tyrwhitt (1775–78), whose text was followed by a comprehensive collection such as Robert Anderson's *A Complete Edition of the Poets of Great Britain* (1792–95), Thomas Wright (1847–51)—so that the poet was always recognized. William Pickering's Aldine Edition of the British Poets in 1845, and a new Aldine—for which Richard Morris edited Chaucer—and Robert Bell's Annotated Edition of the English Poets in 1854–57 begin with Chaucer to make the case for an English literary tradition. These are, of course, not academic editions but books aimed at the educated general reader. They reiterate the judgments of many of England's major poets who were inspired to continue, or rewrite, Chaucer—Edmund Spenser, John Milton, John Dryden, Alexander Pope, and William Wordsworth. Collections of British poets for adults are paralleled by several series of Edwardian children's books that include retellings of major poets—Chaucer, Shakespeare, Spenser, Scott, Tennyson, and Longfellow—often with some quotations.

Chaucer's absence from the mural competition may reflect uneasiness with a poet of the Catholic Middle Ages, necessarily less compatible with the Protestantism of the established Church of England that is so explicit in Spenser and Milton. The nineteenth century echoed the need of the martyrologist John Foxe to explain in *Actes and Monumentes* (1570) how Chaucer escaped from Catholic censure through his subtlety; for he "semeth to bee a right Wicleuian," and to find strong evidence of his Protestantism in "Jack Upland," the *Plowman's Tale*, and in the *Testament of Love*.[9] Both texts were attributed to Chaucer in the sixteenth century, but this was later corrected. Biographies for children usually make a point of Chaucer's connection with Wycliffe through John of Gaunt. The Catholic Emancipation Act had come only in 1829, and efforts made by several retellers of Chaucer for children to confront his religious situation, and to offer reassurances that he stands apart from it, suggest lingering anxiety as a probable cause. An analog is the introduction by the painter Ford Madox Brown (1821–93) of the figures of Chaucer and Gower in his two great paintings of Wycliffe: *The First Translation of the Bible into English: Wycliffe Reading His Translation to John of Gaunt* (1847–48) and *Wycliffe on Trial* (1884–86). Both link the medieval poets to the Duke of Lancaster and present together the writers who established the English language in verse and prose, as does a chapter about the Bible and Wycliffe that precedes H.E. Marshall's three chapters on Chaucer in her literary history for children. However, as we shall see, Ford's *Chaucer at the Court of Edward III* (1851, 1867–68), with its vision of the poet in a context of chivalry, is the painting reproduced in children's books.

The role of children's books in the complex development of Chaucer studies, like the defining of a canon in children's literature, offers a chance for greater understanding of and expansion of both areas. To find errors in antiquarians is inevitable, but David Matthews acknowledges that "the perception of error rests to some extent on our own conviction of our rightness. We see the ideologies of past scholarship with a clarity we do not always apply to our own work."[10] The hope is that recovery of past ideologies will lead to a reconsideration, which should include recognizing strengths in the past rather than simply decrying the limitations and failures of ideologies. Many neglected writers and illustrators, often women whose gender was concealed by using initials instead of first names (a concern/practice repeated by today's enormously successful J.K. Rowling), encouraged the reading of Chaucer. Thus this book will trace and argue a positive contribution by Victorians and Edwardians who brought *The Canterbury Tales* to the nursery and school and, with this "popularization," not only affirmed traditional moral values and contributed to a sense of racial/national identity (shared by Britain, the Empire, and the United States), but also helped to build a foundation significant for the development of English as a literary discipline. Academic discussions at this turn of this century typically express anxiety about the future of English and/or Medieval Studies, so that a return to origins can suggest possibilities to respond to the profound irony in the distress of academics who decry readings of Chaucer that foster popular interests in storytelling, patriotism, and moral virtue and that define Chaucer as genial, common sensible, and extraordinary in his ordinariness and zest for human life.[11] This Edwardian Chaucer has not suited the sophisticated temperament of most late-twentieth-century critics and theorists, who tend to a Whiggish view of history as progress from an inexorable decline to superior knowledge and find reassurance in interpretations that reinforce their own experiences of skepticism and anxiety—which are, of course, recurrent states of mind that are cyclically challenged and supplanted.

There is always a counter perspective, the concept of a Golden Age, a looking to the past as a better time. The Romantics' view of childhood is part of this way of thinking. Wordsworth's concept of childhood as "other-worldliness," a time of imagination in which the child perceives and is close to the eternal but loses such innocence with age, is perhaps the strongest articulation. In *The Prelude*, Book V, Wordsworth describes such "spots of time," and he also lists favorite chapbook stories (Fortunatus, Jack-the-Giant Killer, Robin Hood, St. George and Princess Sabra) that the child loves, for reading them "he forgets himself." Wordsworth is firmly linked to Chaucer, since one of his early efforts was a version of *The Prioress's Tale*, which an American editor (and poet) deemed suitable for a students' reader in 1909.[12] Wordsworth's poetry contains many echoes/translations of Chaucer, "ever-to-be-honoured," whose "affecting parts" he praised in the Preface to the second edition of *Lyrical Ballads*, as "almost always expressed in language pure and universally intelligible even to this day."[13]

It is easy to underestimate Romantic delight in children in the flood of didactic stories produced by Victorians, but it is part of the evidence that many who wrote and illustrated books for children intended them to give pleasure. Connections between moral instruction and delight are well illustrated by one of the earliest and most successful retellings, Mary Seymour's *Chaucer's Stories Simply Told*, published in 1884 by Thomas Nelson, a Scottish Evangelical whose success depended on the juvenile book trade.[14] Nelson's booklist included a cogent recommendation of Seymour's book from *Academy*: "If any one is looking for a 'gift-book' that shall combine profit with pleasure, he will hardly do better than pitch upon this."

The Romantics most cogent to this study are Charles and Mary Lamb, whose *Tales from Shakespear* (1807) were the precedent for retellings of great literature for young people. Their work inspired Charles Cowden Clarke (1787–1877), a personal friend as he was of most of the Romantics, to write *Tales from Chaucer in Prose: Designed Chiefly for the Use of Young Persons* (1833). This first of many books of Chaucer for children recognizes that stories from great literature are better than most tales expressly written for children, both for immediate experience and to motivate later and greater understanding. Subsequent educational theory supports this, and there is evidence that children preferred adult stories to many of the books made-to-order for them. Frances Jenkins Olcott, an American, observed: "Stories from Chaucer are thoroughly enjoyed by children because of the adventure, rapid action, and thrilling plots, while the humane attitude, the genial humor, and wholesome thought of the poet are mentally salutary."[15]

Much has been written about Chaucer's pathos, most eloquently expressed in scenes with innocent children, who are usually more convincing than those in Shakespeare's plays.[16] The strong link between Chaucer and children manifests itself in the frequency with which they appear in *The Canterbury Tales*; one-half of the twenty-four include children or consider the parent-child relationship.[17] Moreover, Chaucer makes the Host describe him in the *Prologue to Sir Thopas* as a "popet" and "elvyssh" (a little doll and abstracted, mysterious, not of this world, perhaps fairy-like [VII.701,703]); these terms suggest young and old and link Chaucer to the child before he tells his first tale. Lerer argues that in the fifteenth century the two tales that Chaucer assigned himself, *Sir Thopas* and *Melibee,* were presented as didactic children's literature.[18] These are not the tales frequently retold for children in later centuries, but there is a continuity in the view of Chaucer as a writer especially suitable and inspiring for children.

Katherine Lee Bates, as editor of an American Series of Supplementary Readers, explains that its name "Canterbury Classics" marks "the memory of the sweetest and most childlike spirit in English song."[19] She is echoing the sentiments of William Morris, a major inspiration for children's literature, especially retellings of sagas and his own stories in *The Earthly Paradise* (1868–70), which imitated both Chaucerian meters and the design of framed stories. Morris published the Kelmscott *The Works of Geoffrey Chaucer* (1896) in collaboration with Edward Burne-Jones, whose illustrations reinforce an emphasis on chivalric elements.[20] In a lecture "Feudal England" (1887) Morris described Chaucer as the creator of "a sunny world even amidst its violence and passing troubles, like those of a happy child ... a world that scarcely needed hope in its eager life of adventure and love, amidst the sunlit blossoming meadows, and green woods...."[21] A pen-and-ink sketch by Edward Burne-Jones, not intended for public display, is perhaps the best icon of the dedication and sentiments of the two friends and collaborators. Dated May 1896, it is titled "Bless Ye My Children." Chaucer, whose name is inscribed in a nimbus, embraces the portly Morris and a lean Burne-Jones, both of whom look exhausted, after completing the Kelmscott *Chaucer.*[22]

Lee Patterson argues the centrality of Chaucer's childish self-image and that the poet uses it "to stage a problematic central to the act of writing," albeit Patterson outlines late medieval interest in the child, conceptions of innocence, the child's closeness to transcendence, and he quotes a key passage from Matthew—"Unless you be converted, and become as little children, you shall not enter the kingdom of heaven" (18.3). Victorians and Edwardians identified many of the same characteristics, but did not theorize that Chaucer was deploying the image to define and subvert. They did, however, identify a childhood in the history of nations—the Middle Ages. Indeed nineteenth-century medievalism is fueled by anxiety and a deep desire to find an alternative to the corruption and terror of the modern world, a wish for change that seemed most likely by a return to an idealized "past" and the recreation of its high ideals, such as chivalry, in the English gentleman and Gothic architecture, especially churches and castles.[23] Both were enriched by "medieval" painting, glass, furniture, and tapestries, and all were described in historical novels, the most popular Victorian genre, set in the Middle Ages. Chaucer for children is a part of this process of idealization directed to many audiences.

Retellings of Chaucer for children anticipate the post–World War I establishment of English studies at university that Terry Eagleton sees as a nationalist response to the Great War, especially the supplanting of Teutonic philology and seeking of moral solace and affirmation in *English* literature.[24] Chris Baldick identified three principal factors that ensured a permanent place in higher education for English literature: the specific needs of the British Empire, expressed in regulations for admission to the Indian Civil Service that stressed English literature and history; movements such as the Mechanics' Institute, Working Men's Colleges, and Extension lectures that advanced adult education; and specific provisions made for women's education.[25] As the Father of English Poetry, Chaucer matched these efforts: he fostered ideals of patriotism through language and history, notably his extraordinary picture of English life and range of storytelling in *The Canterbury Tales,* and through his portrayal of virtuous women, who provided ideals of the role of wife as sympathetic and understanding, thus fostering civilization not least through affirming artistic achievements.

Earlier study of English in the Working Men's Colleges and Mechanics' Institutes, as a kind of classics for the poor man, had advanced in Victorian times, and there is a strong connection with early Chaucerians. Among their many educational endeavors F.J. Furnivall (1825–1910) and Walter W. Skeat (1835–1912) were co-founders of the London Working Men's College. Increasingly major authors in simplified retellings were also part of children's experience unbounded by social class, even though the target audience for many children's books was middle class, certainly the group that set the expectations.[26] The commonplace reality of children's literature is that although the nominal audience is the child, it expresses the concerns of adults, who both write and buy books for children. Moreover, scholars who produced books for adults also wrote for children. For example, Furnivall edited many Middle English texts for the Early English Text Society, including the *Book of Curtesye*, and also wrote the introduction for *Tales of the Canterbury Pilgrims Retold from Chaucer and Others* (1904); F.J. Harvey Darton (1878–1936) was a leading Edwardian publisher and author of many books for children and of the first scholarly history of *Children's Books in England: Five Centuries of Social Life* (1932).[27] His subtitle, cited earlier, defines the crucial role of children's literature as part of what theorists identify as cultural studies, with its offshoot post-colonialism. The extraordinary distinction and significance of children's literature for the English was boldly asserted by the eminent French scholar Paul Hazard: "England could be reconstructed entirely from its children's books."[28]

The period from the late nineteenth century until the end of World War I is often identified as "The Golden Age" of children's literature, a time in which many notable authors (Beatrix Potter, J.M. Barrie, Kenneth Grahame, Frances Hodgson Burnett, E. Nesbit) wrote "children's classics" and transformed traditional expectations. Humphrey Carpenter argues that these authors were creating Arcadias, an alternative world to contemporary English adult society whose views they satirized, and that they produced much celebrated children's fiction.[29] Similarly, Alison Lurie makes a broad case for the subversive nature of major classics of children's literature, while Juliet Dusinberre identifies many connections between Victorian and Edwardian children's literature and the development of modernism.[30]

What is scarcely noted is the concurrent issuing of children's versions of adult literature, especially medieval stories and major canonical works that reinforced traditional values and created an idealized past. As a corollary of the development of the English gentleman, the defining of racial/national identity, and the expansion of Empire by Victorians and Edwardians, there was a substantial, patriotic enthusiasm for medieval narratives—epics, sagas, romances, chronicles, and tales of King Arthur and Robin Hood. Edwardians deemed these stories of "the childhood of the race" especially apt reading for children. Chaucer's role as the Father of English Poetry is crucial, and his stories are a significant part of this canon. The Education Acts of 1870 (England and Wales) and 1872 (Scotland) made elementary education compulsory; thus a large, unprecedented market for elementary school texts quickly developed. The number of schools increased by 50 percent in the first four years, with a rise in attendance of half a million. A corollary was the creation of a National Society for the Prevention of Cruelty to Children in 1885, followed by the

Children's Charter of 1889 to protect them from abuse, and the passage of the Act for the Prevention of Cruelty to Children in 1894.

Preceding these reforms education for many was available only through Sunday Schools, and thus study was rooted in a moral tradition. The Religious Tract Society (RTS) initiated a series of children's books in 1814 and followed with a variety of magazines and books, including some moral tales. Similar efforts of the Society for the Propagation of Christian Knowledge (SPCK) show that increasingly fiction was added to the obvious bibles, catechisms, and primers. Subsequent publishers, particularly Blackie and Thomas Nelson (d.1861), sustained this original Evangelical work. Most of the writers of Rewards books were women, as are retellers of Chaucer for children.[31] An increased market for Reward or Prize books, much used in elementary and secondary schools and in Sunday Schools as well as gifts for birthdays and Christmas, fueled the Edwardian Golden Age of children's books.

Circumstances in the United States differed from those in Britain, but there was agreement about Chaucer's place in the teaching of great literature. Mary Burt, a Chicago educator, for example, largely rejected "the modern school-reader with its ill-assorted, namby-pamby, scrappy selections," identified the typical "goody-goody" books as "a pernicious class of reading," and in short, advocated the reading of traditional texts[32]:

> The truth is that the classics are simpler by far than the great mass of modern writing. They are nearer to children and the childhood of the race. They are the a, b, c of literature and of history, and give the clue to modern thought.... Many teachers have proven to their own satisfaction that young children prefer great classics to weak reading [24, 29].

Like many British writers Burt recognized an affinity between the childhoods of the child and of the race, and she honors nationalism:

> the child can easily see that the work of art which portrays a national life, a religion, is greater than one which shows pettier feeling, Macaulay tells us that religion is at the foundation of the best art, and that national life is at the foundation of religion [37–38].

Burt's "literary landmarks" are worldwide, an early manifestation of multiculturalism that combines English authors with others. Her study, based directly on classroom experience, includes graded charts that give chronology and major writers/texts from the "Age of Myths" to the "Present (Victorian) Age." One major link is "Dante & Chaucer 1300–1400." Burt's pedagogy insists upon a "systematic order," a way of placing knowledge with memorable connections in a mental outline that will serve "as a basis for future reading, either systematic or desultory, a plan by which he can go on educating himself indefinitely and intelligently" (42). There is a poignant urgency as well as high expectations, for she explains that "I am working all the time on the fact that fifty percent of all children who ever enter school leave before the age of ten" (63). As shown in Chapter 6, Burt provides precise accounts of the reading of Chaucer in schools.

The Edwardian Golden Age of children's literature, the decades prior to World War I, is thus rooted in educational reforms, economic developments, and national enthusiasm, and the subtlety of many different treatments and the favoring of specific tales from Chaucer offer insight about the nostalgia and aspirations of English-speaking people at the start of the twentieth century. A strong didactic dimension is both characteristic of children's literature and the early emphasis upon the moral tradition of English literature that initially informed its study. Several eminent Chaucerians, both English and American, contributed to the popularizing of Chaucer for children. Today many academics express anxieties and hostility to "misrepresenting" Chaucer's text, part of an antipathy to any popularization, a simplification through translation and adjusting the Middle English poem.[33] In contrast, Victorians and Edwardians regarded retellings of Chaucer for children as an introduction and incentive to later sophisticated study, upon which to build a lifelong and increasingly advanced reading of *The Canterbury Tales*.

The enthusiastic recovery of the past by antiquarians, the creation of the *Oxford English Dictionary*, and the formation of the Early English Text Society in 1864 led to the editing of many Middle English texts. F.J. Furnivall with Reverend Walter W. Skeat also founded the Chaucer Society in 1868 through the support of academic and educated people from the general public and from the United States as much as England.[34] The first scholarly edition, W.W. Skeat's *Oxford Chaucer* (1894–97), followed; as did his modern translations, an early indication that a popular audience was not incompatible with scholarly objectives.[35] Edwardians depended upon and were inspired by this work. Maurice Hewlett (1861–1923), who began a successful career by writing romantic, and often whimsical, tales of idealized medievalism, sustained the tradition with continuations in *The New Canterbury Tales* in 1901. Early editions of medieval texts led to increased publication of retellings for adults, some of which were subsequently adapted or reprinted in a different format for children. More important was the development of children's books for a major market, both middle-class families and school texts, by British publishers like

Harrap and Nelson for whom an educational list was essential.[36] Parallels in the United States are Rand McNally and Houghton Mifflin. Books and authors were freely exchanged at a time when American literature was deeply dependent upon England, and leading publishers had offices to disseminate books for children throughout the English-speaking world. Chaucer's stories simply told are part of this traditional material; many turn-of-the-century renderings of *The Canterbury Tales,* enhanced with attractive illustrations, sold at a range of prices for modest to sumptuous editions.

The recognition of Geoffrey Chaucer's role as England's greatest writer of the Middle Ages began in his lifetime, and throughout the centuries this did not change. But his advocates moved from imitating poets to an admiring general public to academic study, and in recent decades even *The Canterbury Tales* has been less axiomatically a set text, as signed by loss of its place in the top ten Cliffs Notes.[37] At the start of the twentieth century, a time when there was urgency in the definition of national/racial identity, Chaucer was an obvious author to adapt for children. *The Canterbury Tales,* the quintessential representation of English medieval life and character, became the chosen work. Carefully selected and adjusted, retellings came as separate books and within mixed collections for children. As an assembly of tales, Chaucer's is one of the most sophisticated available, since the stories evoke more complex responses than most heroic legends. Another cogent pedagogical argument is for the ongoing study of an adult original as the child develops increasingly greater understanding. Victorian and Edwardian retellers emphasize Chaucer's excellence as storyteller and his role in the development of the language; his extraordinary embodiment of "Englishness"—love of nature, fascination with work and people, modest self-effacement, and religious interests—exactly suited pedagogical and patriotic hopes. Moreover, Chaucer became a moral force, a primary exemplar at a time when traditional religion was weakening and unity increasingly difficult in a modern society. Both Skeat and Furnivall, Matthews argues, *substituted* Chaucer for themselves to voice ethical values.[38] The appeal of Chaucer was not bounded by class. Thus the wealthy New York Grolier Club in 1900 had "An Exhibition of Original and Other Editions, Portraits and Prints" to commemorate the five-hundredth anniversary of Chaucer's death, while in 1908 the recently founded Everyman's Library offered the general public *Chaucer's Canterbury Tales for the Modern Reader,* a translation prepared and edited by Arthur Burrell.[39] Given this context of adult literature, the appropriation of Chaucer for children was an easy one. Furthermore, up until Israel Gollancz became the first lecturer in English at Cambridge in 1896, leading Chaucerians were not academics. There is an affinity between those who strove to make medieval texts available to adults and retellers of Chaucer for children; both Clarke and Darton, who worked with Furnivall, were publishers.

One enthusiast for medieval ideals who officially influenced political action was Henry Newbolt (1862–1938), whose ballads rivaled those of Rudyard Kipling (1865–1936) in popularity and exceeded them in imperialist fervor.[40] Most notoriously, soldiers in the Boer War spurred themselves on by chanting "Play up, play up, and play the game!" the refrain of his lyric "Vitaï Lampada." Newbolt's early work for children was *Stories from Froissart* (1899), and in his historical romance *The New June* (1909), young knights of Richard the Lionhearted combined chivalry with public school sentiments; for example, by conflating jousting and cricket. Similarly, *The Book of the Happy Warrior* (1917), timed to encourage patriotism in World War I, combines chivalric stories of medieval heroes— Roland, Richard Cœur de Lion, St. Louis, Robin Hood, Bertrand du Guesclin and the Black Prince, Bayard—with accounts of "The Old English School" and "Chivalry Today." Newbolt, who had been president of the English Association founded in 1906 and Controller of Wireless and Cables during World War I, was the man who produced the influential government study *The Teaching of English in England*, in 1921.[41]

Predictably, this Newbolt Report urged that English literature was essential to promote knowledge of and pride in the nation as well as social reconciliation, since its accessibility could resolve class conflicts engendered by earlier emphasis upon the classics. "The literature of England belongs to all England, not to the Universities or to any *coterie* of the literary or the learned: and all may enjoy it who will" (204). Some medievalists decried the loss of comparative philology in the study of Middle English that followed from the Newbolt Report, which solidified the position of English Studies and a "literary" emphasis that relates directly to human experience. But the Report countered the argument that English is a "soft option" at university and stressed its crucial role from the earliest years at school. The simple assertion is that "English is plainly no matter of inferior importance, nor even one among the other branches of education, but the one indispensable preliminary and foundation of the rest" (10). Identified as a necessary reiteration of Renaissance principles of educators who perceived that "the essence of a liberal education is the study of a great literature" (30), the study of English could turn around the modern practices that lost sight of the ideal. According to the patriotic report, for English children no form of knowledge can take precedence of a knowledge of English, no form of literature can take precedence of English literature ... the two are so inextricably connected as to form the only basis possible for a national education [14].

Chaucer's place in education is a prominent one because the report identifies the fourteenth century as the time when Standard English emerged, "the King's English ... the language spoken at the Court, and in Oxford and Cambridge. Through the works of Chaucer it became the literary language of the country" (28). Chaucer's role as a literary figure is both certain and intricate, since his sources, and those of his successors, are identified as "Mediterranean," but "he himself is English of the English," in a line from Anglo-Saxon and Early English writings, which "even if not the sources of the writings of Chaucer, are at least in a true sense, sources of Chaucer himself" (212–13). Here the essence of Englishness, a racial and national identity, is the issue.

The report is almost four hundred pages long and contains details about all levels and procedures, but from "The Summary of Conclusions and Recommendations" comes a succinct iteration of its objectives, pointed by levels. In preparatory (elementary) schools "some acquaintance with English literature should precede the introduction to foreign and classical literatures"; in secondary schools "in Junior Departments, up to the age of twelve, at least one period a day should be devoted to English"; "throughout the Public Schools English Literature should be regarded as entitled to a place in the regular school course, and not be relegated to spare time" (349–50). At the elementary stage, literature lessons were not only to seek "increased command of the language" and "the acquisition of knowledge" but also "appreciation and enjoyment of literature" (82). Care is to be taken to guard against "the mere desultory reading of books"; the intellects of young adults in secondary schools should be worthily exercised through "a close and intensive study of specially selected works in verse and prose, chosen on account of their intrinsic value." Moreover, broad principles of criticism were to be illustrated through frequent reference to "the other creative arts, music, architecture, painting, etc." (16, 118). This acknowledges the crucial role of illustration in collections of Chaucer stories for children, where the text is enriched by the beauty and variety of images.

Appendix III is a "Memorandum ... on ... the Circulation of Books in London Elementary Schools," which concludes with a list of books in "Class A (Those in great and steady demand)." From 1,776 departments surveyed, the scheme found approximately 1,650 titles in circulation, for a number of approximately 2 million volumes. In Class A there are fifty titles arranged in order of popularity; *Stories from Chaucer* is twenty-ninth, while *Tales and Stories from Shakespeare* is number one and *Stories from the Faerie Queene* is forty-six. Other volumes are fairy tales, legends, and many novels; fewer than ten titles, largely fairy tales, are not originally English (374–75). Clearly children in London were already well exposed to English literature, albeit with an emphasis on nineteenth-century writers.

The Newbolt Report, like early criticism of English literature and the practice of selecting books, makes no apology for favoring certain books, for taking for granted that literature is "the most direct and lasting communication of experience by man to men," and that the human spirit is actuated by three motives: "the love of goodness, the love of truth and the love of beauty." An assumed consensus about what these mean led to a confidence that the advantage of the study of literature—along with science, since it was assumed that the scientific ideal and the ideal of human interest are not incompatible—meant that "the child's natural love of goodness will be strongly encouraged and great progress may be made in strengthening of the will" (9).[42] Morality and high sentiment are the ideals, and Chaucer stories for Victorian and Edwardian children epitomized such aims, albeit with today's discovery and advocacy of subversion in literary study they seem problematic.

G.K. Chesterton's *Chaucer* (1932), a late work but still very Edwardian and in agreement with principles of the Newbolt Report, is the apogee of the case that "the ordinary modern Englishman will considerably enlarge his mind by reading Chaucer; and it is my humble desire that he should to some extent be able to read Chaucer, even if he is unable to read Middle English," or in an echo of Dryden, "it would be a good thing to make Chaucer an ordinary possession of ordinary Englishmen."[43] For Chesterton, Chaucer was more than the Father of English Poetry: "He made a national language; he came very near to making a nation.... Chaucer was the Father of his Country, rather in the style of George Washington" (13). Much of his *Chaucer* is an eloquent case for the fusion of the English character and Chaucer, for the "feeling of the curious primeval kinship between England and Chaucer" (202). With this intensely nationalist vision Chesterton naturally favored "a popularized version" (211). "Chaucer is literature and not linguistic study for the learned; that it needs very little to make him popular in the sense that literature can be popular; and that learning is a totally different thing" (214). Moreover, information and attitudes change—"I only note that if the learned are now right, some of the earlier learned were very wrong" (218). The ongoing aptness of this observation is legion, as massive changes in literary criticism and theory generate constant reassessments and revisions.

Dryden's judgment of Chaucer was "Here is God's plenty," and Edwardian retellers chose a variety of ways to present his richness. Children read shorter stories more easily, especially in school assignments, and a selection allowed editing out of tales that might disturb the young. Table 1, "Tales Selected for Collections," found at the back of this book, shows that some tales are much favored, but combinations of different tales can also create a thematic argument. Victorian books, whether for adult or child, were typically illustrated, and illustration is salient in books for children. Thus the initial appeal of Chaucer for children was often as much visual as verbal. Pictures of pilgrims and episodes quickly involve young readers, and several illustrators of Chaucer were among the most distinguished of the period. Their images enhance and clarify the stories and are as much an index to Victorian and Edwardian concerns as the choice and treatment of tales. Table 2, "Illustrations in Chaucer Collections," shows their number and variety.

The Canterbury Tales were an excellent school text to teach stories, to present medieval life, and to further the study of language. Many editions were quite modest. But Chaucer was also often published as a Reward or Prize book, with distinctive illustrations from medieval manuscripts—most frequently the Ellesmere pilgrim portraits, from paintings— Thomas Stothard's *The Pilgrimage to Canterbury* (1806–07), William Blake's *Chaucer's Canterbury Pilgrims* (1810), Ford Madox Brown's *Chaucer at the Court of Edward III* (1851, 1867–68), and with new representations by book illustrators in contemporary artistic styles, especially Pre-Raphaelite and Art Nouveau.[44] No collection is complete; there are numerous differences in the amount of detail included, but Chaucer's greatness as a storyteller is never lacking; in contrast, portraits of pilgrims from the *General Prologue* receive less, sometimes no attention, apart from some favoring as illustration. This, of course, undercuts Chaucer's complexity and much admired irony, but neither is typical of children's literature, which usually deals with surfaces and a strong narrative line. Chaucer's *Canterbury Tales* in storybooks and school texts are often the same except for added lessons and less expensive printing; but Edwardian children also learned about Geoffrey Chaucer from literary histories that were quite sophisticated in presenting an English canon.

Almost all retellers—until very recently—reflect a traditional avoidance of sexuality in children's literature; *fabliaux* are deleted, and objectionable elements in other tales—such as the rape in the *Wife of Bath's Tale*—are eliminated or changed. Chaucer himself acknowledged the likelihood of objections to some tales:

And therfore, whoso list it nat yheere,
Turne over the leef and chese another tale,
For he shal fynde ynowe, grete and smale,
Of storial thyng that toucheth gentilesse,
And eek moralitee and holynesse [I.3176–80].

Victorians and Edwardians follow Chaucer in admitting the need and acceptability of something less than absolute candor of event and language for all readers. Since this issue is crucial in children's literature, it is helpful to begin with a context. Walter W. Skeat, foremost editor of Middle English texts, including the Oxford edition of Chaucer in 1874, after the volume edited by Richard Morris in 1867, is an impressive authority. Skeat identified the two problems straightforwardly and eloquently in his lecture, "The Language of Chaucer," delivered in 1874 or 1875. His points about the licentious quality of the language and the difficulty of reading Middle English are repeated in a preface or introduction in almost every version of Chaucer for children.

> I know of only one serious objection that *can* be made to the reading of Chaucer's *Canterbury Tales* (for it scarcely applies to the rest of his works), and that is one which can be fairly and truly made; viz. that some of his stories are expressed in such free and licentious language as is not acceptable to the taste of the nineteenth century. This objection I admit to be a fair one; but I feel, at the same time, very much inclined to retort upon objectors, that I do not think the literature of the nineteenth century is always better, or always gains by comparison.[45]

The comparison is with modern novels, especially those written for the amusement of women, which Skeat faults for "some of the most outrageous assaults upon good morals ... in the worst possible manner, not broadly and openly, but insidiously and by insinuation." There are many obvious assumptions in this passage that are alien or objectionable at the start of the twentieth-first century when recognition of and references to, much less definitions of, "morals" are no longer agreed upon by society. However, the passage does make clear an alternative set of shared assumptions, ones less strange and offensive to someone whose parents and teachers lived Edwardian childhoods.

Skeat's farsighted discussion of Middle English includes a comparison with Shakespeare, whom he ranks as first poet to Chaucer's second and is assumed to be easily accessible. Much of what is said Skeat identifies as "false pretense and [humbug]" that makes readers fear Chaucer and assume they can read Shakespeare.[46] A summation refutes such "fallacies" about Chaucer:

> [I]nstead of allowing his language to be obsolete and difficult,
> I maintain that is only so in a very limited degree; that the difficulties
> are upon the surface, and vanish the moment that we boldly face
> them; that many of the words which he uses are such as we all ought
> to know well, if we really read, instead of only pretend to read, our
> Bible, our Shakespeare, our Burns, our Spenser. I maintain that in the
> best MSS. (I do not say in the worst), the spelling is intelligible, distinct, correct, and truly phonetic, representing the sound of the word
> with quite sufficient accuracy in every instance.[47]

Skeat delivered the lecture to an adult audience in 1874 or 1875, and, as we shall see, Mrs. Haweis made the same points to her readers in *Chaucer for Children* (1876).

Criticism for adults at the start of the twentieth century, like Robert K. Root's *The Poetry of Chaucer* (1906) and George Lyman Kittredge's *Chaucer and His Poetry* (1915), sustained the medieval and Victorian apologies and were discreet in describing the events in the ribald tales.[48] From Chaucer's variety of subjects Edwardians selected for children the stories that tell of "gentilesse ... moralitee ... holynesse" to provide models of chivalry, virtuous women, and piety. Children's versions of Chaucer offer substantial evidence of the poet's interest and sympathy for women, whether written by men or women. This is part of chivalric idealism so potently rearticulated in Victorian medievalism, but it is also a commonplace didactic purpose of children's literature, whether to inspire boys to be manly and to treat women courteously or to urge girls to be virtuous, self-sacrificing, and patient.[49] Chaucer's medieval religion and attitudes toward the Catholic Church led to Protestant comparisons, typically an argument that the poet was a Lollard, an anticipatory Protestant, and an expression of satisfaction in an English Church that had developed beyond Papist "superstitions." But these sentiments were less frequent than another quality of medievalism deployed to develop "the child's natural love of goodness."

Chivalry and gallantry, much-favored themes in stories from and about Chaucer retold for children, were the ideals for the English schoolboy. A broader context helps to place their importance for Edwardian children. As noted above, Henry Newbolt, an old boy of Clifton College, Bristol, movingly affirmed and promulgated this spirit in his children's collection *The Book of the Happy Warrior* and as public policy in the influential *The Teaching of English in England*. To this it is necessary to add that the public school model prevailed in children's books that were enthusiastically read and embraced across social classes, as the success of school stories demonstrates. Thomas Arnold's ideal of the public school as a place to train character, celebrated in Thomas Hughes's *Tom Brown's Schooldays* (1857), as well as the expansion of education and publishing for children in the nineteenth century inspired a flood of school stories, as is obvious from this section of any antiquarian book shop. Their number and diversity sign the fact that the largest audience was not public school boys, but those who found an ideal image to offset their own grim school situations.[50] The current international and astonishing success of J.K. Rowling's Harry Potter books, which so obviously employ the same devices and situations (albeit Hogwarts School is coeducational and features classes in witchcraft) repeats the phenomenon, and children have been inspired to read. More significant is the fact that Harry and his friends behave like heroes of medieval romance. This is signed by their belonging to the house that embodies the dominant Edwardian ideal, Gryffindor, "Where dwell the brave at heart, / Their daring nerve, and chivalry/ Set Gryffindors apart."[51] The "chums," who are frequently tested, "play the game"—and not just "quidditch"—with courage, skill, and "pluck." They too are the youthful inheritors of the companionship of knights, like the typical hero in the historical novels of G(eorge) A(lfred) Henty (1832–1902)—and his many imitators—that typically urged the same ideals of gallantry, chivalry, and "pluck." The most telling evidence of their widespread acceptance is the initial response to World War I and the way in which the language of chivalry permeated writings about the war.[52] But as reactions against chivalry make clear, there was a dilemma, a threat. Thomas Arnold (1795–1842), whose educational reforms were Christian Socialist, opposed the spirit of chivalry as a spirit of evil, since he discerned in chivalry the qualities of feudalism, tyranny, and class arrogance.[53] Nevertheless, Arthur Hughes's chivalric images in the illustrated *Tom Brown's School Days* (1889) allied the school story with knighthood and Grail quests—Hughes, like George Watts, painted *Sir Galahad.* Thus it is not surprising that the view of Newbolt, which exalted gallantry and chivalry, prevailed.[54] A corollary was promulgating parallel and interlaced ideals of noble women who were ancillary to chivalry and Victorian expectations of gender. Chaucer's tales provide notable examples of ideal women, and collections for children especially emphasized this high sentiment. Among the Victorians Charles Cowden Clarke is the first to retell Chaucer simply for children, and I shall begin with them.

﹏ 2 ﹏

Victorian Beginnings

The tradition of Chaucer for Edwardian children began with one early Victorian, Charles Cowden Clarke, inspired by Mary and Charles Lamb's retelling of Shakespeare for children, and developed with several later Victorians, Mrs. H.R. (Mary Eliza) Haweis, Mary Seymour, Francis Storr and Hawes Turner, and William Calder. Their work defined the objectives and salient characteristics of books retelling the stories of the Father of English Poetry; and they turned the time-honored epithet into a practicality by providing texts, both as home or gift books, rewards, and school texts; often the only difference is in publication costs and supplementary material. Chaucer's stories simply told for children, and usually reinforced with illustrations, urged a widespread reading of Chaucer that was part of the nineteenth-century establishment of a sense of national identity and the study of the English language.

A great Victorian historical painter, Ford Madox Brown (1821–93), early made the point with *The Seeds and Fruits of English Poetry* (1845), a triptych where the central panel features Chaucer and the wings include many later poets. This was a study for Brown's great painting, *Chaucer Reading the "Legend of Custance" to Edward III and His Court, at the Palace of Sheen, on the Anniversary of the Black Prince's Birthday* (1851, 1867–68), which honors only Chaucer, is more glowingly executed, and precisely identifies the text read as the *Man of Law's Tale*. Brown's first diary entry describes how he had an exact vision when he read about Chaucer's importance in the history of the English language: "This at once fixed me, I immediately saw visions of Chaucer reading his poems to knights & Ladyes fair, to the king & court amid air & sunshine."[1] His comments in

23

the catalogue of his Picadilly exhibition, 1865, identify Chaucer (along with Dante) as a

> supremely great mediæval poet.... But Chaucer is at the same time as much a perfect English poet—I am almost tempted to say a modern English poet—as any of the present day. Spelling, and a few minor proprieties apart, after a lapse of five hundred years, his delicate sense of naturalistic beauty and his practical turn of thought, quite at variance with the iron grasp of realism, the deep-toned passionate mysticism, and supersensual grace of the great Italians, comes home to us as naturally as the last volume we hail with delight from the press.[2]

Victorians found in Chaucer an embodiment of both the Middle Ages and timelessness as they admired his national character in appreciating nature and practicality. Those who retold Chaucer for children praise the same qualities; Edwardian writers for children built on this foundation that also supported ideas of educational reformer Henry Newbolt.

Charles Cowden Clarke

Charles Cowden Clarke (1787–1877), son of a schoolmaster at Enfield, was a popular lecturer and author as well as a publisher and bookseller. Although he is Victorian, all the leading Romantics were his friends or acquaintances, most notably John Keats (1795–1821), whose "Epistle to Charles Cowden Clarke" thanks him for his kindness in inspiring a love of poetry and generous friendly conversation that began when as a fourteen- or fifteen-year-old Clarke taught the little boy who was his father's pupil. Charles Lamb was a particular friend; his retelling (with his sister Mary) of Shakespeare's plays for children inspired Clarke's own *Tales from Chaucer in Prose: Designed Chiefly for the Use of Young Persons* (1833).[3] Clarke is best known as a Shakespearean scholar whose many lectures, some published, attracted large audiences from the general public. With his wife, who produced a monumental *The Complete Concordance to Shakespeare* (1845), he wrote *The Shakespeare Key* (1879); *Cassell's Illustrated Shakespeare* (1886) collected their editions of works, biography, chronology, and glossary. However, Clarke began his career with Chaucer, who was the subject of his first lecture at the Mechanics' Institute, Royston, in 1834, the year after he published *Tales from Chaucer*, a book that early made clear his knowledge and understanding of English poetry, subsequently shown in editions for John Nichol's British poets. Clarke's efforts to reach a wide audience are repeated by the Victorian Chaucerians like Skeat and Furnivall.

This first collection was ambitious in coverage; it included the *General Prologue* and ten tales: of the *Knight, Lawyer, Student, Wife of Bath, Squire, Pardoner, Prioress, Nun's Priest, Canon's Yeoman,* and *Gamelyn,* then thought by many to be Chaucer's. Fourteen woodcuts by W.H. Mott and S. Williams provide generous illustration. The images are small, but each is printed on a full page with a quotation from Chaucer. The frontispiece is "The Procession of the Pilgrims to Canterbury," an image so popularized by the paintings of Blake and Stothard as to be an icon of Chaucer as a presenter of English life. Three illustrations are biographical: the title page bears the "Arms of Geoffrey Chaucer" to indicate his noble connections; the "Gateway to Donnington Castle, the last country residence of Chaucer" extends his province beyond London; and "Chaucer's Tomb" affirms his role as Father of English Poetry. These images indicate that the stories are not viewed as separate from their author and his time.

Clarke's selection of tales shows a judgment of what is deemed appropriate subject matter in a children's book—chivalry, patient and enduring woman, magic and fairy tale, warnings against self-indulgent youth and greed, a life of a child saint, a beast fable, and an archetype of adolescent success (albeit not Chaucer's). Two factors are in play, choosing stories for a child audience and changing taste of adults. The latter is not easy to chart, but Betsy Bowden's study of eighteenth-century modernizations of Chaucer leaves no doubt that *fabliaux* were then the tales easiest to find.[4] This preference changes in the nineteenth century when retellings express different standards; and although there are variations, most collections repeat Clarke's choices. Similarly, the episodes chosen for illustration are frequently the same.

Clarke also set a practice of close paraphrase, described as

> to put ... into modern language and into as easy prose as I could, without at the same time destroying the poetical descriptions and strong natural expressions of the author ... to render my narratives as much like *poetical* prose as I was able: and, more particularly, to give them the air of ancient writing newly dressed up.

However, he acknowledges that a later reading of the original will show "how much they have lost by being reduced to my dull prose" (xi), A second prefatory note, "To an Adult Reader," reiterates this description in more-sophisticated language to explain the task Clarke set himself:

> to render my translations literal with the original, to preserve their
> antique fashion, and withal to give them a sufficiently modern air to
> interest the young reader. I was to be at one and the same time "mod-
> ernly antique," prosaically poetic, and comprehensively concise [xiii].

The language may sound quaint, but he indicates the limitation of any
translation, recognizes the audience (not a sophisticated academic one),
and the role of popular texts.

Clarke offered "To My Young Readers" a book of moral value with
three objectives:

> [F]irst, that you might become wise and good by the example of the
> sweet and kind creatures you will find described in them; secondly,
> that you might derive improvement by the beautiful writing (for I
> have been careful to use the language of Chaucer whenever I thought
> it not too antiquated for modern and young readers); and, lastly, I
> hoped to excite in you an ambition to read these same stories in their
> original poetic dress when you shall have become so far acquainted
> with your own language as to understand, without much difficulty, the
> old and now almost forgotten terms [xi].

This Introduction sets a precedent, for it combines a brief biography—
with some improvisation such as Chaucer's being entered as a student at
Cambridge and at Oxford, with no record of which college at either (xv)—
and a critical appreciation, mostly quotations from William Hazlitt
(1778–1830) about the authenticity of Chaucer's voice ("His poetry reads
like history"), his power of description, and contentment "to find grace
and beauty in truth" (xx). The climax of Clarke's biographical sketch is
Chaucer's position

> at the court of Edward III, a prince as eminent for his patronage of
> genius as for his romantic valour. In this gay region of chivalry, mirth,
> and gallantry, surrounded by wit and beauty, he started upon the full
> career of life…. A handsome and modest young poet moving about a
> gallant court is a beautiful picture for the mind to contemplate [xvi].

Chivalry and gallantry were, as previously noted, ideals of Victorian
medievalism advocated for the public schoolboy—and other Edwardian
school children for whom their ideals provided a model. Clarke's picture
of Chaucer at court is an analog to Ford Madox Brown's vision in his
painting; both express the sentiment epitomized by Daniel Maclise's *The
Spirit of Chivalry* (1845), so eloquently described in a review by Charles
Dickens:

Is it the Love of Woman, in its truth and deep devotion, that inspire you? See it here! Is it glory, as the world has learned to call the pomp and circumstance of arms? Behold it at the summit of its exaltation, with its mailed hand resting on the altar where the Spirit ministers. The Poet's laurel crown, which they who sit on thrones can neither twine nor whither—is that the aim of thy ambition? It is there.[5]

That Chaucer was retold for children in this Victorian context, is obvious from both Clarke's choice of and treatment of tales, often reinforced by the illustrations. The woodcut for *The Knight's Tale* shows Emily and the Queen weeping before Theseus, an image of knightly strength that can be mitigated by the humility and compassion of women. Clarke's lesson is for all "young persons," not one gender; women are essential for chivalry, since male valor often stems from women's vulnerability, poignantly evoked in another woodcut that graces the *Man of Law's Tale*, where a distraught Constance gestures toward the ship that is to take her to Northumbria. An image of the oppressed mother is not reiterated for the *Clerk's Tale*, which signs instead the dutiful daughter and wife. Griselda stands modestly, her head bowed, between Walter and her father as her future husband explains that she is to "well understand" that the men have agreed about the marriage.

Clarke's paraphrases are fairly full, especially of exciting narrative. In the *Knight's Tale* the description of the tournament is rousing pageantry, but philosophical reflection is less evident. Thus the conclusion eliminates the First Mover speech to reach the happy ending quickly, when Theseus "after a decent process of time" for mourning, calls all together and asks, "Why are we sad, that good Arcite, the flower of chivalry, has departed with high honor from the thralldom of life?" (52). Theseus urges Emily to wed her knight Palamon, since he has loved and served her well. Their marriage is the wish of Theseus, "a warrior" and "King of Athens," as the opening line identifies him (21), and his "whole council" assented to his wish. Here is a congruence of Victorian and medieval customs of mourning, marriage, and hierarchy. It is reiterated in the *Clerk's Tale* and illustrated by the woodcut that shows an elegant Walter pledging to Griselda, clad in a folk-peasant dress with apron, as her father gapes in amazement.

The appropriateness of such sentiments in children's literature is marked by a continuance in subsequent books. Clarke's version of Chaucer's *Knight's Tale* survived, as did its role in fostering chivalry. Robert MacIntyre included his *The Story of Palamon and Arcite* in *Tales of Romance*, published in a Junior Modern English Series by Harrap in 1932. This collection for school use is representative and essentially Edwardian;

it reprints favorites from books in earlier series, such as E.M. Wilmot-Buxton's *Olger the Dane* and Eleanor Hull's *The Story of Deirdre,* as well as modernizations of Malory, Layamon, and *Don Quixote.* Here Chaucer's *Knight's Tale* is part of the tradition of ideal chivalry known through medieval romances, tales of stirring action, whose splendid storytelling endears them to young folks (12). The exercises for students include questions that require thoughtful responses, such as whether Theseus acted justly and how Arcite exemplified chivalry. One activity is to "Draw a plan of the lists described in the story, inserting and naming each of the details mentioned," and the final part deploys nineteenth-century medievalism: "Compare this description with that of the lists at Ashby-de-la-Zouche in *Ivanhoe*" (224). Thus Chaucer's role in the formation of English is linked with a devotion to the Middle Ages inspired by Sir Walter Scott's novel, which through countless editions for children incited them to the same romantic ideals in the United States no less than in Britain. Selections from Clarke make up *A Child's Book of Chaucer* (1927), which has three items: *Prologue, Knight's Tale, Man of Law's Tale.* The editorial choices reiterate the Victorian/Edwardian view of Chaucer as a teller of stories of chivalry and high sentiment. Brodie reprinted this book as late as 1950.[6]

When he deems it necessary, Clarke modifies Chaucer's text to mitigate impurity. Hence the Wife of Bath has no Prologue, and the initial scene is evasive: "a handsome and vigorous young bachelor knight, who … saw before him a young maiden, whom in a transport of willfulness and brutality he ill-treated" (97); however, when the queen orders penance with the chance of life, Clarke renders Chaucer's "knight" as "ravisher" (98), which is bolder than subsequent retellers for children. Nevertheless, the illustration is of the folk motif likely to fascinate children, the meeting of the knight with the loathly lady or hag, which combines humor with apprehension. Clarke's elimination of *fabliaux* reflects a reticence about physical functions, as does his cleansing of details in other tales. Thus Pertelote in the *Nun's Priest's Tale* recommends not "som laxatyf" (VII.2943), but "some cooling herbs" to treat Chanticleer's choler and melancholy (139). The woodcut is one of the most apt for children's literature in the tradition of Aesop; Russell waits while Chaunticleer crows. There is a sprinkling of explanatory notes, several from Tyrwhitt's edition, but many written by Clarke himself, of which two are notable. The first concerns Chanticleer's exploitation of his knowledge of Latin to insult his wife: "The impudent wag! he knew that Dame Pertelot was no scholar, or she would have told him that the translation of the saying was, 'In the beginning woman was man's confusion'" (142). The second is an assertion of Protestant over medieval Catholic belief and practice, a recurrent theme.

In the *Canon's Yeoman's Tale* Clarke glosses an "annualler" as "a priest employed solely to sing annuals, or anniversary masses for the dead, *without having any cure of souls*" (italics added, 177). Again the illustration reinforces Clarke's judgment, as the canon notes how the priest sweats over the coals and offers a cloth, thus creating the moment for sleight of hand. In contrast, some reassurance is offered by the illustration for the *Prioress's Tale;* the abbot at the coffin of the little clergeon, asks how he can help, and the background includes an altar, many crosses, and men in religious garb. Few images of children are more familiar to Victorians than the untimely deaths of the very young and concomitant ways to manage grief or subliminally to warn against bad behavior—subject matter made familiar by publications from the Religious Tract Society. The meeting of the rioters—fashionably dressed and showing pride, gluttony, and anger in their demeanors—and the old man that accompanies the *Pardoner's Tale* is in the latter category. As we shall see repeatedly, retellers of Chaucer for children often found ways to comment on decorum, and the *Pardoner's Tale* was an exemplum.

Like many others, Clarke used the *Squire's Tale* to show Chaucer's place in the tradition of English literature by summarizing Spenser's continuation in *The Faerie Queene* (IV.ii and iii), which takes more pages than Chaucer's tale. It also provided the pictorial image, the cart drawn by a lion, that enhances the sense of magic in a tale here concluded with "all ... happily accorded ... all loved and were beloved alike" (124). In contrast to this glowing resolution is another vision of chivalry, one in which the fight against evil knights is protracted. The *Tale of Gamelyn,* assigned to the Cook and widely accepted by Victorians as Chaucer's work, is a male Cinderella story with obvious pertinence to a young audience, who can find in the mistreatment and trials of the younger son a mirror of adolescent experience. Clarke does not stint in his account of the youth's impetuousness and initial self-indulgence as well as his naiveté. The woodcut is iconic, a familiar image from stories of the outlaw Robin Hood. The youth Gamelyn attacks his enemies with a staff; already the bishop has fallen from his chair and a monk lurches away from the table. Not all subsequent collections included this non–Chaucerian work, perhaps because it is devoid of interest in women, unusual in Chaucer's stories.

There was no second edition of *Tales from Chaucer in Prose: Designed Chiefly for the Use of Young Persons* until 1870, perhaps because of Clarke's own rival two-volume *The Riches of Chaucer.* However, a reissue of Charles Cowden Clarke's *Tales from Chaucer Told for Young People* in 1947 demonstrates the continuity of belief in Chaucer's role as the Father of English Poetry and the viability of his stories; the publisher was aptly named The Heritage Press. Significantly, Marchette Chute's *Geoffrey Chaucer of England*, which has been much used in schools, was published in 1946. This popular biography, written to delight and reassure, finds shared traits between the twentieth century and the fourteenth century, "a distant mirror," as in Barbara Tuchman's later history. Chute notes many anxieties and hardships but still finds Chaucer's time a "cheerful, civilized, tough-minded century, with a lively sense of the ridiculous."[7] Similarly, J. Selby Lowndes's *Canterbury Gallop* (1945), an engaging juvenile novel about a lost son whose beautiful voice makes him a success first as Chaucer's minstrel then as a chorister at Canterbury Cathedral, combines paraphrases and characters from *The Canterbury Tales* with social and economic history.[8] With World War II came an increase in patriotism that was expressed in children's literature by the reprinting of traditional stories of heroes, such as Guy of Warwick, and other local legends.[9] The Heritage Illustrated Bookshelf's new edition has one significant deletion, the *Prioress's Tale*. The medieval tale's depiction of Jews made it objectionable in the context of the horror of the Holocaust. New rich-color portraits of pilgrims (1946) by Arthur Szyk add a modern look, while emphasizing character over story.[10]

Clarke's *The Riches of Chaucer* (1835) is very ambitious; its long descriptive subtitle declares conformity to a recognized Victorian sensibility, "in which his impurities have been expunged, his spelling modernized, his rhythm accentuated, and his obsolete terms explained."[11] Clarke begins his Preface with a defense against criticism of his efforts. By presenting Chaucer's text in modern verse he is going far beyond his initial prose retelling to advance a further level toward the objective, "to read these same stories in their original poetic dress," that he gave "To My Young Readers" in the first book. There are aids: accents to facilitate pronunciation, "a few explanatory notes," and a glossary of Middle English words at the bottom of each page. Lines with "impurities" are replaced by ellipses. For example, in the *General Prologue* are deletions of four lines about the Summoner that describe his lechery ("As hoot he was and lecherous as a sparwe," I.626) and his giving his concubine for a quart of wine (I.649–51); the comment on the Pardoner's sexuality ("I trowe he were a geldyng or a mare," I.691); but in glossing the Wife as "gat-tooth'd" (I.468), Clarke's note adds that "the real meaning is unsettled" (73). The Host's blessing of the Physician's "urynals and jurdones" in the Prologue to the *Pardoner's Tale* (VI.305) are eliminated (263), as are his nine ribald lines (VII.3450–59) to the Nun's Priest in the Epilogue to his tale so that Clarke's version reads as a repeated thank-you: "This was a merry tale of Chanticleer…. But, Sir, fair fall you for your Tale" (301). Cuts in the *Nun's Priest's Tale* reduce examples (VII.3112–49) and eliminate the cock's sexual pleasure ("Al be it that I may nat on yow ride," VII.3168; 294).

Although *The Riches of Chaucer* is far more sophisticated than *Tales from Chaucer*, Clarke still ends his preface with an exhortation to "my young friends (for to you principally do I, of course, address myself) let the loadstars of your literary voyage be the standard writers of the old times" (1: xi). This reiterates the opening apologia for presenting Chaucer for the modern reader, an early answering of objections to modern sophistication. Perhaps Clarke's most significant intention is to gain an audience of young women; certainly his elaborate Victorian decorum gives insight to current views:

> I proposed to omit all those tales and casual passages of ill-favored complexion, which, if retained, would infallibly banish the book from the very circles whither it was directed, and whence I hope to hear of its welcoming—I mean those ornaments of this civilized age, and patterns to the civilized world, the ingenuous, intelligent, well informed, and artless young women of England. I would fain hope that in the general fermentation of mind now going on here, that amidst all the voyages that are making in search of the *useful* in life—all the circumnavigations for the substantial, that the really ornamental (for that is "useful," seeing that it conduces to a refined and gentle civility, and consequently to happiness) will not be wholly lost sight of in the race. Let not our poetry be quite forgotten, and above all, our old poetry: let not the eloquent simplicity—the only well-wearing eloquence after all—(like simple mechanism) the sudden, and electrical pathos of old Chaucer; the universal code of humanity in Shakespeare; the gentle fancy, languishing voluptuousness, and religiously poetical faith of Spenser; the divine afflation and Atlantic roll of Milton;—let not the works of these giants become the subject of mouth-honor only; let them not be trolled over the tongue, and after bolted; but let them be healthily prepared, ruminated, and thoroughly digested;—when their ethereal fumes will ascend into the brain, and prompt the mouth to "speak great things" [1:x].

Albeit rhetorical flourishes and gastronomic metaphor are overblown, and demarcation of gender reactionary by today's standards, Clarke's pointing to his audience as female and view of women as "ornaments" and "patterns" of "this civilized age" explain in part his choices of tales with an emphasis upon the pathetic, feminine over coarse, masculine stories. Another factor was that "English literature occupies a more prominent position in the education of girls than of boys," according to a Schools Inquiry in 1869.[12] Skeat's observations about young women's reading and studying English persist in Newbolt's Report on *The Teaching of English in England* in 1921.

The title page of *The Riches of Chaucer* also announces "A New Memoir of the Poet," an expanded biography that still praises Hazlitt's incisive criticism but also quotes extensively William Godwin's *Life of Geoffrey Chaucer* (1803), especially the importance of the poet's relation to John of Gaunt and John Wycliffe.[13] Clarke's other authorities are the Renaissance antiquarian John Leland, Speght's edition, and Urry's *Life*, and the Life in Bell's edition. A long extract from Froissart builds the chivalric emphasis (1:6–8n). Religion is a more complex issue. Clarke discusses Gaunt's ambition, which led him to espouse Wycliffe's reform attitudes toward the clergy, and considers the questioning of Chaucer's authorship of *Jack Upland* and *The Ploughman's Tale* from "affected zeal for his reputation or from religious partisanship." He quotes John Foxe's rationale that Chaucer was a Wycliffite but yet escaped ecclesiastical censure, follows Gaunt's changing views after Wat Tyler's rebellion, and concludes with evidence of Chaucer's Roman Catholicism in the belief in transubstantiation in *The Testament of Love* and in the Retraction, which he deems a change of opinion unworthy of serious consideration since made at the end of life "when neither mind nor body can be in its full condition of elasticity" (1:16–22). Clarke's summary judgment is that whatever Chaucer's response to Wycliffe's doctrines, he was a *reformer*, not a *seceder;* not least because "the man of imagination is seldom calculated to maintain an up-hill struggle in the cause of reform" (1:44).

This Romantic view of the poet—albeit refuted by the young Wordsworth and Shelley—followed a curious, complex analysis of Chaucer's physiognomy and character:

> The person of Chaucer was of middle stature, in advanced years inclining to corpulency.... His face was full and smooth, betokening regular good health, and a serene and cheerful frame of mind. His complexion was fair, verging towards paleness: his hair was of a dusky yellow, short and thin; that of his beard grew, or rather perhaps it was fashioned into a forked shape, and its color was wheaten ... the general expression of his countenance combined a mixture of animation, of lurking, good natured satire, of unruffled serenity, sweetness, and close thought....
>
> His features, as in most instances of sincere and transparent natures, were an index of his temper, and this comprised a mixture of the lively, grave, and modest. Yet was the gaiety of his disposition more prominent in his writings than in his general demeanor....

> His youth was not altogether free from the indiscretion natural to a
> man surrounded by the beauty and wit of an admiring court ... [evi-
> dence of loyal courtship of wife] ... his constant behavior towards
> women, and his exalted admiration of them, at once exempt him from
> being a coarse or common intriguer.... Many of his tales are question-
> able in their morality ... but it is strongly doubtful, (coarse as they
> are) whether they would so surely sap the structure of a well-educated
> young mind as many productions of some modern writers, and which
> are nevertheless found in almost every bookcase in the kingdom
> [1:41–43].

Again Clarke concludes with an apology for the appropriateness of
Chaucer as reading for young people. His Chaucer is essentially the genial
man and poet, with a stress upon modesty; hints of characteristics unac-
ceptable to Victorians are admitted and explained. One can only specu-
late what the mixed readership of adult and child made of some tantalizing
hints; however, there is no doubt that he is Chaucer's advocate, with a
solid summary of professional achievements:

> The career of Chaucer, from whichever point we may view it, assumes
> a character greatly elevated above that of ordinary men. He was a
> poet, a philosopher, an astronomer, a logician, a linguist, a politician,
> a theologian, a humanist, a gentleman [1:43].

The accolade "gentleman" both concludes and summarizes the aspirations
of Victorian society. Nineteenth-century fascination with biography developed early in children's literature with lives of heroes, saints, and modern accomplishments of "bold deeds" in professions. Clarke's Life of
Chaucer is of this type, with increased judgments of tales.

First, although *The Riches* is in two volumes, Clarke declares his own
wonder and admiration and asserts that it is on *The Canterbury Tales* that
Chaucer's fame reposes (1:31). Certainly this is true of the poet's place in
children's literature, which may explain why Clarke's first evaluation is of
the *Nun's Priest's Tale*, "allowed by all judges to be the most admirable fable
(in the narration) that ever was written." He praises the *Knight's Tale* as
"a splendid succession of gorgeous scenery" and the *Squire's Tale* for being
"told in the fullest inspiration of Oriental imagining," and he finds the
Pardoner's Tale "both striking and original.... Death ... equal in vividness
of coloring to any portrait in Dante or the Greek dramatists." But most
attention goes to two stories of noble women, the *Man of Law's Tale* and
the *Clerk's Tale*. Constance's story is "one of the loveliest of his tales," the
work of an "earnest" author, "eloquent in his pathos" so that readers do
not hold its improbabilities in their minds. "Nature, truth, and steadfastness

in love, shine forth from her heart, and rivet the attention and sympathy of the reader in a remarkable manner." However, Griselda's story is "the finest in point of severely beautiful writing," and Clarke's praise of it reiterates his Victorian elevation of women, the conviction that they are the civilizing force to lift man's nature:

> The whole conduct of the heroine is a fervid hymn in praise of patience, forbearance, and long-suffering. [Clarke offers to any who deny the tale's worth] ... the three grand points upon which the story is constructed, viz.—those of fidelity to her promise; strength of principle in maintaining it; and stubbornness of principle in loving her husband "through good report and through evil report." ...That the marquis was unworthy of the love of such a woman, is but the type of every day's occurrence, and corroborates the fidelity to the nature of the narrative [1:46–50].

There is, then, no feeling of the need to allegorize expressed by Chaucer's Clerk and his academic inheritors. Clarke's analysis of the *Clerk's Tale* is an exemplary reading that is an unmitigated extrapolation of ideal behavior suitable to modern living. This contrasts with the fifteenth-century simplification of the *Clerk's Tale* in the Huntington Library Manuscript 140, which appends the lyric *Truth* to extend the didactic message of self-mastery beyond the domestic sphere.[14] Those who find Clarke too naive and didactic have the additional evidence that with a simple reference to the *Prioress's Tale,* he concludes, "the choicest of the Canterbury Tales may be said to have been enumerated."

He was not, however, averse to including some tales not deemed "the choicest." The first volume of *The Riches of Chaucer,* which is *The Canterbury Tales,* almost repeats the selection in *Tales from Chaucer;* but Clarke increased complexity by adding the tales of the *Friar* and *Franklin* and accuracy by taking out *Gamelyn.* This meant new illustrations by W.H. Mott and S. Williams: an altercation among the Summoner, Devil, and the Old Woman, which has implications of devil-like indulgence in a corrupt church; and Aurelius pleading with Dorigen, a dark aspect of love in chivalry and a hint at modern flirting. One consequence of Clarke's increased sophistication, a use of lines of modernized verse, is the omission of Spenser's continuation, and thus the original woodcut, which is replaced by one of Canacee, an appealing vulnerable maiden, conversing with the hawk in a tree to evoke the magic of romance and show a Victorian lady in a park or garden.

The second volume contains *Troilus and Creseida,* five parts of the *Legend of Good Women, Queen Anelida and False Arcite,* isolated passages

The poor woman curses the greedy summoner in W.H. Mott & S. Williams' wood-cut for *Friar's Tale* in Charles Cowden Clarke's *The Riches of Chaucer* (1835). This tale's morality suited Victorian didacticism; justice comes quickly when the devil—shown in the guise of a yeoman—tempts and traps the dominant officer of an eccle-siastical court. There is also a lesson about the difference between what one says and what one means.

from *The Assembly of Fowls, The Book of the Duchess,* selections from *The House of Fame,* allegorical characters from *Romaunt of the Rose,* a number of Ballads, and poems no longer attributed to Chaucer (*Flower and the Leaf, Chaucer's Dream, The Complaint of the Black Knight*). The extended works is an unusual Chaucer for children; however, other children's writ-ers modestly imitated such breadth when they included lyrics with the *Canterbury Tales.* Clarke's two volumes were successful enough to war-rant editions in 1870, 1877, and a reprint in 1896. Concurrently, R.H. Horne's modernization of *The Poems of Chaucer* (1841) suggests a grow-ing interest for adults, even though Walter Pater's dismissal makes the opposite point. Seeing Horne's effort, Pater "remarked that he had heard of the Canterbury Tales, but did not know that they were considered of sufficient importance to be modernized."[15] Many translators and pub-lishers, parents and teachers, did not agree.

Mrs. Haweis

The second major Victorian retelling is Mrs. Haweis's *Chaucer for Children: A Golden Key* (1876); Chatto and Windus published a second edition in 1900.[16] Mary Eliza Joy Haweis (1852–98) was the wife of a vicar who was active in publishing. Although she later wrote *Beautiful Houses* (1882), her initial effort was that of a mother, since the eagerness and intelligence of her son inspired a confidence that children could read and respond well to Chaucer. Her first Chaucer book included Middle English and modern translations, substantial biographical material and information about the Middle Ages, and meticulously detailed illustrations that showed her fascination with medieval costume. *Chaucer for Children: A Golden Key* was a great success, widely and favorably reviewed, and Haweis followed this with a book designed for pedagogical use, *Chaucer for Schools* (1881). Next was *Chaucer's Beads: A Birthday Book, Diary, and Concordance of Chaucer's Proverbs or Soothsaws* (1884), a sign of Chaucer's presence throughout the year.[17] Her conception and execution are sophisticated, a reflection of the growing depth of medievalism and Chaucer studies.

An embossed cover of an original edition of *Chaucer for Children: A Golden Key* immediately attracts; its five scenes, with daisy decoration and an explanation, suggest variety. Two are male images of love—a battle between Palamon and Arcite amidst Cupid's arrows, and Aurelius's offering Dorigen his flaming heart—and one is maternal, a baby, suitable to Griselda or Constance. The other two are didactic warnings—a demon leads away a summoner, and skull and crossbones surmount the rioters of the *Pardoner's Tale*. Among the many efforts to present Chaucer to children, this is the most complex and advanced; Haweis relies upon and cites current scholarship, quotes a substantial amount of Middle English, and provides her own elaborate illustrations with commentary. The 1900 edition compares lines from Skeat's recent *The Complete Works of Geoffrey Chaucer* (1894) with earlier editions of Thomas Tyrwhitt (*The Canterbury Tales of Chaucer*, 1775–78), Robert Bell (annotated *English Poets*, 24 vols. 1854–57; new ed. 29 vols., 1866), and Pickering's Aldine Poets (1845; 1866 and 1874); she also refers to Furnivall's work and publications of the Chaucer Society.

Haweis expresses great confidence in the curiosity and skills of the child reader; her stress upon traditional moral values signs her book as Victorian, and these persist as Edwardian ideals. She was "encouraged to put the book together by noticing how quickly my own little boy learned and understood fragments of early English poetry" (xi); her dedication to "My Little Lionel" resonates with Frances Hodgson Burnett's *Little Lord*

Fauntleroy (1885), especially in the drawing of a long fair and curly-haired boy in lace-trimmed blouse. The book suggests a remarkably clever and keen lad or a doting mother, since it argues that Middle English is not too hard to understand: mother and child can read it aloud after considering a few basic directions about the language (*"if you pronounce the words so as to preserve the rhythm* all will be well," xii), even though complete understanding would require more exceptional knowledge (xvi). Haweis reiterates aesthetic delight in Middle English: "you will soon see how much prettier and more musical it sounds than our modern tongue, and I think you will like it very much" (13). In fact, the book offers some likelihood of success; like Clarke's *The Riches of Chaucer*, it has features used in editions for today's undergraduates and other adults. Double columns print Middle English verse with a modern verse translation, unusual words are glossed in the margin, and notes at the bottom of the page explain details of medieval life. Haweis makes substantial selections from Chaucer's links and tales and prose synopses, of varying length depending upon the tale, for the missing portions.

"Chaucer the Tale-teller" gives the reader an approach to Chaucer that Haweis had already signaled in the opening Foreword:

> Chaucer is, moreover, a thoroughly religious poet, all his merriest stories having a fair moral; even those which are too coarse for modern taste are rather *naïve* than injurious; and his pages breathe a genuine faith in God and a passionate sense of the beauty and harmony of his divine work. The selections I have made are some of the most beautiful portions of Chaucer's most beautiful tales [xii].

With typical nineteenth-century interest in physiognomy, her essay also ventures a psychological analysis based on Chaucer's appearance:

> You may see how good and clever Chaucer was by his face; such a wise, thoughtful, pleasant face! He looks very kind, I think, as if he would never say anything harsh or bitter; but sometimes he made fun of people in a merry way. Words of his own, late in life, show that he was rather fat, his face small and fair. In manner he seemed 'elvish,' or shy, with a habit of staring on the ground [3].

Combined with this conflation of medieval and modern is an appeal to patriotism; Haweis urges admiration for the Father of English Poetry and briefly describes historical circumstances: dwelling place, costume, London (the fourteenth and nineteenth century maps point continuity [5]), court connections, and diplomatic missions. She views *The Canter-*

bury Tales enthusiastically and optimistically and finds Chaucer a genial man:

> full of cheerfulness and fun; full of love for the beautiful world, and full of sympathy for all in trouble or misery. The beauty of Chaucer's character, and his deep piety, come out very clearly in these tales, as I think you will see…. There was a large-heartedness and liberality about Chaucer's mind, as of one who had mixed cheerfully with all classes, and saw good in all. His tastes were with the noble ranks among whom he had lived; but he had deep sympathy with the poor and oppressed, and could feel kindly even to the coarse and wicked. He hated none but hypocrites; and he was never tired of praising piety and virtue [11–12].

There is no doubt about Haweis's Protestant Evangelical judgment of Chaucer's religious beliefs: "Chaucer's personal distrust and contempt for the contemporary Church and its creatures was the natural and healthy aversion of a pure mind and a sincerely religious heart to a form of godliness denying the power thereof—a Church which had become really corrupt" (33).[18] This leads to praise of Chaucer's "perfect artistic thoroughness" that, in spite of his aversion, kept him from giving an immoral or imperfect tale to a nun or friar, who would have been unlikely to incriminate themselves publicly!

Five tales—of the *Knight, Friar, Clerk, Franklin,* and *Pardoner*—well illustrate the high sentiments that Haweis finds in Chaucer, and subsequent collections often repeat her selections. She follows each tale with "Notes by the Way," in which she delineates moral intentions and shows some critical acumen. Her remarks are thoughtful, an example of Victorian sensibility and evolving theory about the use of adult classics for children's literature, with several key arguments.

Haweis's main point about the *Knight's Tale* is an objection to those who fail to find Palamon and Arcite very different characters, and she eloquently argues for Arcite's nobility, praising his "power of self-control and brave heart" and his death-bed sacrifice that is "a sign of forgiveness" (56). The combative young men, who sacrifice their friendship for love of Emelye, are the center of interest, partially because Haweis is uneasy with "How idealized, and how idolized, the passion of love had grown to be" in medieval times (45n). The narrative runs continuously, with almost half as direct quotation (with a parallel modern version). Haweis's favoring of description shows her fascination with costuming and nature over dialogue, which she more often gives in prose paraphrase. An exception is the meeting of the heroes in the woods, with Palamon's fierce speech (41).

Although Haweis paraphrases Chaucer's account of the great tournament, the rich description remains. Her abridging heightens action and deletes philosophical reflection; Theseus's Prime Mover speech and the wisdom of Egeus are eliminated, but not a description of Arcite's bier and funeral, since for her he is the worthy hero, the one who dies young at the moment of triumph.

Two tales told by pilgrims employed by the medieval church stretch Haweis's moral judgments. The *Friar's Tale* is a popular legend; and although it does not discourage swearing, it makes a distinction in an age when oaths were common. "The rough moral deduced was admirably suited to the coarse and ignorant minds of the lower orders" (64). A concern with common vices is the issue in the notes for the final selection, the *Pardoner's Tale*, when Haweis identifies "the practice of men drinking and playing themselves bare in the taverns, … the resort of all the refuse of the people." Thus she abbreviates issues of the *Pardoner's Prologue* to tell the story of the three rioters, who "were probably young men who had ruined themselves by folly and license, and whose besetting sin, surviving all it throve on, urged them to any and every crime for the sake of renewed gratification. Their end is beyond measure frightful." This is the severest of Haweis's Victorian judgments, and a didactic warning, well gauged for youth. In spite of some disapproval Haweis sustains her great admiration of Chaucer: "The extreme beauty of this poem, even in a technical sense alone, is such that I lament the necessity of abridging it" (99). This refers to the Pardoner's initial preaching against sins, subsequent swearing, and the final apostrophes against sins and the Pardoner's attempt to dupe his hearers. The actions of the three rioters are complete, almost entirely in Middle English, with modern verse parallel, so that Haweis has a crisp tale of warning, a model often repeated in subsequent Chaucer books for children.

Between these two tales come two others that consider women's situations, the *Clerk's Tale* (which is in every collection for children) and the *Franklin's Tale*. The former is the only tale for which Haweis retains Chaucer's division into parts. The first four (of six) are mostly prose summary, with verse largely reserved to key speeches, such as Griselda on obedience. The final portions, Griselda's being put away for a new wife and the reconciliation of the family, are mostly in verse. For Haweis the tale is one of "tender pathos," and like Clarke she reads it realistically: "The definite human interest running all through it points to some living Griselda…. Resignation, so steadfast and so willing, was the virtue of an early time, when the husband was really a 'lord and master'" (82). Haweis's illustration of "Griselda's Sorrow" does not soften the combined

"Griselda's Sorrow" as her child is taken from her is vividly evoked by Mrs. Haweis, who both wrote and illustrated *Chaucer for Children* (1876). The image combines the threat of violence in the attendant's dagger and the terror of the child with a grieving Madonna; it also includes small details (toys, shoe, a dog with a bone seen through the window) to engage the child's attention The *Clerk's Tale* was much favored in retellings for children, usually with greater emphasis upon the humble and obedient wife.

horror and resignation of her surrender of the child; she sits immobile, like a grieving Madonna, the sergeant looks very fierce and holds a dagger to the child that he has tossed over his shoulder and whose outstretched arms beseech the mother (73). A note explains that noble families typically put their children with other families: "The removal of Walter's children from the mother was *not* an outrage: but concealing their fate from her was" (71). The analog of the public (boarding) school is inescapable. Although a comparison with modern circumstances would suggest Griselda was mad and that her husband should be hanged, Haweis concludes that the tale in its own terms makes a point: "When almost everybody gave way habitually to violent emotions of all sorts, those who could rein in a feeling were held in high esteem. Perhaps Walter himself may not have been wantonly cruel, but only so bewildered by these unaccustomed virtues that he could not trust their sincerity without experiments" (83). As a gloss of Victorian expectations of decorum in society and an assertion that the Middle Ages lacked sophisticated restraint, this authorial intervention both judges severely and attempts to rationalize. Haweis follows her simplification by admitting that she deleted the last six lines, "as the ironical directions to wives to be bad wives would be probably not understood by a child, and superfluous if they were" (83).

The *Franklin's Tale* is largely a prose summary, with the magician's role in verse; cutting is extensive—as when Dorigen's laments take but a sentence. The notes make another strong judgment about gender; if praise of Griselda's patience and endurance—at best repressive and at worst abusive—troubles many feminists, Haweis's analysis of Dorigen may be even more distressing:

> One of the most interesting illustrations of the singular morality of women's transition state from a position of slavery to one of equality with man, is to be found in this curious but beautiful tale: a tale which in any other age could scarcely have been popular.... It is seen that woman, from being regarded as a mere chattel, like horse or dog, came to be unnaturally exalted; and, as new movements often outshoot their mark and go too far, she came to be held as something god-like and ideal, the moving spring of all heroic virtues. Valour, courtesy, self-control, obedience, were taught by her, and she could give no higher guerdon than herself [91].

This continues Haweis's earlier note about the *Knight's Tale* and how women were idealized and idolized, the power of love in rough days, especially as inspiration of the arts: "her encouragement of all that was aesthetic, her influence over men, and therefore the impetus she gave to the higher life, must never be underrated" (45). She concludes:

> The *Franklin's Tale,* with its pathos and earnestness, passing at times into burlesque, is as quaint and instructive as an early effigy on some cathedral door.... A certain soft and refined luxuriousness seems to hang like a gossamer veil over a sentiment of genuine and vigorous chivalry, carried too far for our 19th century notions, but, like the generous mistakes of youth, none the less touching [91].

This fascinating gloss suggests the tension caused by the New Woman of *fin de siècle,* who elicits both admiration and anxiety, a will to suppress. It also shows the central role of chivalry in both the Middle Ages and its adaptation in medievalism. Victorian severity returns in Haweis's final warning against "giving the smallest inlet to wrong dealing."

In addition to textual analyses *Chaucer for Children* includes the author's eight color pictures, printed by Edmund Evans (1826–1905), and

"Dorigen and Aurelius in the Garden" is a romantic scene typical of Victorian medievalism. An illustration for the *Franklin's Tale* in *Chaucer for Children* (1876), it suggests Mrs. Haweis's affinity with Walter Crane, one of several famous artists printed by Edmund Evans, renowned for his skilled production of color.

thirty–one woodcuts. All illustrations are derived from medieval manuscripts, painting, and sculpture. Haweis includes specific "Notes on the Pictures" and "Notes on the Woodcuts," since the book's visual interest rivals the verbal.[19] That Evans was the printer is a mark of distinction, for he was renowned for his color-printing and contributed to the success of many distinguished artists. He early recognized the skills of Randolph Caldecott and Walter Crane, whose toy books he commissioned and printed. Evans was also one of the first to recognize Kate Greenaway's talent and to print several of her books; and it was he who printed almost all of Beatrix Potter's books for Warne, using the three-color half-tone process that he had perfected for delicate watercolors. As for the text and biography, Haweis acknowledges dependence on key authorities, such as the dramatist and antiquary James Robinson Planché's *The History of British Costume* (1834), the antiquary Henry Shaw's *Dresses and Decorations of the Middle Ages* (1843), and Frederick William Fairholt's *Costume in England* (1846), for her illustrations.[20] Behind these antiquaries' work lay Joseph Strutt's *Complete View of the Dress and Habits of the People of England* (1796–99). Haweis's frontispiece is directly related, for she does her own version of Thomas Stothard's *The Pilgrimage to Canterbury* (1806–07), an archetypal picture of the processional group that relied upon the portion of Strutt's work devoted to "Traveling Dresses of the 14th Century." Haweis shows the Host, who is pointing to Chaucer, assembling the pilgrims outside the Tabard, indicated by a sign in the upper right corner. Chaucer (after the Hoccleve portrait) and the Wife are the only mounted figures and are just behind the Monk and Prioress, at the center of the picture. An added interest marks this space; a boy holds the rein of the Knight's horse in one hand and a toy in the other, with a playful dog at his feet—a direct appeal to the illustrator's audience. The other pilgrims are the Friar, Summoner, Pardoner, Second Nun, and Franklin. This selection relates to the tales Haweis includes, but the woodcuts that introduce each portrait in the *General Prologue* give an image of each pilgrim. Haweis's devotion to costume leads her to identify details and elaborate upon their significance in notes on the page and in short essays at the end. Opposite this group image of the frontispiece is the title page with a woodcut of jousting at a tournament and the caption "Doth now your devoir, yonge knightes proude!"—a line from the *Knight's Tale* (I.2598). Both are calls to chivalry, a major theme enhanced by some abridgments as noted above.

The final section of *Chaucer for Children* expands beyond *The Canterbury Tales,* for it is a selection of lyrics, given in parallel columns of original and modern verse, that bring the reader back to Chaucer himself. First

"Mine Host Assembling the Canterbury Pilgrims" is an exciting frontispiece for Mrs. Haweis's *Chaucer for Children* (1876). She combines her devotion to details of medieval costume with lively action while showing the variety of persons on the pilgrimage—including an added boy with his dog that provide the point of view of her audience.

there is the "Complaint of Chaucer to his Purse," and the notes include Furnivall's speculation about whether Chaucer might have been involved in alchemy. Two *rondeaux* and a *virelai* are perhaps "ditties and songs glad." But the last point reaffirms Chaucer's noble character, initiated by the "Good Counsel of Chaucer" that urges truth. Haweis cites Furnivall as authority that "this pathetic little poem" was a response to Chaucer's being expelled from the Customs offices, and she argues that

> his month of power in Parliament ruined him. It is pretty certain that some vote of his, while sitting for Kent, caused his dismissal from office, and thus he ruminates on worldly ambitions. It is impossible, in reading these melancholy and stately lines, not to feel that they ring true, and betray the half-sarcastic disappointment of a well-meaning man, the resignation of a religious man, and the faith in right-dealing bringing its own reward of a thoroughly honest man [105].

Like earlier statements about Chaucer the man, this interpretation of a lyric shows Haweis assuming knowledge of both event and response to it as part of a typical Victorian focus on character. The last verse, given also in prose, sums up the pilgrim's way. While it introduces philosophical considerations more appropriate to an older audience, this conclusion does not change her judgment of the genial Chaucer, a great storyteller.

Chaucer for Schools (1881) was her book "for older readers" and incorporated the extensive responses to *Chaucer for Children*, including more-recent theories about Chaucer's life and work. Haweis retains the parallel texts of Middle English and modern verse translation and explains her intention to "reprint a large portion of the juvenile edition with new matter, but without the various colored illustrations and woodcuts" (ix). Schoolbooks were typically produced somewhat modestly, in an era when much attention and substantial payments to artists characterize children's books, to set them apart at a time when many adult books contained pictures. The "new matter" shows a stronger didactic purpose for a book designed for study; it adds several bolder judgments, changes the selection of tales, and includes pedagogical aids. In the introduction, Haweis expands her view of Chaucer's religion to make a strong case for Protestantism and thus lower the risk of Catholic influence. To earlier observations about Chaucer as a religious poet, she adds:

> His *Parson's Tale*, tampered with and interpolated as it doubtless has been by some orthodox Catholic scribe, is as full of Wycliffism and true Protestant feeling as many other portions of the *Canterbury Tales* are full of satire against the corruption of the Church: and Chaucer may be said to have striven as hard to propagate with his pen the faith of the new religious views as Albert Dürer strove with his pious pencil, long before Luther sounded the note of victory [x].

Changes in the tales selected also indicate further "Protestantizing." *Chaucer for Children* had included the *Friar's Tale* and the *Pardoner's Tale*, which showed abuses in the church but were also compelling narratives about sin and the supernatural, vivid pictures of a medieval Catholic ethos. Haweis substitutes a few lives from the *Monk's Tale* (Ugolino, Zenobia, Croesus, and Holofernes) and the *Nun's Priest's Tale*, "probably a floating popular *fabliau*, like others used by Chaucer to sharpen his own tool of satire and delicious humour" (139). Despite some confusion of genre, her notes point to Chanticleer's recognition in the midst of his terror of the ludicrous quality of his situation, an example of Chaucer's knowledge of human nature, a much esteemed quality.

Finally, Haweis replaces the *Franklin's Tale* with the *Man of Law's*

Tale—given in prose translation. She thus keeps an example of noble womankind, albeit she still finds medieval ideals unsettling. Constance is a singular character who does not provoke the anxieties aroused by Griselda's subjection and Dorigen's ambiguity.[21] Most importantly, in this religious romance, Haweis develops her own analysis of religions, adding attitudes to different faiths and tolerance. She explains Constance as ethereal:

> Carefully, and even tenderly as Chaucer has touched off the figure of the meek and holy Christian Princess, it remains thin and filmy in its spiritual beauty, like a fair visitant from another sphere indeed—save in moments, as when he pictures her hushing the fretful babe [160].

Some subversive tendencies surface when Haweis finds the old Sultaness a much more intriguing character, "a living figure," who appeals to human fascination with the imperfect as ideal figures do not. Further comment about Chaucer and religion follows:

> That Chaucer was a religious man cannot be doubted—that he was a strict or narrow one, may fairly be. His theological views in this tale reflect the ignorant general prejudice against foreign forms of thought, in which, of course, he had been brought up: not his own personal hatred, which only comes out against meanness and hypocrisy. It was, in fact, the educated, not the instinctive enmity [161].

Thus she frees Chaucer from the confines of the Middle Ages and finds in him prescience of modern belief. This develops into an explanation of the similarity between Mohammedan and Christian bigotry and medieval lack of understanding that Mohammedans opposed Christians as Christians opposed Jews because each saw the professed religion as "superseding" the earlier faith: "An advanced creed cannot give way to an obsolete one, which it has outgrown" (161). This glosses Victorian understanding of what should be taught—the advance of Protestantism announced in the opening.

The pedagogical apparatus of *Chaucer for Schools* includes materials that recur in many later schoolbooks. "Glimpses in Chaucer" offers five points to guide students' reading: the individuality of characters; the medieval fashion of portraits; Chaucer's highly respectable position in society, his probable shortsightedness, and the presence of "endless little pointed allusions, personal and political, with double meanings and hints which we cannot now decipher" (xiv). There are confident underlying assumptions of class and biography but also some recognition that the knowledge and attitudes of the Middle Ages and Victoria's reign are not the same. This mixture curiously simplifies and provokes. A table of historical events, with two columns, "at home" and "abroad," for the years 1300–1400, is an addition to much of the historical and social background in the "Chaucer the Tale-Teller" of *Chaucer for Children,* here divided under topics: Chaucer's time, work, home, London, appearance, court life, position, adversity, prosperity, politics, and life work. The list of topics shows Haweis to be a comprehensive editor.

Of greatest significance is an expansion of the case for Chaucer's place in English literature that is not in the volume prepared for her son. Here we see how children's literature, especially lessons taught in school, initiates recognition and an understanding of the English tradition and the essential role of the Father of English Poetry, which even challenges Shakespeare for primacy:

> Chaucer is, in fact, the first, and in one sense the greatest, of English poets. His knowledge of life, his breadth of sympathy with all classes of people and all modes of thought, his inexhaustible fancy, and his consummate art place him intellectually on a level with Shakespeare; and we must remember that without the first great man the second might never have existed. Moreover, though Shakespeare claims to have founded our modern drama, Chaucer founded the whole fabric of English poetic literature, and there is no doubt, so dramatic are many of his poems, that had a secular drama been called for in his day, Chaucer would have been a dramatist [3].

This is a major addition to Haweis's first evaluation of Chaucer's character, much of which is repeated here. The schoolbook lays a foundation for the appreciation of a national tradition, strongly urged in literary histories for children by H.E. Marshall, Henry Gilbert, Amy Cruse, William J. Long and Eva March Tappan, which are discussed in chapter 7.

Reviewers responded to *Chaucer for Schools* very positively.[22] *Academy* "hailed it with pleasure," praising "Chaucer the Tale-teller" as "the pleasantest, chattiest, and at the same time one of the soundest descriptions of the old master, his life and works and general surroundings, that have ever been written. The chapter cannot be too highly praised." The book is the "best means of introducing young pupils to the study our first great poet" (*Scotsman*) and will attract "not a few children of larger growth, who have found Chaucer to be very hard reading, even with the help of a glossary and copious notes" (*Echo*). *School Newspaper* deemed, "The book is a mine of poetic beauty and most scholarly explanation, which deserves a place on the shelves of every school library." A new edition of 1899, published posthumously, has only a few modifications, an added frontispiece (a drawing of the Hoccleve miniature) and a Chaucer autograph from Entries of the Customs. From *Chaucer for Children* were added the *Pardoner's Tale* and the "Minor Poems," enhanced by "Good Counsel" and "Balade of Gentilesse" and "Proverbs." Several "Fragments" appealed to a love of nature and the sea, traits much touted in the English character: "A Vision of a Garden" from *The Parliament of Birds* and "The Daisy" and "The Sea-Fight," part of the Antony and Cleopatra section, from *The Legend of Good Women*. Clearly books of Chaucer for children had become essential.[23] Other retellers lacked Haweis's high expectations, especially of ease in reading Middle English, so that their books for children offer less challenge but no less enthusiasm.

Mary Seymour

Mary Seymour lacks Haweis's academic sophistication, but *Chaucer's Stories Simply Told* (1884) expresses a modest confidence in the child's capacity to read the original; having given an assurance that "it is not so difficult to make out this quaint Old English as might be supposed at first glance; we grow accustomed after a brief trial," she interlaces a few passages of Middle English, often didactic summations that are thus made prominent.[24] Seymour offers a few general points about spelling and provides marginal definitions for italicized difficult words in each quotation. Her very clearly written book retains much of Chaucer's detail and was popular in schools; an American educator, Mary E. Burt, cited it as "Simple enough for third, fourth, and fifth grades" and priced at $1.25.[25]

Seymour's introductory "Story of Chaucer's Life" is typically Victorian in an emphasis upon his close ties to John of Gaunt (which possibly explain his years out of favor and want) and role as a court favorite, so that "he could give us living pictures of knightly honor and courtesy, of truth and worth and hearty piety" (xii). Much of her biography is an analysis of character very like Haweis's view of a genial and moral Chaucer. Seymour describes "a man of sympathy with suffering, a man of cheerful mind and practiced patience, whose love was always on the side of good and virtue, and who hated nothing but the mean, the deceitful, and the untrue" (xii). Knowledge of Chaucer's heart comes from "the noble deeds and high aims, the generous self-sacrifice and the patient waiting on God, which he has drawn for us" in characters—Griselda, Custance, Arcite, and Arviragus—and many of his "descriptions of women are life-like" (xii–xiii). Haweis's psychological analysis of Chaucer based on his face is paralleled by Seymour's creation of a perfect Anglo-Saxon racial type—"his complexion fair and pale, his hair deeply golden of tint and very luxurious" (ii)—that resembles the hero with Viking forebears so popular in juvenile historical novels. A final characterization comes through quoting Chaucer's lines—his love of books, his following of earlier writers, and expression of "a spirit of simple faith far removed from the spirit of the present day, which seems to delude itself with the idea that to question revealed truth, and to reject the old land-marks, are proofs of a superior mind and an expansive intellect" (xiv). Thus Seymour looks to Chaucer as an alternative to Victorian loss of belief, an impetus for medievalism. Finally, she hopes that readers will not stop short with her "'retold tales,' meant only as an introduction to the original work" (xv).

Chaucer's Stories Simply Told is one of the more comprehensive collections, for it includes the *Prologue* and sixteen tales, one of which combines two; *Chaucer's Tale* is both *Sir Thopas* and a much longer and illustrated *Melibeus*. The other tales are told by the Knight, Man-of-Law, Wife of Bath, Friar, Clerk, Squire, Franklin, Doctor, Pardoner, Prioress, Monk, Nun's Priest, Second Nun, Canon's Yeoman, and Manciple. Seymour favors several didactic tales rarely retold for children. Her version retains all the examples in the *Monk's Tale*: "I will bewail in a sort of tragedy the misfortunes of those once of high degree who have fallen from their place, and may never hope to regain it" (152). This sounds a bit close to a pamphlet of the Religious Tract Society, with which Victorian children's literature began, and the death of a child, the boy saint in the *Prioress's Tale,* is a similar match. Chaucer's *Melibeus* and the *Second Nun's Tale* of Saint Cecilia, like the *Doctor's* story of the martyred Virginia that is almost as unusual, all build up the nobility of women that is a major emphasis in Seymour's collection.

The frontispiece depicts pilgrims, but not in procession; the group of sixteen figures is at "The Halt near 'The Watering of St. Thomas.'" The Prioress holds a prayer book as she sits—with two dogs curled at her feet, an animal appeal for children, as is the boy in the right corner who ties his shoe laces—and the Nun beside her holds a rosary. At the center is an animated Wife, also seated and looking toward a thoughtful Knight. A somewhat abbreviated *Prologue* names all of the pilgrims; most are cogently described, but not the Reeve and Miller (9). Thus Seymour suppressed pilgrims who told tales most "lamentably coarse—with a coarseness that no desire nor effort may attempt to disguise" (xii), just as she deleted lines like the description of the Pardoner's sexuality. Clearly it was unnecessary for her to translate Chaucer's apologia about correctly repeating tales, however churlish. A modified exception is the quarrel of the Friar and Summoner, provoked when the Friar identifies the summoner in his story as "not only a spy, but a thief also" (60). However, the Host "disliked all this quarrelling and ill-feeling and was glad to call upon another of the company who seemed at peace with every one" (70), and Seymour continues with a polite link to the *Clerk's Tale*.

Some judgments of pilgrims have resonances of nineteenth-century society: the Friar's many gifts come from "an undue love of popularity" (5), and the Merchant is obsessive about making money. Chaucer's detail that children run away when they see the stern face of the Summoner becomes a compliment to the audience with the addition "this always augurs no good, for little folk are keen observers and judges of character" (9). The Clerk's salient quality ("And gladly wolde he lerne and gladly teche," I.308) is a model for decorous conduct in the schoolroom: "this rare charm — he was quite as ready to learn from others as he was to inform them concerning subjects which he understood better than they did" (6). There is also a hint of the classroom when the Host asks his hearers to "signify it by holding up a hand" (11; cf. "Hoold up youre hondes, withouten moore speche," I.783). Predictably this woman reteller of the 1880s who praised Chaucer's lifelike portraits of women, pictures the Prioress and Wife without irony or ambiguity. The Prioress "was very cheery and light of heart, kind, too, of disposition; therefore she was not absorbed in thought of self" (4); while the five-times widowed Wife "was not weighed down by sorrow, but was very lively and talkative," and enjoyed her money, clothes, and travel.

E(dith) M. Scanell, an English woman who specialized in genre painting and portraits of children and exhibited frequently between 1880 and 1921, notably in Manchester and Liverpool, provided the sepia illustrations that reinforce the book's feminine emphasis or an interest in children. The *Knight's Tale* is unusual in having three illustrations: the classic Emelye in the garden (18) and the "Espousals of Palamon and Emelye," in which she modestly looks down (34), and a male image "The Rival Cousins — Palamon Rushing from Concealment" and Arcite very much a lamenting lover in the wood (24). The text, in contrast, focuses on the tournament and the scenes of death and funeral. The *Clerk's Tale* has only one illustration. the traditional "Griselda Bereft of her First-born" (80); here she sits on a Gothic chair with a look of horror on her face, while the woodsman with the baby on his arm pulls the curtain to leave.

The most unusual choice of episode to illustrate is for the *Man of Law's Tale*: "King Ella Beholding his Son for the First Time" (48) in a scene where women serve food and drink to male company (48); later collections favor pictures of Constance in her boat. The appeal to an audience

"Arthur's Queen Propounds a Difficult Question" establishes the knight's quest to discover the answer to "What is it that women most desire?" in the *Wife of Bath's Tale*. The caption reminds the audience that the tale is set in the time of King Arthur, and E.M. Scannell involves the child reader by placing two boys at the center of the picture, a device she used several times in Mary Seymour's *Chaucer's Stories Simply Told* (1884).

of boys continues in the picture for the *Wife of Bath's Tale*: two boys sit at
her feet when "Arthur's Queen Propounds a Difficult Question" to an
apprehensive knight (50). Similarly, central to the illustration for the *Pardoner's Tale* is "The Boy Answering the Request of the Inebriates" (128)
in a tavern scene whose other occupant is a somber-looking man. The caption
focuses attention on the temperance issue, so cogent for Victorians.
The lure of sin is perhaps most subtly depicted for the *Friar's Tale:* "The
Summoner Masking His Unjust Demands" (68); a bold and well-dressed
man with staring eyes gestures to an old woman that holds her hands in
supplication, while reclining in the background is the yeoman devil whose
narrow face, mustache, and slouch hat are worthy of Victorian melodrama.
The other two illustrations tell of woman's situation. One, "The Meeting
of Dorigen and Aurelius" in the *Franklin's Tale* (114), is quite peculiar; in
a scene outside the castle walls both are smiling, as she curtsies to him,
while on the side a more faintly drawn couple look on apprehensively. A
favoring of such womanly subservience is signed by the use of the two
figures on the cover, gold stamped on a handsome green cloth with a
brown framing and foliage that ties the cover to the spine, which has the
single figure of Emily in the garden. The remaining illustration, which
has no parallel in later collections, highlights *Chaucer's Tale*: "Prudence
Seeking to Comfort Melibeus" (144); he sits on a chair, his right hand
covering his eyes, while she stands solicitously beside him, one hand on
his shoulder and the other palm up as she lowers her arm. The image well
suits her advice: "I pray you, overcome your own heart, and reflect that
nothing becomes a great lord so well as great mercy and forbearance. Let
men praise you for your gentleness and pity; then shall you have no reason
to repent your dealings with others" (150). This summarizes Seymour's
characterization of Chaucer and advocacy of the ideal of patience
in adversity, usually epitomized by Griselda.

However, there are complex and counter statements. In the *Wife's Tale*
the knight endangers his life because "riding by a river-side, and seeing
a beautiful maiden walking on its banks, he fell suddenly and violently in
love with her," and the king hears of it. One reply to the question about
woman's most desired thing is "perfect freedom to do her own will" (51),
but the answer given to the queen is unconditional—"entire sovereignty
over their husbands or over their lovers" (54). At the center of the tale is
the lesson about what makes a gentleman, and the groom perceives that
the old wife's words are true and "a kind of rebuke to him" (56), again a
model for good behavior. The clearest adjustment for children is an explanation
that "the age and ugliness had only been a disguise lent by the
elf-queen that so the courtesy of one of Arthur's knights should be put to

"Prudence Seeking to Comfort Melibeus" has an unusual subject, since *Chaucer's Tale of Melebeus,* seldom read by adults, appears rarely in collections for children. But Mary Seymour abbreviates it effectively in *Chaucer's Stories Simply Told* (1884), and E.M. Scannell's picture of a compassionate and sympathetic wife supports the tale's appeal to Victorian ideals of domestic relations.

the test" (58), which returns to the opening paragraph and identifies fairy tale.

The severity of the *Prioress's Tale* is quite a contrast; it is strongly anti–Semitic: "the Jewish men of that city were known to be cruel and bad; many a foul deed had been perpetrated in that part." A "'vile Jew'" slays the child (137), and each Jew says "No" to the distraught mother and "passed on coldly, nor felt in his hard heart one spark of pity" (138). The concluding sentence, "The Jews were punished for their wicked deed with the severity it deserved" (140), is disturbingly absolute. By cutting Chaucer's prayerful conclusion and return to Marian devotion Seymour maintains harshness and mitigates Catholic elements, frequently as offensive to Victorian Protestants as were the Jews.

This was compatible with the Evangelical commitment of the publisher T. Nelson, who issued many books with religious content: hymns, descriptions of the Holy Land, and a Living to Purpose Series with biographies of admirable persons and lessons to be learned from "earnest" and "noble" lives. Seymour's *Chaucer's Stories Simply Told* is in a small series Classic Stories Simply Told, which included her *Shakespeare's Stories Simply Told: Tragedies and Historical Plays* (1883) and *Shakespeare's Stories Simply Told: Comedies,* and three books of stories (Old Greek, Old Roman, days of King Arthur) by Charles Henry Hanson. This series affirms a confidence in the uplifting nature of literature that many other retellers of classics promoted.

Francis Storr and Hawes Turner

Concurrent with the previously described women's efforts to make Chaucer available in the schools was the work of Francis Storr (1839–1919) and Hawes Turner, who first published *Canterbury Chimes, or Chaucer Tales Retold for Children* in 1878 and an enlarged edition in 1914 with evaluative prefatory material that marks the development of Chaucer's significance to the study of English. Both were scholars of Trinity College, Cambridge, where Francis Storr the younger was well established through his books about language and translations from French and German. He later translated Sophocles, but he gave further time to children with *Fifty-two Stories of Classic Heroes* (1910), one of several uniformly numbered collections published by Hutchinson. Storr and Turner first proved to their satisfaction that the children they knew in family circles were delighted to hear Chaucer's stories, a corollary to Mrs. Haweis's domestic experience. Their approach is a pragmatic one of making available a medieval author who is inaccessible, even to most adults, in his original language and whose detailed learning is sometimes too sophisticated for beginning readers. Storr and Turner were keenly aware that recently expanded general education meant an opportunity to increase the study of English language and literature but recognized a need for stories of higher quality than were currently available for children. Like Clarke and Haweis, they admire Chaucer as a storyteller and believe that children will understand and be delighted by the tales.

Their approach to translation takes a view more pedagogical than Haweis's initial maternal enthusiasm for little Lionel's brilliance. Storr and Turner begin with the statement that Chaucer is "one of the few great story-tellers of the world, and many of his tales are such as children must delight in" (v).[26] They state that making Chaucer's stories available is the more urgent since "there is so little supremely good literature within the reach of children" (v). This is a salutary reminder of the state of children's literature in the last quarter of the nineteenth century, before the Golden Age of splendid and mass production of books for children. The same judgment sadly still applies to many of today's children's books. Victorians, who drew a less-bold line between books for adults and children, as is evident in the devotion to family reading aloud, in many ways provided greater opportunities for children to learn about literature.

Storr and Turner, unlike Haweis, make no attempt at Middle English; they admit that this language, which often deters adult readers, "to children [would] prove an insurmountable difficulty" (v). Their attitude, more like Seymour's, prevails among other children's versions, even though several still offer sample passages in Middle English. Moreover, "occasional coarseness" (not specified) makes some tales unsuitable. "A translation or paraphrase of selected tales is then the only way of making Chaucer at all accessible to children, and this is the task which we have attempted" (v). Storr and Turner try to preserve as much of the original poetry as is possible in prose translation, even Chaucer's "sunny humour," which can only be faintly kept. Nevertheless, liberties are taken: some paraphrasing as well as translation, addition of occasional modern touches, and free cutting of mythology and astrology. They are confident about their work, which has already "passed muster" with "many a childish audience when told by the fire-side" (vi)—a reminder of the "Children's Hour" immortalized in Longfellow's poem.

Storr and Turner have further expectations; they voice the resounding argument for ongoing learning: "We trust that this version of the 'Canterbury Tales' will lead children who may read it to turn later to the rich original, there to find a splendid amplification indeed, but not a contradiction of their old story-book" (vi). In contrast to much educational theory today that urges current "relevant" stories, Storr and Turner make a case for the ongoing reading of major canonical authors. There is no pretense that children are ready for the full original text, but there is confidence in a positive response to stories of universal appeal; they see a strength in reading literature that is not written expressly for children.[27] Moreover, they have no anxiety that an early encounter with a simplified text, a popular version, dishonors Chaucer.

An appeal of the selected tales is their appropriateness for the intended audience. An introduction tells "How we rode to Canterbury, and who the Pilgrims were," and there are six tales: the *Knight's* for chivalry, the *Man of Law's* for a constant woman and religious devotion, the *Nun's Priest's*, a beast fable always favored for children, the *Squire's* for magic gifts and exotic Oriental lands, the *Franklin's* also with magic but some obvious moral challenge, and the tale of tried youth, *Gamelyn*, given to Chaucer instead of *Sir Thopas*. The edition of 1914 adds the *Clerk's Tale* of *Patient Griselda* and the *Pardoner's Tale* of *The Three Revellers and Death*. Sometimes a gloss adds to translation and paraphrase, as when the *Squire's Tale* finishes with a direct address and a challenge to young readers: "[You will want to hear about the wonderful horse of brass and the brave deeds of Cambuscan, and how Algarsyf wooed and wedded the fair Theodore. Alas, the tale is left half told; who shall end what Chaucer began?]" (139). The Introduction to the *Man of Law's Tale* describes the *fabliaux*: the Miller's is "a vulgar tale, and not a bit like the Knight's, but still it was full of fun"; the Reeve's story was of a Trumpington miller cheated by two Cambridge students and so he paid the Miller back. "The tales were good of their kind, but not such as you would care to hear, so I will leave them out and repeat the tale which I heard from the Lawyer, whose turn came next" (88). At the end is praise for the Man of Law, who "did great honor to the Church of Christ" (108). In comparison, the *Franklin's Tale* offers a kind of sophistication. With a stereotypical assumption of woman's insight, Storr and Turner gloss that Dorigen knows that Aurelius loves her, since a woman can tell even if a man does not declare himself; decorously they delete Aurelius's "mad prayers and vows to the gods in whom he trusted."

The Victorian edition is a solid book, a red cloth cover, with four pilgrims (Knight, Physician, Pardoner, Clerk) stamped in gold. Woodcut illustrations from the Ellesmere manuscript show additional pilgrim portraits, while Hoccleve's portrait of Chaucer is the frontispiece. Storr and Turner argue that these "give a truer idea of the personages of the Prologue than such modern pictures as Stothard's, or even Blake's, and we believe that children will not be offended by the bad drawing, while they will be pleased by the real power shown in these seriously-meant grotesques" (vi). This counterpoints the epigraph of lines from Keats that indicate Romantic enthusiasm for "old piety and glee." The enlarged edition of 1914 adds as a frontispiece, the Hoccleve portrait, a further emphasis upon medieval images.

But the most significant part of this edition for the study of Chaucer for children is the added new preface, which evaluates the development of the study of English by children in schools. The changes that have occurred, through expanded primary education and the publication of juvenile books, are extraordinary:

> The first edition of "Canterbury Chimes" dates back to 1878, and today it would be nearer the truth to say that there is not an English author of preeminence, capable of being brought within the comprehension of children, whose works, either in the form of translation, paraphrase, or abridgment, have not been adapted for school use or reading at home. Children, if they are so minded, or if their pastors or masters ordain, can now peruse the masterpieces of English literature from "Beowulf" to "The Earthly Paradise," from "Gulliver's Travels" to "Waverly" [ix].

These popular books are "in great and steady demand" in the list for London Elementary Schools in the Newbolt Report; children's versions are in several Edwardian series, from rather expensive editions such as Jack's *Stories Told to the Children*, Harrap's *Told Through the Ages*, and Blackie's *Stories Old and New*, to cheap school texts from Nelson, Macmillan, Houghton Mifflin, and others. Opportunities for children to read canonical English authors are diverse—home, school, and Sunday School.

For Storr and Turner the change has been profound and hugely significant:

> The growth of a new kind of literature for boys and girls has followed on a development of English education—hardly less remarkable than that which took place at the Renaissance. "English" now figures in the curriculum of every school in the kingdom, and English literature is gradually vindicating its claim to rank as a serious study to be pursued by all, whatever else they may learn, a study for which neither the Classics nor Modern Languages are any substitute [x].

Again this Chaucer storybook anticipates the aims of the Newbolt Report for children. Such an early introduction to the canon of major English authors and books contributed to creation of a university program. As discussed more fully in chapter 5, an American professor, Katherine Lee Bates of Wellesley, deplored the absence of such juvenile training, without which college students were "barbarians." Finally, it is important to recognize that Edwardians did not see such youthful study of a canon as elitist.[28] Storr and Turner explain that their enlarged edition is cheaper than the original Victorian offering and intended to "serve the needs, not only of the lower forms in Public Schools, but also of the upper forms in Primary Schools, where literature (too often in snippets or of second-rate quality) has always formed part of the curriculum" (x). They recognize that since the publication of their first book, there have been some dozen adaptations of *The Canterbury Tales,* and they identify Margaret C. Mac-Caulay's as the closest translation of Chaucer. The reference to grade levels shows that some flexibility was possible in timing, and a variety of versions meant a choice; there is no longer a question about whether children will read Chaucer, but at what age and which version.

William Calder

The evolving formation of a canon of Chaucer stories simply told for children explains the impetus for a collection that came between the two widely spaced editions of Storr and Turner. William Calder (1869–1945) in *Chaucer's Canterbury Pilgrimage* (1892) distinguished between the "fairly well known" *Prologue* and the "little known Tales and Incidents of the Journey" and was presented "in a fairly popular form to young folks and ordinary readers" in the hope that it would inspire them to read the original. Calder's judgment is that by studying the riches of the *Canterbury Tales,* they will "become rich themselves in their knowledge of beautiful stories, illustrative of high and noble thoughts, and expressed in verse whose melody has never been surpassed." His anxiety is that Chaucer's "masterpiece" will be neglected because of academic appropriation, signed by excessive notes even for the *Prologue,* and a "thought that the verse is antiquated and difficult to read, while the fact is, that after a little practice, the beautiful musical flow of the lines, sweet yet firm and vigorous, constitutes one of the main charms of the poetry." Although he echoes the optimism of Haweis, Calder's explicit concern is that the editorial work of the Chaucer Society and the Early English Text Society, while important and much to be praised, is also dangerous; the risk is that Chaucer's poem will be "regarded as of mere dry philological value, and that his splendid power of characterization and the fascinating interest which, as a story-teller, he is able to command, are being largely lost sight of." In short, the issue is whether Chaucer will be studied primarily for language or as literature, as a popular or an academic author. Calder extends his appeal by quoting lines from Longfellow on the title page and citing his phrase "the Poet of the dawn" along with "the Well of English undefil'd" in an introductory sketch; he also links the *Canterbury Tales* to Evangelical children's literature by dedicating his book to "Right Rev. James Macgregor, Moderator of the General Assembly of the Church of Scotland." Like all retellers, Calder writes to sustain and expand the popular audience, even though he recognizes that an epitome by its nature "must always be more or less unsatisfactory, and the poet's quaintness, his skilful management of minute details—in a word the charming *personnel,* which pervades the poetry all through, must be largely sacrificed."[29] Candidly he admits that an epitome is not the same thing as the original Middle English text but confidently he claims its merit.

What is different about his approach is stated on the title page: "Epitomised by William Calder." To illustrate precisely his efforts, he prints the *Prologue* in Middle English (21–54), with final -*e* marked and the French accent (`) for stress, and a "Paraphrase of the Prologue" in modern English (52–100), with a few notes, more readily used than his final glossary, mostly of Middle English words that he is translating. A comparison of the two prologues shows Calder's high sentiments, and a few descriptions will indicate how he both retains Chaucer's essence and infuses Victorian values into male ideals exemplified in the Knight, Clerk, and Parson.

> Like a true knight, he was reticent as to his achievements ... the soul of honor, the perfection of kindliness and consideration of others, brave in war, prudent in counsel, modest in demeanor, and dignified in speech and action. We one and all of us decided there could be no more honored representative of the glory of England than he, and that he was indeed "a verray perfight gentil knight" [60–61].

As in his biographical sketch, Calder assumes the Chaucer persona to enter the narrative to affirm nationalism and unanimity of judgment. Later, this even leads to an un–Chaucerian use of the personal pronoun: "I felt far more interest in another member of our company, a Clerk rich in all the qualities which render their possessors the leaders of culture in their day ... like all high-minded and generous students, glad to give others benefit of knowledge" (72). For the Parson he has an evangelical sympathy: "what a contrast his life and work presented to those of the self-seeking ecclesiastics of his day, whose main considerations were the most effective way to assert their dignity, and the best means of acquiring wealth and power! ...I felt the greatest respect" (86–88).

Victorian attitudes about female character are clear in two pilgrims. The Prioress's French is "that of the better class of French refugees"; she is sentimental—shown not in an "enthusiastic desire on her part to improve the condition of her fellow-creatures; but ... in the way she pampered some pet dogs"—and has "many little feminine affections," but she is courteous to all, and thus they feel it is an honor to have her in the company (65). Calder's thorough modernizing is for "another member of the fair sex with us," the Wife:

> a very lively lady ... perfectly ready, on all occasions, to exhibit her charms ... comfortably attired with broad hat, well-fitting riding-habit, booted and spurred, she rode along perfectly at her ease, and quite resolved to make the most of her holiday ... five times at church door, each time accompanied by a bashful man ready to acknowledge her sway, and to be bound to her by the blissful bonds of matrimony [81–82].

A generalization that all five husbands were "bashful" is perhaps most revealing of nineteenth-century uneasiness with the "new woman" of independence that Alison anticipates, not least in her attire and flirting; "blissful bonds" is ambiguous.

Calder's concentration on the *General Prologue* sustains school emphasis, but he intended *Chaucer's Canterbury Pilgrimage* to expand knowledge beyond this remarkable galaxy of characters. Thus the epitome of "The Incidents of the Journey" includes a mention of each tale and teller, including material from the links, often fuller than the tale, as in the *Canon's Yeoman's Prologue*, but very abbreviated *Pardoner's* and *Wife's Prologues*, since the two tales are especially strong, quick narratives. Like other Victorian and Edwardian writers, Calder evades the improprieties of the *fabliaux*. The Host, "like a sensible Englishman, who wished to keep things smooth, made a virtue of necessity" and let the Miller tell his tale—reduced to an account of three in their tubs aroused by a "hullabaloo"—but intervenes because "the tale though well worked out and very laughable, is too gross to be reproduced here" (131). In fewer than five pages, Calder also epitomizes the tales of Reeve and Cook, who is assigned *Gamelyn*. Later, he identifies the *Shipman's* as "not one of the great tales," but another satirical *fabliau*, as is the *Merchant's* (207). Bracketing by subject without seeing artistic achievement relegates all to cursory treatment. The Host later intervenes because of the Frere's violent language (158) and loses his temper at the end of the *Pardoner's Tale* (206).

Although Chaucer's showing of human folly "in a manner much more direct and open than is customary nowadays" (6) requires careful selection for young people, the high moral integrity of his character is never an issue:

> He was evidently a man whose heart's delight was in all that is "true, and honest, and lovely, and of good report," and who hated with the full strength of a noble nature whatever is base, and mean, and double-dealing, and oppressive; and the cowardly bully who unworthily uses the circumstances of his position for the purpose of causing unhappiness to others, along with the tools whom he finds mean enough to be willing to play into his hands, have never in all the range of our English literature been subjected to greater castigation, or held up to more deserved opprobrium, than by him [6].

Bullying, the vice singled out for censure, is legion in school stories and juvenile historical novels whose heroes are often champions to defeat the bullies who oppress the community. Calder makes typically nineteenth-century assumptions about the author and deploys them to make moral points. He asserts that little is known of Chaucer's biography but is confident about the poet's attitude to his work as Comptroller of Customs in London: "No doubt his commonplace duties, though conscientiously performed, would be irksome to him; but we know that he heartily enjoyed the good things of this life when he had them, and that he had one great pleasure which never failed him—his delight in books" (8). Again the moral point suits the ideal schoolchild, and it is echoed in a reading of Hoccleve's portrait: "comfortable-looking, with a very kindly if somewhat judicial cast of countenance, and eyes of a dreaming nature, indicating complete absorption on his part in the subject which for the time occupied his thoughts, and much absent-mindedness towards everything else" (11). A miniature of the Hoccleve portrait is part of the capital that begins the "Introductory Sketch."

Calder concludes his account of the genial Chaucer with a paean to the poet who borrowed from others but greatly improved what he found; this enriched his readers, presently marked as much in need of an affirmative and consoling view of the world.

> The longer we read Chaucer, the more we love him; and the reason is that, feeling as he evidently does, genuine pleasure in his work himself, he strives with all his might to add to ours by means of his sparkling liveliness and joyousness, his kindliness, his modesty, his love of nature in all its moods, his devotion to work, his sweet and pure versification, his rich command of apt illustration, his open-air

> directness, his practical good sense, his dignified self-possession, his
> knowledge of the world, his kindly humour, his great dramatic skill,
> his brilliant power of characterization. His rich fancy has done much
> to introduce us to another world of beings, who are ever with us to
> cheer and enrich our lives—friends to whom we can always go for
> amusement and solace, and encouragement, and warning; ... a noble
> galaxy of ideal beings, a rich treasure-house, possessing which no one
> can ever be really poor, or ever quite alone [14].

Portraits are the essence of the great authors in English literature, a
national tradition that began with Chaucer, the first to present divisions
of middle-class society, the ordinary people and life of the streets, not
abstractions or chivalry: "All the members of his group are thoroughly
English in their nature and habits, and our interest in them will ever continue to be fresh and permanent because they are true idealized repre-
sentatives of ordinary human nature such as we find it every day around
us." Calder further explores the tension between Victorian ambition and
uneasiness when he acknowledges that Chaucer presents life "with the joys
and sorrows, the laughter, the tears, and the long periods of colorless exis-
tence which we must all pass through"; his pilgrims can be "discourag-
ing" because they show how many "betrayed their trust," but others
"counted it their highest privilege 'to drawé folk to heven by fairéness'"
(18).

   Just how crucial it is to read Chaucer is affirmed when Calder praises
the two Romantic pictorial representations of the pilgrims—the processional paintings of Stothard and Blake, of which engravings are now very
scarce—but asserts that they "cannot surpass Chaucer's word-painting"
(17). The fold-out frontispiece is a sculpture modeled by Henning of
Stothard, a gray bas relief in a frame of leaves and grapes. Other illustrations are engravings of the Tabard Inn (52 and 102) and of the choir
of Canterbury Cathedral (258). These continue the book's somber appearance, dark blue cloth with minimal gold stamping: a small device of
Chaucer's coat-of-arms in the upper left corner of the cover and the author
and title on the spine. Thus the physical appearance of the book favors
the "ordinary readers" more than the "children" whom Calder identifies
as the audience for his epitome.

   The collection has ten tales, each bearing a descriptive title, in some
completeness: *Knight: Palamon and Arcite the Two Noble Kinsmen, Man of
Law: Story of Constance, Wife of Bath: The Knight and the Fairy, Clerk:
Patient Griselda, Squire: Cambynskan, Franklin: Dorigen and the Sunken
Rocks, Pardoner: The Death Slayers, Prioress: The Martyred Child, Nun's
Priest: Chanticleer and Dame Pertelote,* and *Manciple: Phoebus and the Crow.*

The subtitles, as in later collections, stress the characters or identify fairy tale and beast fable. The *Squire's Tale* is presented as an Eastern adventure, related to Marco Polo and the Great Khan (176), and it includes Spenser's addition. Children's interest in bird and beast stories may explain the unusual presence of the *Manciple's Tale* that also leads well to the treatment of the Parson, whose sermon it is "impossible to outline" (236) and to Chaucer's Prayer and Retraction, rarely included and here offered with some question as to what to think. Although Calder has assumed the Chaucer persona with confidence, he finishes with "Who knows?" (238), another sign of Evangelical belief, here an incompatibility with medieval otherworldliness, which goes beyond the awe inspired by the *Prioress's Tale* (208) or the accessibility of the Monk's definition of tragedy (215).

Calder's dedication to chivalric ideals finds its fullest appraisal in an introduction to the *Knight's Tale*: "This is the grandest of all the tales, and exhibits in the highest degree the gifts for which, as a *raconteur,* Chaucer was especially distinguished—splendid descriptive powers, genial humour, and lifelike portraiture" (106). Some quotation in Middle English is interlaced, as it is in the *Wife's Tale,* which begins when the knight is "disgraced by doing a shameful deed" (152). As always, Griselda is exemplary, "steadfast and true to the last" (173). Of all Chaucer's stories, hers receives treatment in a variety of forms and in collections not exclusively of *The Canterbury Tales.*

Chaucer in Mixed Collections

Collections of Chaucer for children did not, of course, prevent retellings of some of *The Canterbury Tales* in books not exclusively devoted to him, and their greater selectively gives an insight to what was deemed suitable. Like single-author collections, mixed collections favor the *Knight's Tale* and the *Clerk's Tale* to affirm Chaucer as a poet of chivalry and noble womankind. Both are in David Murray Smith's *Tales of Chivalry and Romance* (1869), a collection of exciting adventure and an introduction to the richness of English literature. Smith acknowledges that the idea "to reproduce, in a form appreciable by the young people of the present time, a number of the very best stories with which their elders are familiar" was original to Charles and Mary Lamb's retelling of Shakespeare; but their tales "give only the most meagre outline of the prominent incidents," while he has attempted "to reproduce the whole plot, and all the most prominent characters."[30] The first two of Smith's nine tales are Chaucer's *Palamon and Arcite* and *The Patient Griselda*. Next are two retellings of Shakespeare, followed by two stories from Froissart, and three from *Le Morte d'Arthur*.[31] The name of the publisher—Virtue—signs the volume's purpose. Smith achieved his objective in narratives that are smooth and continuous, and generally close to Chaucer's original detail, but he makes some adjustments. In the *Knight's Tale* Chaucer's opening line "Whilom, as olde stories tellen us" (I.859) becomes "In ancient times, when people still prayed to their Pagan deities—Jupiter, Mars, and Venus—" (1). It may seem that religious explanation replaces literary tradition of storytelling, but Smith is also being economical because he deletes the subsequent prayers of the three young people to these gods, as well as Duke Theseus's "First Moevere" speech. Vivid descriptions of knights in shining armor, lists for the tournament, and the fury of combat dominate the text and three of the six black-and-white engravings: Theseus interrupting the combat of Palamon and Arcite (17), the lists shown as a ruined classical amphitheater (20), and Arcite mounted on a dangerously rearing horse as he "leads his hundred knights through the gate of Mars" (25). But there is also a stress upon mourning, from the first heading that shows the three grieving and pleading queens (1) to the final death scene of Arcite, beside whom kneel his companions while the ladies stand in sorrow (32). Victorian preoccupation with death makes these images cogent. Smith alters Chaucer's concluding prayer, "And God save al this faire compaignye! Amen" (I.3108) to worldly change of fortune and a happy ending in the present world: "and this mournful history, which began with battle and death, ends with peace and melody and all joyfulness" (32).

Similarly, Smith adapts the ambiguous "Lenvoy de Chaucer" for the *Clerk's Tale* to a direct exhortation that embraces both men and women: "her story is still told to teach us, every one in his degree, to bear adversity with constancy and with uncomplaining humility" (68). This follows from several adjustments to mitigate the cruelty of Marquis Walter's testing and the horror of Griselda's apparent callousness in surrendering her children. Chaucer's Clerk asserts that trying a wife unnecessarily and causing fear and suffering is "yvele" (IV.460); Smith softens this to "but whether it was her mild patience that provoked him to tempt her to disobey, or whether it was that he might know how really good she was, I cannot tell" (47). Yet when Griselda agrees to give up their daughter (IV.498–500), her feelings and decorum, correct for a Victorian lady, are defined: "though her heart was wrung with pain, yet she looked up with a countenance that was unmoved. Neither in her speech, nor in her manner did she seem to be in grief" (49). Where Chaucer's text refers to the husband's "wikke usage" and desire publicly to tempt his wife to the limit (IV.785–91), Smith rationalizes Walter's behavior: "Had he not known with certainty that she loved her children most dearly, he would have thought that there was some evil or cruel hardiness in his wife's nature.... But the marquis well knew that, after himself, Griselda loved her children more than all the world." Walter is explained as the kind of person who when he has "taken up a certain purpose will follow it out to the end" (55). Chaucer's seven lines of summary praise of Griselda's virtue (IV.753–59) become a full paragraph about her patience in adversity that concludes "No man can bear himself in humbleness as a woman, or can be half so true" (61). The *Clerk's Tale* is a tablet upon which to write ideals of feminine behavior, the counterpart of male heroism, which explains its popularity, as does its universal message. Smith's adjustment is analogous to the conclusion of the *Clerk's Tale* in Huntington Manuscript 140 that adds the lyric *Truth*. In both, children are the audience, and Chaucer's address to wives becomes a lesson about humility and patience for all humanity, whether in the fifteenth or nineteenth centuries.

Somewhat resembling Smith's *Tales of Chivalry and Romance* is a collection made at about the same time in the United States by a woman writer whose primary objective was to introduce her child readers to the riches of English literature and to provide appealing stories. Romance, not chivalry, is the theme in *Stories from Old English Poetry* (1871), written by Abby Sage Richardson (1837–1900).[32] There are brief biographical introductions for the three principal authors in a collection of sixteen stories that begins with five from Chaucer ('the Father of English poetry,'—think what a title that is to wear for four centuries and a half!" 1–2) and ends with seven from Shakespeare. The others are Renaissance authors: Spenser with the conclusion of the *Squire's Tale* and the *Adventures of Fair Florimel*, both from *The Faerie Queene*; John Lyly's *Campaspe and the Painter*; Robert Greene's *Friar Bacon's Brass Head* and *Margaret, the Fair Maid of Fresingfield*. Shakespeare is the major figure, and Richardson's Preface to the Gentle Reader describes her excitement as an eight-year-old child when she discovered two small volumes of his plays in an old chest in the garret; these greatly expanded her usual reading in a time when there were very few books for young folks. (She owned only the Bible, *Pilgrim's Progress*, and *Arabian Nights' Entertainment*.) She concealed her find and read secretly lest she lose the pleasure of *Macbeth, The Winter's Tale, The Merchant of Venice, Romeo and Juliet*, and *King Lear*. This memory and her later experience of telling the stories to her son inspired the writing of *Stories from Old English Poetry*. The level of reading is high, as with many in the nineteenth century, but the stories are humble when she identifies the romance tradition as a popular one, notably that Shakespeare found inspiration in chapbooks and "old tales and legends which he had heard" (142). The favoring of romance resembles early fiction written for the Religious Tract Society.

Chaucer's inspiration comes more generally from the time in which he lived, "the days of romance, of crusades, and tourneys … plenty of material for stories" (3). Predictably, Richardson is interested not in the pilgrim tellers but in their stories. Indeed she says nothing about a pilgrimage: "Each story is supposed to be related by one of a party of travelers who are journeying together"; only the first is identified as "told by a knight" (4), perhaps to favor appeals of chivalry and aristocracy. Richardson's view of Chaucer the man differs from that of the Victorians in England. She provides an American context by noting that he was "born over one hundred and fifty years before Columbus discovered this continent. It is so long ago that all things about him are uncertain, except that he was a great poet. That will stand, I hope, while the English language lasts" (2). Unlike Haweis and Seymour, Richardson says nothing about the original Middle English verse. However, she shares their belief in the relation of appearance to character ("Chaucer is said to have been very handsome, and I fancy it is true, since his beautiful works must have made him beautiful" 4); this is helpful, since she next quotes a description of him as short and lean that is not very flattering. Most emphasized are Chaucer's success at Edward III's court and his association with John of Gaunt. The latter's significance is that he favored "Wyclyfe, the great preacher, who fought stoutly against the bad and ignorant priests, and tried hard to make the Church better." Chaucer's disgrace at court and flight to Hainault came because he favored the reformer, a praiseworthy religious view: "Wyclfye was a very noble, fearless man, and it is one of the best things we know of Chaucer that he was on his side" (3). Behind this advocacy lies Protestantism, strong in New England. Richardson is not concerned with Chaucer as the presenter of the national character, a partial explanation of her exclusion of the *General Prologue*. In fact, she is generally dismissive:

> His poetry is old-fashioned now—much of it unfit to read. But in many of his verses, especially when he describes nature, we seem to see the daisy or the dewy grass, or smell the odor of new-mown hay in country pastures, and hear the cattle lowing, and feel the fresh air blowing from woods and fields [4].

Here is the Romantic poet of nature, one especially appealing to the predominantly rural United States, so that Richardson's retellings often contain fine descriptions of nature.

The five stories are: *Two Noble Kinsmen* (an allusion to the play now attributed to Shakespeare), *The Pious Constance, The Knight's Dilemma, Patient Griselda,* and *The Story of Candace.* Richardson's method is to simplify and focus on cogent detail to make the stories accessible and a good read. Thus Constance's character is shown in an opening paragraph that explains that her character makes people forget her beauty and call her "Constance the *good*" (20), her religious devotion is signed when she is characterized as "so pious and devoted that she was willing to go if it would make Syria a Christian land" (22), but she does not utter the prayers of Chaucer's Constance. The evil Donegild, instead of identifying Constance as an "elf" come by charms or sorcery (II.755), terms her "a witch" who gave birth to "a horrible, fiend-like creature" (27–28). Richardson specifies that Alla, who has gone to Rome "on a Christian pilgrimage," is "from the North-land" (50–51). Details like these frame the center of interest which is Constance's twice being put in a boat in exile because heathens defame her in resentment of her Christianity, a situation analogous to nineteenth-century tales of missionaries. Instead of Chaucer's prayers and questions about fate as she sails in a rudderless boat (II.438–508), Richardson ensures a swift engagement of young readers with a combination of hardship and excitement:

> Fancy her, tossing about on the wild sea, amid waves and winds, all calm and pale, with her little crucifix, which she always wore round her neck, folded close to her bosom. So she sailed on drifting past many shores, out into the limitless ocean, borne on the billows, seeing the day dawn and the sun set, and never meeting a living creature. All alone on a wide ocean! drifting down into the soft southern seas where the warm winds always blew, then driving up into frozen waters where green, glittering icebergs sailed solemnly past the ship, so near, it seemed as if they would crush the frail bark to atoms [24].

The scene illustrated shows Constance stranded on the English shores: she kneels with bowed head in the prow of a ship into which move armed men (24). Faced with a second voyage she pleads that her innocent son remain for his father's return, but then "through the street she walked, the people following her with tears, she with eyes fixed on heaven and the infant sobbing on her bosom" (29). Such compression is a substitute for Chaucer's unforgettable description of Constance's pale face, prayers to Christ and Mary; spared extreme pathos, the young reader goes quickly to an exciting description of the dangerous longer trip and a straightforward account of reunion and reconciliation.

With a similar focus on the big moment, Richardson's rendering of the *Knight's Tale* reaches its high point in a vivid description of the tourney:

> Now the heralds have cried aloud the charge, and the trumpets and
> clarions have blown, and the drums beat, and the fierce onset begun.
> The lances shiver, swords gleam, the maces ring heavily on steel hel-
> mets. Now this brave knight is unhorsed, and meets his enemy in
> fierce grapple; now one is trampled underfoot; now clouds of dust
> hide all like a thick smoke; here they struggle unfairly and are led to
> the stake, till the affray is over; there one is borne bleeding from the
> field [16].

This reduces significantly Chaucer's account (I.2599–2634), but keeps
the excitement and color of the chivalric engagement and its fierce effects.
Similarly the philosophical consideration, fully expressed in Theseus's
First Mover speech, and the magnificent funeral are rendered as a paragraph of grief that ends when maidens at Arcite's bier cry, "Alas, alas!
Arcite, why didst thou die thus? Hadst thou not gold enough and Emelie?"
(18). The only illustration, untitled, shows the two men in prison, looking through bars at Emelie (7), "fairer than May, and sweeter than the
roses (6) ... yellow hair garlanding her head" (16), an archetypal heroine
of romance, albeit unaware of the male gazes.

In the *Wife's Tale* adjustments aver a theme that physical beauty is
not the only kind, nor is it to be privileged. The knight with a dilemma
is named Sir Ulric, and the old crone he meets is memorably ugly: "so
hideous a hag wrinkled and toothless, and bent with age. One eye was
shut, and in the other was a leer so horrible..." (35). Chaucer's complex
exposition of "gentilesse," secured by many authorities, is replaced by a
scene in which the knight, who sits with his back to his bride, "could but
confess that her voice was passing sweet, and her words full of wit and
sense ... could not help being moved by the beauty of her conversation,
which surpassed the beauty of any woman's face he had ever seen. Under
this spell..." (39) he is content with her as she is. The aura of fairy tale
is thus enhanced, before the now both beautiful and wise bride explains
that the "enchantment" that made her old and ugly could be removed
only when a knight would both marry her and "yield to my will" (40).
This is more forcefully put than the reply given the Queen and verified
by the court ladies: "the thing of all the world that pleaseth women best,
is *to have their own way in all things*" (37). However, the most interesting
modification is that the woman has a beauty of conversation, more compelling than physical beauty. Richardson repeats this shift to women's
intelligence in *The Story of Canace*. Where Chaucer's *Squire's Tale* has a

stanza of apology for lack of rhetorical skill to describe her beauty
(V.34–41), she reports that Canace is "already noted for her learning,"
content with her books, and thus given the ring "so that by its aid she
became the wisest princess in Europe" (59). The retelling's "graceful union"
of Chaucer's incomplete tale and Spenser's conclusion required alterations,
notably deletion of the falcon's sad tale of betrayed love and addition of
a tournament that is the set piece of romance, as in the *Knight's Tale*; here
it leads to a happy double wedding of pairs of brother and sister and a
model of friendship.

Richardson alters *Patient Griselda* more radically, for she substitutes
elements from the ballad and play, popular versions after the Middle Ages.
Thus Walter hums the song of King Cophetua and the Beggar-maid—
an engaging story celebrated in Tennyson's short lyric (1842) and in
Edward Burne-Jones's great painting of 1884—as he sets out to hunt, a
favorite activity evoked with memorable sound effects: "tootle-te-tootle
went the huntsmen's bugles; clumpety-clamp went the horse's hoofs on
the stones, and out into the green forest galloped the royal hunt" (43).
No passage is more obviously aimed at child readers.

In this version Janicula has a son, Laureo, who is studying in Padua,
so that Griselda helps her father at basket weaving. In an extraordinary
elaboration, they sing a "glorious labor-song" with the refrain "O sweet
content!" and a chorus:

> Work apace, apace, apace
> Honest labor bears a lovely face;
> Then, hey nonny, nonny! hey nonny, nonny! [44–45]

Richardson thus advances an ideal of the American work ethic. To mark
her status Griselda "still clad in her russet gown" rides to the palace gates
to marry the Duke and returns home in the same dress after years of
"cruel" treatment caused by the "demon of distrust" and "demon of sus-
picion." As in the ballad, the birth of twins instead of a daughter and then
a son speeds the narrative. More telling is the treatment of Griselda as
an obedient wife and an intensely emotional mother. Devotedly she cares
for her babies herself and initially believes that Walter has sent Furio to
make her engage a proper nurse. When she learns that he has ordered the
children removed because his people

> murmur that an heir of base origin shall grow up to rule over them.
> ...the sorrow of Griselda would have melted the tough flint to tears.
> She prayed with moving words, she shed such flood of tears, she gave
> such piteous cries of agony, that Furio, tearing the children away with

> a strong effort, ran from the room with the screaming infants, his own
> face drenched with weeping [51–52].

This dramatic scene intensifies the wonder of Griselda's subsequently
meeting Walter without reproach. After twelve years of marriage Walter
says that he would wed again, but he brings the two children home for a
happy ending. Griselda's swoon lasts for some time, and when she revives,
Richardson makes a final observation about female beauty:

> radiant with happiness, all the beauty of her girlhood seemed to come
> back to her face. Nay, a greater beauty than that of girlhood; for soft-
> ened by heavenly patience, her face was as sweet as an angel's…. And
> to all ages will her story be known, and in all poetry will she be
> enshrined as the sweet image of wifely patience, the incomparable
> Griselda [56].

Religious allegory has no place in this version where class, the work ethic,
wifely obedience, and motherly love make Griselda a model to explore
women's situation.

A similar adaptation was made by Ascott R. Hope, the pseudonym
for A. R. Hope-Moncrieff (1846–1927), a journalist with many interests
who wrote prolifically. *Patient Griselda* is one of nine titles in *Stories of
Old Renown* (1883); most interestingly, it was chosen specifically for the
child reader. The first edition is elegant Victorian, but subsequently Gresham printed it in an inexpensive series of collections of folk and historical tales and customs.[33] Half of the stories, with texts unchanged, are also
in Hope-Moncrieff's large collection *Romance and Legend of Chivalry*
(1883) for adults, which was in the Gresham Publishing Company's series
Myth and Legend in Literature and Art that spanned many cultures and
with additional volumes after World War I. This extravagant Edwardian
book, green cloth covered with highly decorative stamping in gold,
included a "History of Romance" and sixteen romances (Arthurian,
Charlemagne, Spanish, and noncycle); it is also a repository of chivalric
images, eight plates in color of paintings by famous artists and twenty-
seven monochrome plates. Although the critical survey might have limited interest for young readers, the stories and pictures are typical children's
literature—and echo the mixed medieval audience for romance. *Stories of
Old Renown* features tales of challenged youth and alters the strongly
male interest of *Romance and Legend of Chivalry* by adding stories that
praise women. *Patient Griselda* is the fourth story, after *Guy of Warwick*,
whose adventures conclude as a pious hermit. But Guy dies moments after
his wife recognizes him, an end similar to that of *Geneviève of Brabant*

who dies soon after being reunited with her husband. This lady is falsely accused by a doubting husband and banished to the forest with her son.

In such company *Patient Griselda,* which is divided into three chapters, may be read as a cheering story, since she lived for "many years in prosperity with her husband and children" (115). This version announces the evils of male authority in the opening line: "In the old times, when men played the master harshly and poor women and children had often much to bear from them, there lived in Italy a great lord named Walter, Marquis of Saluces" (94). Chapter two is titled "The Cruel Trials of Griselda," and Walter's decision to try her comes to him as "a mad thought" (102). Reassured by Griselda's humility, he "was full of joy and love for his wife. None the less he persisted in carrying out his harsh purpose" (103). Walter, "cruel-seeming" (104), "cast down his eyes for shame" (106), and "marvelled more and more at this steadfast patience of his wife ... at times cut to the heart by her gentle resignation" (107), yet persisted with the prospect of another marriage before finally declaring, "I have made thee endure more that ever woman endured, and never woman has proved herself so noble through all" (114). Unlike many other retellings, this one includes the religious interpretation of the original to declare and universalize the moral:

> The memory of her constancy has been handed down from age to age as a lesson to us all how to bear adversity, for if a woman could be so patient towards a mortal man, should we not receive humbly all that God sends us? Great, truly, is the love and patience of woman, but when was woman ever so sorely tried as this Griselda! [116]

Thus Ascott R. Hope both exhorts children to Christian resignation and admiration for humble endurance and at the same time reassures them that such testing is not part of contemporary Britain. This sophisticated handling is reinforced by the illustrations of Gordon Browne (1858–1932), one of the greatest illustrators of the time, skilled and astonishingly productive. His drawing is dynamic and yet painstakingly careful. Among the most intriguing images are the headings of chapters in *Stories of Old Renown,* and for *Patient Griselda* they are especially strong commentary. The first is one of sheer excitement: a young man pulling back on the reins of a rearing horse (94), while the last shows a somewhat stiff marquis with head raised and arm extended in declaiming gesture (109). However, chapter two presents a literally two-faced Walter; he bows slightly as he holds a mask before his face, while a modest Griselda looks down (101) in a recapitulation of an earlier stern Walter in a half-page drawing (106). Four separate images of Griselda reinforce her story: as a shepherdess with her

THE CRUEL TRIALS OF GRISELDA.

"The Cruel Trials of Griselda" are softened by Gordon Browne's heading for *Clerk's Tale* in Ascott R. Hope (i.e., A.R. Hope-Moncrieff), *Stories of Old Renown* (1883). Walter's mask alerts the reader to pretense and reassures that there will be a happy ending.

crook standing in a wild landscape (97), pensively kneeling before a crucifix in a chapel (108), standing sadly beside a huge partially shown column (112), and the end piece, lying dead (116). The single full-page illustration is an archetypal "Griselda is deprived of her child" (102); the departing male holds a young child in his arms, while she stands behind in sadness, her arm lifted to a high window sill (102). As in a chapbook, these nine pictures illustrate the text at almost every opening.

Indeed chapbooks and ballads, two forms of popular literature for several centuries, contributed to widespread interest in Griselda's story and sometimes displaced Chaucer's *Clerk's Tale* as Victorian adaptations drew upon a complex tradition that also included a Renaissance play. Four versions exemplify the connections. One early to recognize a potential in retold classics for children was Sir Henry Cole (1808–82), an energetic and distinguished Victorian and a patron of the arts, who, as "Felix Summerley," deliberately set out to challenge the dominance of the American Samuel F. Goodrich (1793–1860), whose "Peter Parley" books, purveyors of facts, were designed to increase understanding with little concern for the "fancy, imagination, sympathies, affections" that were served by "tales sung or said from time immemorial."[34] As the father of numerous children, Cole began with a pragmatic wish to give children something less limited and relentlessly didactic, and he stated this clearly in the prospectus for the exquisite books originally published by Joseph Cundall in 1843–44 at great expense—prime examples of Victorian extravagant bookmaking. A decade after Clarke's first retellings of Chaucer, the first stories of "anti–Peter Parleyism" to redress the balance were fairy tales—always a center of controversy about what is "suitable" for children—the form often urged in Chaucer stories for children. Cole had the position to challenge Goodrich; his career as a civil servant included drawing upon his work at the newly institutionalized Public Records Office to write a series of handbooks about major public buildings in London and being a force for the creation of the Great Exhibition of 1851—he was a friend of the Prince Consort. Cole became the first director of the South Kensington Museum (Victoria and Albert) and included among his literary friends Thomas Love Peacock and John Stuart Mill. Cole also produced the first English Christmas card. His *The Home Treasury* was followed by *Gammer Gurton's Famous Histories*, expanded as *Old Story Books of England*, edited by "Ambrose Merton," that is, William Thoms (1803–85), a scholar and antiquarian who served as deputy librarian at the House of Lords, founded *Notes & Queries*, and is usually credited with inventing the term "folklore." Thoms's special devotion to romances and chapbooks partially explains the inclusion of *Patient Grissel*, which is the eighteenth-century chapbook printed at Aldermary Church Yard, a factory source for some of the most successful and elegant examples of this popular literature directed at the newly literate adult audience but also appealing to curious collectors like Samuel Pepys. John Newbery's decision to produce chapbooks specifically designed and marketed for children—with gender-determined gifts of a ball and a pincushion—came from his knowledge that children were reading the chapbooks he printed for adults, so that the chapbook is a primary example of the easy flow between adult and child audience.[35] An analogous recognition of gender is indicated by Thoms's addition of chapbook favorites that feature women to balance genders, at least nominally, as part of the midcentury development of books designed for boys and girls.

This is obvious in the choice of *Patient Grissel,* "a pattern for all women." Albeit less worrying than Haweis's illustration, John Franklin's "Grissel Consents to Give up Her Child," is severe and not reassuring for a child: a stern messenger stands with his left hand outstretched and his right grasping the hilt of his sword; a seated Grissel looks up sadly with pleading eyes, while her arms encircle the toddler daughter who kneels on her mother's lap with arms pressed against her bosom.[36] The image was not used in a subsequent simplified rendering, in much larger type, of six of the Ambrose Merton stories as *Nursery Stories and Pictures for the Young* published in 1878. *Patient Grissel* is here with four traditional English heroes *Guy, Earl of Warwick; Sir Bevis of Southampton; Tom Hickathrift, the Conqueror; King Hal and the Cobbler* (a ballad in verse), and *Peter the Goatherd* (a more modern story of Sittendorf that includes travel back in time to Frederick Barbarossa). Nevertheless, the cover features boys, images of military figures—guardsmen and a sailor—and a flag and lion, emblems of Empire, reiterated in a small flower device of rose and thistle beside the title.[37]

Parallel to the chapbook tradition is one of ballads, dating back to a text first printed before 1596 in Thomas Deloney's *Garland of Good Will. Old English Ballads* (1888) shows explicit continuity; John Franklin's engraving of the messenger taking the child accompanies the ballad (272), and a headnote refers to "Chaucer, who (in his 'Clerk of Oxenford's Tale') first made known the tale to English readers."[38] "Patient Grissel" is number twenty-eight in a collection of forty-five. The fourteen-line stanzas quickly tell the story, of which the essence is the same. But there are differences, some already noted in Richardson's retelling. The Marquess is first attracted to "a proper maiden, as she did sit a-spinning" because "She sang most sweetly, with pleasant voice melodiously, / Which set the lord's heart on fire" (269). Most crucial is the explanation of Walter's cruelty; the tests are a response to the snobbish taunts of his people:

> Against his faithful wife,
> Whom most dearly, tenderly, and entirely
> He loved as his life;
> Minding in secret to prove her patient heart,
> Thereby her foes to disgrace;
> Thinking to play a hard discourteous part,
> That men might pity her case,— [272]

At the final feast he restores their children, chides the members of the court who envied her, and lauds "patient Grissel, my most constant wife" (278). Here the daughter and son are twins and taken away together as babes; twins increase folkloric interest—albeit the illustration becomes inaccurate—and reduce the stress of two abandonments. A further softening is the mother's parting: "She often wishes, with many sorrowful kisses, / That she might help their harms" (272). The ballad is thus a populist rendering in which the marquess never doubts Griselda and tests her only to teach his people a lesson about virtues of patience and constancy. Brevity and lack of ambiguity are more reassuring for children, but Griselda's story did not please all.

Grace Greenwood, pseudonym for Sara Jane Clark / Mrs. S.J. Lippincott (1823–1904) was an American whose response to Merrie England was ironic and whose typical treatment of traditional stories was to question conventional attitudes. She was one of the first women in the United States to become a regular journalist and frequently expressed feminist sentiments. This is the context of her rendering of "Patient Griselda" in *Stories from Famous Ballads for Children* (1859), fourteen prose retellings of ballads and four full-page illustrations by Billings.[39] "Patient Griselda" is the first, and the subject of the frontispiece. Billings shows a demure maiden seated at her distaff outside the cottage and perceived by the Marquis of Salusa who has ridden up on his white horse. But Greenwood's rendering subverts both image and story. Griselda begins as a quite independent young woman, perhaps because Greenwood stresses her mother's role to abate the male dominance of father and then husband. This Griselda "was very much surprised, but not overcome" (3) that a fine court figure entered her "homely bower"; when almost immediately, over brown bread and milk, he proposes marriage, her response is to state her peasant origins and conclude, "Surely thou dost jest" (4). The marquis's accompanying "gay young knights" offer congratulations, "but they laughed behind her back at her rustic air and russet gown—the rogues!" (5). At court the proud and aristocratic family's condescension is matched by Greenwood's ridicule of their tracing a lineage to their own separate Eden (8). The prospective second bride is a proud, haughty, crafty schemer who had hoped to be the first wife. Griselda's enlarged family also includes a brother, who accompanies her when she is recalled to the palace after fifteen years as exiled wife; his spirits offset her modest patience: "with a fiery glow in his swarthy cheeks, and an angry flash in his eyes; for he loved his fair sister, and fiercely resented her wrongs" (16). The objections of an American to European snobbery and aristocracy partially explain such additions, for Greenwood allows herself to ridicule "more than one great lord, with an immense pedigree, and a brilliant string of titles streaming after his name, like the tail of a comet" (18). Her interpolations must have given pause to the wealthy Americans traveling to Europe in pursuit of culture and aristocratic connections.

Nevertheless, Greenwood is more feminist than republican. She objects vigorously to the essential Griselda story, the testing and proof of a

> wife's patience and constant love. This plan has been greatly admired and commended, especially by poets; but I cannot say that I approve of it at all. From beginning to end I think it was most unkind and ungenerous. I must confess, too, that I cannot altogether admire Griselda's wonderful "patience." In my opinion she had altogether too much of a good thing [10].

The reference to "poets" and Greenwood's spelling "Griselda" indicate that she has Chaucer in mind. That there should be universal approbation of the docile female infuriates her, yet she adds details of sympathetic characterization. In a moment of spirit before Griselda calms herself and surrenders the twins, she "burst into tears and sobs, and wrung her hands wildly" (11), and she is so sad that she no longer sings when she returns to her parents' house. Griselda's mother offers incisive advice, urging her not to return because "Thou owest that wicked man no duty, now that he has put thee away" (16). Greenwood creates a family drama in which the peasants have sensible understanding, speak daring words, and are not intimidated by royalty; these details intensify the extremism of Griselda's reactions and behavior, since the story demands meek submission. Members of the court think, weep, declare her "an angel, and no mortal woman!" (18), and rejoice in the happy reunion; but Greenwood's final railing is only slightly mitigated by a wry self-analysis:

> Now, if I had been Griselda, I am almost sure I would have drawn back at this, and said, "Pardon, my lord marquis, but this must not be. Thou didst never truly love me, if, having no reason to doubt my constant affection, thou couldst, for a mere whim, so cruelly rend my heart, and so severely try my patience, through these long years. I cannot be again thy wife. Give me my children, and let us part in peace."
>   But then I should have spoiled more than one quaint old ballad and charming romance, and robbed the husbands of many generations of a valuable example to hold up before their wives. So, on the whole, I suppose it is as well that I was not in "Patient Griselda's" place [20].

One characteristic of medievalism is the counter argument of those who were depressed or annoyed by it. As Théophile Gautier (1811–72) exclaimed, "Again the middle ages, always the middle ages! Who will deliver me from the middle ages that are not medieval? The middle ages of cardboard and terra cotta—medieval in nothing but name."[40] Many thus respond to the Victorian Gothic Revival in its ample manifestations, but as the variety of children's literature that redeploys medieval stories like *The Canterbury Tales* shows, reasons for celebrating the Middle Ages were quite varied, and often admirable. For example, Gautier was seeking the absolute in art, and medievalism led to some of the finest examples of Victorian historical painting and to the subsequent creation of similar images, like George Frederick Watts's *The Happy Warrior* (1884?), acclaimed as early Symbolist and Art Nouveau. Retellings of Chaucer had a part in this process, and for Edwardians it began in the nursery.

✣ 3 ✣

Chaucer in the Nursery

That Chaucer belonged in the world of children's literature is concretely demonstrated by his portrait image in the Nursery of Cardiff Castle, built by the third Marquess of Bute, who used part of his great fortune, made from the Cornish mines, to create a medieval space. His medievalism was unusually intense, even by Victorian standards, for he converted to Roman Catholicism in 1868, three years before he engaged the architect William Burgess to turn his vision into building. Chaucer is present in both the adult and child worlds of the castle. The octagonal Beauchamp Tower (fifteenth century and 1877–84) with its splendid wooden flèche was chosen for a favorite family space, and the "Chaucer Room" has a statue of the poet over the fireplace as well as wall decorations of birds and "Good Women"—made very popular through the efforts of John Ruskin, William Morris, and Edward-Burne Jones. Over the doorway of the Nursery (c.1879) are two tile medallion portraits; one is Aesop, and the other is Chaucer, both authors appropriated for children. The walls are tiled, the lower portion in a Morris-like decoration of green squares with gold center. Above this, around the room, is a tile frieze with characters (and sometimes a hint of story) from fairy tales and a few literary classics popular for children. The third Marquess of Bute was very much a man of wealth who could indulge his medieval interests, but many children had books of Chaucer to read.

Stead's Books for the Bairns Series

The small collection that probably best demonstrates Chaucer's broadest appeal to Edwardians is the most modestly produced, *Stories*

78

from Chaucer, Being the Canterbury Tales in Simple Language for Children (1903). It was number 83 in the Books for the Bairns Series, published with rose-colored paper wrappers, that sold for one penny and carried advertisements inside. With these little books the editor W.T. Stead (1849–1912) made simplified versions of great literature available to the thousands of poor children who were not well-educated and in need of something easy to read and of an alternative to the didactic offerings of the Religious Tract Society and the Sunday School Union. Such cheap "paperbacks" paralleled chapbooks and penny dreadfuls but strove for higher quality and a wider range of interest.

The original series, published from March 1896 to June 1920, numbered 288.[1] Each item has sixty pages and measures four-and-a-half by seven inches. Stead tried to put a picture on every page and usually printed the text (except plays) in double columns. The range of titles is remarkable: many fairy tales, both familiar and less well known (from Japan, Persia, India, Australia, as well as European, and some as plays), nursery stories (both traditional and original), stories for Christmas, *A Story-Book of Country Scenes.* There were also many books of history, such as *Favourite Stories from English History* (spanning from the Conversion of the English to the siege at Lucknow), but also to explain current events, notably in 1902 *The Crowning of the King in Westminster Abbey: Why and How It Is Done* and the imaginative *"I Wish I Were the King," or Harry's Dream,* giving detailed explanations and pictures for the upcoming coronation of King Edward VII. Similarly, World War I was marked; for example, in 1914 *Stories of Christmas Among Our Allies* and in 1916 *Stories of the Great War.* Most significantly, there are versions of the major works of English literature, and Chaucer is one of the earlier issued.

W.T. Stead, an Englishman despite his choice of a Scottish name for his series, was a journalist, pacifist, and social reformer who became "the foremost publisher of paperbacks in the Victorian age." A man who preached a Christian way of life, Stead had as his objective—several times stated in forewords to books in the series—to overcome the separation of rich and poor by making books available to all classes. The price of one penny per book made for success; within a year, sales reached 150,000 a month. Stead sailed on the *Titanic* and was one of the many who died when the ship sank, but his legacy was a great and long-lasting one. Just as Stead recognized that his own professional success was possible because he had books—specifically the *Dick's Penny Shakespeare*—when very young, so Allen Lane, who enthusiastically read Books for the Bairns as a child, got from them the idea for the Puffin Series, and the first paperback children's books were published in 1940 by Penguin Books. Children's literature would be immeasurably poorer without the ideals and energy of W.T. Stead.

Stories from Chaucer, illustrated by Edith Ewen, has at least one black-and-white picture at each opening, so that the effect is reminiscent of chapbooks, seventeenth- and eighteenth-century precursors of Victorian paperbacks for children that continued into the nineteenth century. The cover has a half-page picture of ladies (in henans) who are dressing Griselda. The Preface is nostalgic about the fourteenth century and optimistic about its social ease: "Never again, I fear, will Merrie England see the friendly social gathering of knight and squire, of stately dame and low-born cook ... spending the evening together in listening to such tales as these." Thus in spite of their "quaint and curious language" Chaucer's short stories are familiar and appealing and the primary interest. Pilgrimage is simply defined as a medieval custom and portraits are brief. Stead identified fairy tales as children's favorite reading, and each of the eight stories begins, "Once upon a time" or "There was once." The choice of tales reflects the combination of romance and religion that is characteristic in medieval manuscripts and in nineteenth-century views of chivalry, as in the Victorian favoring of Galahad among the Knights of the Round Table, both in literature and painting.

Edith Ewen illustrated only two Books for the Bairns, #93 *Stories from Chaucer* and #92 *Tales from Shakespeare*. The *Knight's Tale* has factotum images, pictures such as decorated *Guy of Warwick* chapbooks: Emily in the palace garden, Arcite's Dream (in bed with a messenger), the Death of Arcite (a small scene of combat and grieving), and young lovers Emily and Palamon. Making adjustments to the *Wife of Bath's Tale* is always more complex. Here the action begins: "As she was very pretty, the knight stole a kiss from her, and King Arthur, being the soul of chivalry and honor, punished all such offenses with death" (17); in the illustration "The Knight's Offense" a lady shrinks from a menacing knight who has got off his horse. But there is a lighter touch in "What the knight saw in the wood"—fairy maids in a circle, and a half-page roundel of the knight and hag. There is also an Edwardian delineation of gender: "Women liked to have the upper hand in their own homes, both over their husbands and the rest of their households" (19–20). Nevertheless, in an adjusted *Franklin's Tale* Dorigen "Meekly consented to be his [Aurelius's] wife, telling him how her husband had agreed to give her up rather than let her break her word" (42). The implication is that divorce is preferable to adultery. Most striking are the facing illustrations: "Magician stretched out his wand over the sea" and "Dorigen wept and bemoaned herself."

As previously noted, the *Clerk's Tale* made the cover; this picture is repeated, with scenes of Griselda carrying water on her head, and with her daughter, here a very bright baby. This interest in children recurs in another illustration, the "Arrival of the Strangers," that has both a girl and young boy. Magical elements in the *Squire's Tale* tie it to fairy tale. "Princess Canacee and the falcon" sit in the wood, she looking like Snow White; a later half-figure holds the bird, and there is a bold "Falcon and Hawk."

The final three stories are all religious. The *Man of Law's Tale*, as with Haweis, heightens the importance of devotion. At Constance's trial, where she is shown kneeling, a voice states, "Thou has maligned a daughter of the Holy Church, and how can heaven be silent?" (46). The first picture shows a lady with her attendants; then she is "Adrift on the Ocean," before a last reassuring family group when "The King Finds His lost Wife and Son." The *Pardoner's Tale* tells only of the three rioters, without the elements of sermon except for a direct address to the audience: "No doubt you are feeling very sorry for the poor fellow who was being so treacherously plotted against by his companions, but he himself deserved no pity..." (54); the moral is clear, "The love of money is the root of all evil." The *Priest's Tale* has several pictures of the farmyard and the cock; here the narrative is swift, with little detail about the dreams but some additions to the moral: the widow put up stone walls, and the Cock lived happily with his seven wives, "amusing the little chicken son many a wet afternoon, with the wonderful story of his escape from the fox" (60). This tidy plea for the delight of Chaucer's engaging stories seeks empathy from the bairns who read the books and shows a model for parental storytelling.

Kelman in Jack's Stories Told to the Children Series

Much more up-market than the Books for the Bairns Series were T.C. and E.C. Jack's nursery books in the Stories Told to the Children Series, which sold for one shilling and six pence, or in a cheaper version for one shilling. The "dainty volumes" measure four-and-a-quarter by five-and-three-quarter inches, little books for little hands as Beatrix Potter insisted. Each has eight original colored illustrations. The most elegant form was cloth with one of the pictures pasted on the cover, framed in gilt stamping, including an Art Nouveau design derived from Charles Rennie Mackintosh, a sign of the role of Scotland in British publishing and education. The one-shilling version had ornamental boards, black-stamped lettering and a simpler picture or decorative device.

The series includes one of the earliest, simplest, and most often reprinted Chaucer volumes. Written by Janet Harvey Kelman with pictures by W. Heath Robinson, *Stories from Chaucer* was published in February 1906. Thus it was one of the first books in the series, listed as #3 and preceded only by *Robin Hood* and *King Arthur*. This shows both a recognition of Chaucer's place in literary history and that English identity is a primary criteria for the series. Stories Told to the Children, along with two uniform but shorter series—Stories from History and The Children's Heroes—are a testimony to an Edwardian ideal of giving children the great stories of Western civilization—biblical, classical, medieval, and modern.[2] To these two shorter series, Kelman contributed, respectively, *Stories from the Crusades* (1907) and *The Story of Chalmers of New Guinea* (1905), both about religious dedication and evangelization beyond Britain. More remarkable is that Kelman, who lived in Edinburgh, also exhibited (1900) with the Royal Scottish Academy. Like Beatrix Potter, she drew skillfully from nature; her pictures adorn several nonstory books for Jack's Shown to the Children Series—*Butterflies* (1906), *Flowers* (1906), *Trees* (1908), and *The Sea-Shore* (1908). The variety demonstrates how publishers assigned several titles to the same person.

W. Heath Robinson (1872–1944) was the youngest of the "Three Musketeer" artist brothers and a successful illustrator of children's books for several publishers, notably Hodder and Stoughton, and Constable. Early in his career he showed the influence of Art Nouveau and produced illustrations for books like *The Arabian Nights Entertainment* (1899), with Helen Stratton, *Hans Andersen's Fairy Tales* (1913), and *A Midsummer Night's Dream* (1914) as well as popular original fantasies *The Adventures of Uncle Lubin* (1902) and *Bill the Minder* (1912). *Stories from Chaucer* belongs to this period. Robinson's initial delight in the wonderful shapes in nature and in human eccentricities gave way to a fascination with machinery, and he became a successful comic artist who ridiculed its triumph in an age of science.

Kelman's brief introductory note identifies Chaucer as "a grave and gentle man," who rode with a company of pilgrims and wrote down the stories "in quaint old English words," the meanings of which would not be clear even with effort. She makes no attempt to convey the whole; there are no prologues or links. Kelman simply presents "four of the most beautiful of all those stories that Chaucer tells us big people loved to hear, when the world was young." This time was "Very long ago, when children still walked softly through the Greenwood to surprise the fairies" (vii). As in Stead's Books for the Bairns, opening sentences sustain the linking of Chaucer to fairy tales; two stories begin "Once upon a time," and one starts "Very long ago there lived." The four tales are "Dorigen, the story by the Man of Land"; "Emelia, the story by the Man of Might"; "Griselda, the story by the Man of Books"; "Constance, the story by the Man of Law." The names of characters give prominence to women and put the story before the teller, but there is a curious balance between woman as subject and man as definer. Kelman's renderings of the stories enhance traditional male expectations about the virtuous behavior of women and fulfill Dickens's view of the spirit of chivalry with its love of woman that inspired truth and devotion. Her identification of the Knight as the "Man of Might" points to the strength of knighthood, which passages in other stories develop.

Griselda, pictured on the cover and repeated inside (52), is an icon of the volume's values. The young woman recalls a Pre-Raphaelite figure even in the muted colors of her blue gown amid a background of soft greens, creamy rose, and gray that show the influence of Art Nouveau.[3] While her sheep graze at the right side, she sits on a rock and looks toward a knight who is mounted on his white horse. The caption signs her humility: "She rose to curtsy to him." Griselda's story is one of admiration for Walter, a worthy knight. This picture illustrates one of the earliest descriptions in which Griselda looks toward the white towers of the castle: "She thought that their master was the best and greatest man in the world. She knew that he was kind also, and courteous" (52). Walter is a man pleased by "the free life of the forest and the hunt," but he accepts his responsibility to wed. A second illustration, in the vibrant red, green, blue of Pre-Raphaelite painting, shows Griselda's devotion. Again she is seated, now holding a baby, but she still gazes upward at her husband, "Lord Walter came into the room" (61). Kelman somewhat mitigates the evil of the Marquis's doubts and testing of his wife's obedience with an indication that his resolve is weakening. When he orders their son taken, "[H]e could not look at his wife lest he should not have the heart to do as he wished" (65). The final scene of reunion reassures with a heightening of Griselda's embracing of her children; however, wifely devotion still dominates: "Then she looked at Lord Walter, and said, Death cannot harm me now, since thou lovest me still'" (72), before she speaks to the children. The concluding paragraph notes "the gay voices of happy children as they played with, and cared for, the old grandfather whom their mother loved so dearly," but the last sentence describes how Griselda constantly meets the eyes of Walter to be reassured "again and yet again that he trusted her utterly" (73). The gaze of lovers is central to this story's imagery. Indeed Kelman's retellings gain clarity through her use of recurrent images, a correlation of her visual art.

"She Rose to Curtsy to Him" focuses on Griselda as a sherpherdess who sees the marquis on his white horse. The figures are widely separated to sign both social difference and romantic longing in the *Clerk's Tale*. This is one of W. Heath Robinson's eight illustrations for Janet Kelman's *Stories from Chaucer Told to the Children* (1906), a "nursery book" originally intended for very young readers, but whose stories and illustrations were reprinted in several encyclopedias.

The story's ideal is of female devotion to the knight husband, albeit he is not always worthy, but it begins in the opening account of the dutiful daughter's care for her helpless father Janicola and regret that she cannot make his life easier. "Griselda was not unhappy though her life was hard, because she was so glad that she could serve her father and show her love to him, forgetting about herself and her own wishes" (52). This teaches a child obedience and obligation to a parent. Griselda uses religious language to agree to Walter's terms: "Lord, I am not worthy of this honor" (58), that echoes the penitent's prayer before receiving the Eucharist ("Lord I am not worthy to receive you, but only say the word and I shall be healed") and Mary's acceptance in the "Magnificat."

Similarly, the story of Dorigen stresses wifely dependence. The frontispiece shows a solitary lady looking out to sea but recognizing that none of the ships brings back Arviragus, her devoted lover and husband, who is also an ambitious knight. After a year at home, he grew restless: "He felt that no true knight had a right to live on quietly at home, with nothing to do except to order his castle and to hunt. So he sailed away to England that he might win honor and renown in the wars there" (3). Later Aurelius recognizes Arviragus as "a worthy knight" and "his great honor." Kelman's most striking revision is of Aurelius's desire; he asks Dorigen for the beautiful jewel that she wears on her breast. The jewel is an image for a woman's chastity, later described as rare, given at birth, and dazzling. Dorigen's mother explained the jewel's worth and its power to give her joy but also warned that its loss would destroy her beauty and cause her to be isolated (8). The hardness of the jewel links it to the rocks, "grisly and black and fearsome as before," whose restoration in the final scene Dorigen and Arviragus see as the sunlight strikes her jewel that "shone more brightly than of old" (25). The chivalry of Aurelius's conversion to nobility balances the Magician's amazing powers.

Emelia's story offers greatest opportunity for chivalry, and Robinson's illustrations point to this. In the first a young woman in a garden of red roses looks away toward a distant white tower. Her abundant auburn hair and long neck, emphasized by a necklace, and her green shawl suggest the "stunners" of Dante Gabriel Rossetti, albeit with softer colors. Although this child's version eliminates the proud virginity of Chaucer's heroine, emotions, even passion, dominate this retelling of the *Knight's Tale*. Here the tournament is reduced to a single page, and the action to a line: "Through the bright sunshine they fought, advancing here, and beaten back there, till at last Palamon was hurled from his horse and taken prisoner" (46). Interest lies not in the deeds of chivalry but in the response to it: "In the eagerness of the fight Emelia had begun to like the warriors who fought for her, and her liking grew ever stronger as they showed their worth. When Arcite rode towards her with glowing face she was proud of him, and leant forward to welcome him gladly" (47). This is stronger than the "friendly eye" cast by Chaucer's Emily, a response explained as women's following Fortune (I.2679–82). That response comes later in the child's version, which insists upon a proper period of mourning; "After two years Theseus sent one day for Palamon and Emelia" (48). He still wears the black of mourning for Arcite, but she, having ceased to mourn, is in white, once again "Emelia the Radiant." After she weds Palamon, Emelia tells how "she had looked at the prison in the morning mist, and murmured to herself the names of the captive princes, 'Palamon and Arcite, Palamon and Arcite'" (49). Only in the final paragraph does Palamon, after "many years of joyous life had passed over their home," tell Emelia that he had first seen her on that morning. Male reticence, then, contrasts with feminine attraction. Thus although Emelia was heard to murmur on the day of the tournament that she would prefer to wed neither (46), she had a distinct interest in one of her suitors. For Kelman, chivalry manifests itself in moving a young woman to intense admiration of a male hero and encouraging praise of him after they wed.

The story of *Constance*, in contrast to *Dorigen*, admits that a husband can be "pitiless" (105). This accusation of Alla is false but necessary to show the worthiness of the woman, which Robinson's first illustration makes explicit: "To them she seemed a martyr" (80) is a Roman scene with costume that echoes Justinian's Theodora, but also is current Art Nouveau with hints of Japanese influence. The gray-blue cloth has a bold pattern of white flowers in red circles. A pensive Constance, eyes lowered and chin resting on her left hand, stands tall, an elegant figure, behind whom are the poor and pilgrims, and beyond them the white architecture of the Rome of Antiquity to which she bids farewell. Such a picture elaborates the story, which Kelman fills in with details to answer a child's questions about the voyages—lists of provisions and careful explanations of food and drink available while at sea. In a curious episode as Constance sails past Italy (89–90), she attaches a crown to the anchor in an attempt to stop the boat, but it is swept away and ultimately reaches the coast of Northumberland. Kelman similarly expands Constance's voyage with her little son. Five years pass not unhappily, since they are together, and the mother devises entertainment and instruction for her child: "Through the long days Constance told him many tales of heroes and of saints" (107). With these Edwardian favorites, a good mother prepares her son for a life of chivalry; early storytelling forms character. Robinson's illustration "When her boy lay asleep she knelt at the prow" (108) has lovely Art Nou-

In "To Them She Seemed a Martyr," W. Heath Robinson's decorative design of Constance's dress combines Art Nouveau style with the classical architecture of Rome. The *Man of Law's Tale* chronicles journeys through the Mediterranean and on to Britain, an exciting romance with adventures at sea and on land. As a study of religious and cultural conflict, as well as a story of a noble woman and mother devoted to her child, it is one of four tales in Janet Kelman's *Stories from Chaucer Told to the Children* (1906).

veau curves in Constance's back and the prow of the ship, while a triangular section of sail cuts to the center. Her gown is boldly patterned, and the colors are intense. Like Griselda, Constance is a model of devotion, but almost equal attention is given to Alla's grief and love. The point is that both parents care for their child, a reassurance for the nursery audience. The conclusion expresses Edwardian patriotism, for the happy family return to Northumberland, where they are joyfully greeted, and the last words are cries of "May the Prince live!" (114); Britain, not Rome is home, with a return from a distant part of empire. The future lies with the young boy who will carry on the traditions of the nation.

Stories from Chaucer was intended for very young children. This partially explains its greater attention to women, since traditionally the role of the mother is most crucial in the first years of life. Two illustrations show young women looking toward the knight in armor on his steed. Another, with a male figure in the foreground, repeats the idea of longing. Palamon sits by a pool of water, thinking of what he can do after escaping; in the distance is the mounted knight Arcite, now at the court disguised as Philostrate (39). The accomplished male is not pictured, at least not as a knight. There is an illustration of the Magician standing on the shore in Dorigen, but he is in a mist, hands raised as he looks out to sea (16). Fulfillment and the accomplishment of knights come in books intended for older children, such as those of F.J. Harvey Darton, J. Walker McSpadden, Emily Underdown, and Percy MacKaye, which are discussed in chapters 3 and 4.

Kelman's Stories from Chaucer were widely disseminated; for example, Historias de Chaucer, Quentos de Canterbury was printed with Robinson's illustrations in Barcelona in 1914. But the widest audience was in the United States, where children could read the stories both in a single volume of the Told to the Children Series, sold by E.P. Dutton for fifty cents, and through popular children's encyclopedias, which were typically organized conceptually not alphabetically. Three stories—Dorigen, Emelia, and Griselda—were reprinted among Classic Tales and Everyday Stories, volume three in The Young Folks' Treasury (1919).[4] The exclusion of Constance suggests Protestant avoidance of its Catholic religious sentiment. There are only two of W.H. Robinson's illustrations: Dorigen looking out to sea and Griselda with her baby and husband. This encyclopedia enjoyed continuous publication; for example, as The Bookshelf for Boys and Girls (1948) that culled items from The Young Folks' Treasury and The Boys and Girls Bookshelf, mostly published between 1909 and 1919. Kelman's Chaucer stories come, rather nicely, at the center of volume six, Famous Stories and Verse, with four new partial page, black-and-white illustrations by Franké.

Three are for the *Knight's Tale,* the largest being "The Tournament." Others are a duel and Emelia as a maiden in sunlight. For *Dorigen,* he shows a couple pointing to a swirl of rocks. The one full-page color illustration is the original W. Heath Robinson's "Dorigen" (opposite 150). But here the image is in a frame with pale blue line drawings of a magician, a knight in armor, and a castle. Thus the encyclopedia's illustrations add martial interests that broaden and heighten the chivalric content, a surer appeal to boys.[5] With repetition in encyclopedias Kelman's Edwardian nursery *Stories from Chaucer* had a much expanded readership and an additional respectability long after their first appearance.

The Delphian Course

Encyclopedias for children in many ways resemble those for self-improvement of adults, especially in how they presented Chaucer. One example, *The Delphian Course,* published by the Delphian Society of Chicago in 1913 in nine volumes, is subtitled: *A Systematic Plan for Education, Embracing the World's Progress and Development of the Liberal Arts.*[6] An introductory explanation cites the educational reform of Charles W. Eliot, editor of *The Harvard Classics* (1910): "from the total training during childhood there should result in the child a taste for interesting and improving reading, which should direct and inspire its subsequent intellectual life" (1:x). A "Council of Review" included academics from many universities and Hamilton Wright Mabie, essayist and a major figure in producing books for children. The course is comprehensive, that is,

> the subjects which are now offered in the curriculums of our leading colleges and universities—history, literature, philosophy, poetry, fiction, drama, art, ethics, music. Mathematics, being in its higher forms essential to few, has been omitted; languages, requiring the aid of a teacher, and such sciences as make laboratories necessary, are not included. Technical information has no place whatever in such a scheme. The branches of human interest which remain are those of vital importance to everyone [1:xi].

The place of the Middle Ages is signed by the frontispieces, in five of the nine volumes pages from a fourteenth-century French Book of Hours are in color. The history of the period is identified as "Age of Chivalry" (4), volume 5 is primarily "Medieval Stories" (most are national epics) combined with the "Story of Music" and a larger section of articles about "The Conduct of Life." Volume 8 surveys English history in forty-eight pages and devotes nearly 400 pages to English poetry and fewer than 100 to Western Europe (France and Germany); the significance of English literature for an American audience is paramount. Chaucer's independent spirit "lives through the 'Canterbury Tales,' the first masterly exhibition of contemporaneous English character" and thus the beginning of "a real literature" distinct from "the glamour of the heroic past." While much is forgotten or neglected, "the 'Canterbury Tales,' in veneration of the Chaucer period, is prescribed in schools and colleges" (8:50). A brief review of language in the fourteenth century and a noting of major works and followers introduce Chaucer, who "stands pre-eminent as the Father of English Poetry" as his immediate successors recognized. His power comes as "the master delineator of human character which never changes ... portraits as fresh and true to-day as when he penned them five centuries ago" (8:60). This judgment does not differ from the retellings for children. The principal selection is *The Prologue*, in Middle English without a glossary, and with discreet cuts as for the young. The *Knight's Tale* is paraphrased with an interlace of modernized extracts by Mrs. Haweis, some of which are in her earliest *Chaucer for Children*. Two lyrics, "Chaucer to his Empty Purse" and "Good Counsel of Chaucer," conclude the section. Again the emphasis is upon chivalry, the loss of material fortune, and steadfastness, all concepts urged for children. The Delphian ideal in "an age characterized by intensity, strenuous effort and tireless exertion" was to develop "insight into the mystery of life ... a love for things worthwhile increases" (1:ix, xiii).

Carolyn Sherwin Bailey

In spite of such high sentiment, judgments about acceptable stories, as well as the treatment of honor and adult behavior, are not always predictable. An adaptation of Kelman shows how there was deviance from the accepted norm. Carolyn Sherwin Bailey, in *Stories of Great Adventures* (1919), part of the American For the Children's Hour Series, is such a work.[7] Its language and artlessness suggest the young reader; the two Chaucer tales, *Patient Griselda* and *The Rocks Removed*, both focus on woman's response to hardship, though male knights are largely responsible for most of what happens. Nevertheless, the reassuring image of woman is missing. Bailey's titles suggest the influence of Darton, but essentially she paraphrased Kelman, simplifying to an iteration of events with very little descriptive detail and nothing of Kelman's subtle understanding of Chaucer. Bailey changes the characterizations of the principal heroines and shifts the moral emphasis, so that the story is much harsher. Griselda is sentimentalized and given intense maternal feelings: she dreams of how the baby girl will grow up to ride beside her father and make him proud (147). Walter does not talk to his wife, but sends "an evil looking guard" with a message that her lord is to be obeyed. She "tried, at first, to snatch back the baby, and then she remembered the promise" (148). Similarly, she rejoices in the son who replaces the lost child and expects this heir to please his father. This time she tries "to cover the boy with her own body" before the guard takes him with drawn sword and then reminds herself of the wedding promise. Griselda's more emotional responses continue; when Walter tells her that he will wed another, she weeps but bows her head to hide the tears. She exercises discipline, but not before she has expressed something other than perfect obedience. After early resistance, even physical action, there is little emotion at the end. Walter's moral is pompous: "I have tried your patience and faith as no lady's were ever tried before, and you have proved my faith in you. Be no longer sad ... for your patience is rewarded" (153).

If Bailey's Griselda is an assertive woman, her Dorigen behaves in ways that are sexually ambiguous, or at least provocative. The May dance at which she meets Aurelius is "a country dance"—perhaps an appeal to provincial American readers—and Aurelius is "admired by everyone because of his youth, and strength, and good looks. They did not know the evil hid in his heart" (156). Dorigen notices the handsome young squire, thinks him "a graceful boy, or the image of Pan, the god of out-doors.[8] Seeing her interest, Aurelius made bold to speak" (156). His request, as in *Stories from Chaucer,* is for "the beautiful jewel that she wore on her breast." At first amazed, Dorigen notes the preciousness of the jewel (here a pearl) and recalls her husband's delight that she wore it on their wedding day, and she refuses emphatically. "Then a thought came to Dorigen. Aurelius still waited, kneeling at her feet, and she spoke to him again softly and looking about to see that no one heard her" (157). This suggests impropriety, albeit in the next paragraph she avows concern about being separated from her husband, when she asks Aurelius whether he can remove the rocks. Bailey supports this reading with the sentence, "Dorigen shuddered to think that she had even offered to part with her jewel" (158). Chaucer's account of the Magician's demonstration of his skill includes his showing of Aurelius's lady dancing (V.1199–1200). Here she is no longer wearing "the clear white jewel on her breast." Further, the magical jousting knights are of King Arthur's Round Table, and the fairest lady whom all struggle to win is Dorigen (159). These additions introduce sexual fantasy and obscure the allegory of the jewel for chastity. After the rocks disappear, Aurelius meets Dorigen on the shore and grabs her arm: "'Give me your jewel, my lady. I have accomplished your desire,' Aurelius demanded" (160). In another abrupt shift Dorigen starts, grows pale, and is sick at heart, since she "never dreamed that her foolish demand could be complied with" (161). Moreover, Arveragus's insistence that his wife keep her word states that he loved his wife's jewel as deeply as he loved her. Finally Aurelius is moved by such truth and a recognition of Arveragus's "knightly honor," so that debts are forgiven. With the rocks restored, the loving couple live in the undimmed light of her jewel. Bailey lessens the simple innocence and clear moral values of *Stories from Chaucer* at the same time that her style is less subtle. Publication in the United States and a date at the end of World War I may explain the differences. As the novels of Henry James make clear, American young women behaved more "freely" than their European counterparts, and the Great War completely changed social and moral assumptions. Bailey wrote just as the Twenties, the decade of extraordinary changing morality, particularly freedoms for women, forever altered expectations of private and public behavior. *Stories of Great Adventure* shows a significant deviation from the high standard of many memorable collections, especially those aptly termed "extravagant" because of their beauty.

❧ 4 ❧

Edwardian Extravagance
for Youth

The dedication of Edward Burne-Jones and William Morris to Chaucer, brilliantly expressed in the Kelmscott *Chaucer* that was published in 1896, is unsurpassed. But many imitators contributed to the taste for extravagantly beautiful books that were both a tribute to the author and a display of bookmaking skills. This could be for private or public delight and indulgence, as two examples demonstrate. Only fifty copies were printed of *The Prologue to the Tales of Geoffrey Chaucer*, as a final note explains:

> The printing of this book was begun in July and finished in December of the year of the Diamond Jubilee of Queen Victoria 1897 by St John Hornby & his sisters with some little help of Cicely Barclay at the Ashedene Press Herts. For private circulation only amongst their friends and neighbors[1]

The illustrations are facsimile woodcuts from the earliest printed edition, Caxton's *Canterbury Tales* (1478, 1483, 1484), itself extraordinarily beautiful and crucial to the first English printer's effort to make available all of major vernacular English works. Hornby's tribute to Queen Victoria thus reaffirms national pride and confirms Chaucer's importance in the nineteenth century. The text is W.W. Skeat's from the Clarendon edition.

Very similar in intent, but commercially printed is *The Prologue to the Canterbury Tales of Geoffrey Chaucer* (1909) with designs by Ambrose Dudley.[2] It also prints Skeat's text, but the illustrations, twenty original designs, are very different and are a principal reason for the book. In the frontispiece "In Southwerk at the Tabard as I Lay" Chaucer stands on a balcony of the inn to look down upon several mounted pilgrims—Clerk, Wife, Knight, Squire, Franklin, as well as a Cook with pans and a Miller with bagpipes—while the Pardoner and Summoner are among a standing group and the Prioress rests. A framed title page shows nine riding figures with details in the borders—a row of daisies and bells and on the broader left side Chaucer stands reading. The first page has the eighteen opening lines with a left border (ram, birds, tower, and pilgrim) and a heading of the wind Zephirus. Subsequent designs vary—ten full-page illustrations and as many marginal frames, single or combinations of pilgrims—each bringing to life details from Chaucer's descriptions. Four are especially notable: the Physician with books, phials, a skeleton, and mortar pots (facing 18); an elegant Wife of Bath walks out from a church (a boy carries her train!) and smiles as she is observed by onlookers (facing 20); a Plowman in the field with his oxen tips his hat to a bareheaded Priest who is visiting the parish (facing 22); a wild-eyed dramatic Pardoner, with a wallet full of relics, enthralls many listeners (facing 28). Such books offered a rich introduction to Chaucer for adults, and publishers provided comparable rewards for children.

Confident expectations that children should and would continue to read stories from Chaucer meant that Edwardian publishers concurrently produced books of retellings for children older than the nursery audience served by a writer such as Kelman in Jack's Told to the Children Series. Those in the junior school had a wider choice, both of sumptuous editions (often given as rewards/prizes or for Christmas or birthdays), and of modest school texts with more elaborate social and historical information. Early twentieth-century educators recognized the great appeal to children from eight to twelve years old of stories of adventure, heroic and legendary figures; since national epics, sagas, and romances are the popular texts, the Middle Ages is a dominant interest.[3] Major authors are the other source of traditional literature for children, and Chaucer is among the favored authors in series and collections made for this audience. His role as Father of English Poetry partially explains inclusion, but his gifts as a storyteller and choice of material, much readily allied to fairy tale and folklore, are also cogent. Stories like the *Knight's Tale*, the *Squire's Tale*, and the *Wife's Tale* belong to the realm of secular romance in which King Arthur was supreme. Moreover, the *Clerk's Tale* and the *Man of Law's Tale* presented heroic virtue in women in what may be called religious romances.[4] These most frequently included tales sustain their popularity already observed in Victorian books. A salient advantage is that women play significant roles and also are noble, as they frequently are not in Malory, another much favored text (with proper adjustments) for youth. Three especially beautiful and influential Edwardian Chaucer books, by two British and one American author, two men and one woman, differ notably in emphases but not in extravagant details of book production.[5]

F.J. Harvey Darton

No writer in the Edwardian period was more committed to children's literature than F.J. Harvey Darton (1878–1936), who had influence both as an author and as a publisher. Indeed, as previously indicated, his *Children's Books in England: Five Centuries of Social Life* (1932) first defined the significance of children's literature. Darton, who was committed to medieval stories, probably wrote *The Seven Champions of Christendom* (1901), issued *Tales of the Canterbury Pilgrims* (1904) using his name, and then followed this success with *The Wonder Book of Old Romance* (1907). He wrote and published many other books, but these three contributed to the vogue of chivalric stories for children. Darton's Chaucer tales also appeared in an abridged small book that resembles the Stories Told to the Children Series. There is a less-expensive American edition, and several of his Chaucerian tales appeared in anthologies and an encyclopedia.

The original *Tales of the Canterbury Pilgrims* is extraordinarily handsome, black cloth stamped in gold. The title is at the top of the cover, most of which is filled with a splendid procession of equestrian pilgrims, adapted from the Ellesmere miniatures. The figures, each identified by a name written in the spaces between the horses' legs, cross in four rows, alternately from right to left. Trees along the sides and grass across the bottom frame the cover, while the tops of a row of larger trees separate the title from the pilgrims. Chaucer and the Host are on the spine, with the title and "by F.J.H. Darton/illustrated by H. Thomson." Darton's name does not appear on the cover, which is signed with the initials "H.T."[6]

Hugh Thomson (1860–1920) was the most popular illustrator of the period in black-and-white, and his drawings for *Tales of the Canterbury Pilgrims* are lively and varied. Thus the richness of Darton's text is matched by the fullness of Thomson's pictures, fifty-three in all; twenty-six are full-page illustrations, two half-page, fourteen headings with decorated capitals, eight headings only and two capitals only, and one small inset picture. Thomson, who early worked with Randolph Caldecott, was respected for his use of accurate period details and delicacy of line, with a style that can be identified as "genteel."[7] However, Thomson's imagination is more complex than this suggests. For example, he introduced humor in a slapstick brawl as heading for *Gamelyn* (58) and in a man's early rising in a capital *T* (294). He also makes didactic points about the consequences of sinful behavior, most vividly in the heading for the *Pardoner's Tale*. Three elegantly dressed rioters gamble and drink, watched by a cowled figure of Death with his scythe; below, Death wearing a black hat and swinging his scythe fills the open capital *T*. The Death figure serves childish pleasure in things that are "scary," as references to food and drink frequently play to audience interest. Thomson shows several cogent scenes: a maid filling the Host's tankard (xix) and a manservant carrying a platter of meat to an expectant plump Franklin, "Epicurus' own son" (232); both look Victorian and might adorn a Dickens novel. More Chaucerian but still resembling a cartoon is the Pardoner, watched by the mounted pilgrims, having his cakes and ale (135). Most curious is a scene from a link, when the drunken Cook becomes so angry at the Manciple's taunts that he cannot stay on his horse. Thomson pictures the difficulty as pilgrims hold him steady (269). Both text and image make clear the cumulative nature of sinful behavior, but Thomson's caricature and the expressions of several pilgrims in the picture are another social commentary. As an experienced book illustrator he skillfully captured narrative moments.

Darton's inclusion of material from the links expresses fascination with personality as well as a wish for completeness, and Thomson's pictures of pilgrims are often quite subtle. The only processional scene is a reverse one, a back view of the pilgrims, except for the Host who turns in his saddle as "They saw the spires and battlements of Canterbury before them" (275). But many full-pages focus on a pilgrim or two, with others in the background. The pairings are often relevant; for example, the Wife and Clerk, opposing points of view in their treatment of gender and decorum—an anticipation of Kittredge's identifying a group of tales as the "Marriage Group"—are first (6), while the Wife, crossing social lines, also rides opposite the Knight, who seems to pose his question to her (29). Chaucer and the Host, who share orchestration of *The Canterbury Tales* and "waists as fairly shaped" (105), are the other interesting pair, along with a moment only attributed to Chaucer—exploited by Percy MacKay (as discussed in chapter 5) in which the Wife asks the Prioress to walk in the garden (288). The episode, like Lydgate's arrival (285), belongs to

The Pardoner's Tale

The Three Revellers and Death.

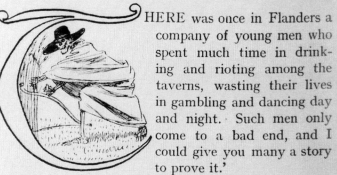

'HERE was once in Flanders a company of young men who spent much time in drinking and rioting among the taverns, wasting their lives in gambling and dancing day and night. Such men only come to a bad end, and I could give you many a story to prove it.'

The Pardoner was unable to forget his business. He broke off to warn the pilgrims at great length about the

"The Three Revellers and Death," *The Pardoner's Tale*, is an example of the complexity of Hugh Thomson's design for F.J. Harvey Darton's *Tales of the Canterbury Pilgrims* (1906). The three revellers play at dice on a board on a barrel, and one holds high his tankard, to suggest the sin of drunkenness along with gambling. In the background hovers the figure of Death/Time with his scythe; he reappears in the opening capital cutting the grain with his scythe. Pages like this juxtapose words and image, an example of how children's literature so much depends upon both author and illustrator.

the disposition of pilgrims after they arrive in Canterbury. Several full-page illustrations simply represent details from the *General Prologue*: the Prioress with her dogs, the Miller with his bagpipe (15), Friar Hubert performing as a musician (161). More ingenious are the placing of the equestrian Cook figure, his hat doffed into the letter *L* below *Sir Game-lyn* (58), and a brilliant extension of letter *I* into a tree trunk about which fairies swirl, attracting the attention of the knight who rides in full armor at the start of the *Wife's Tale* (152). Thomson's skill with chivalric figures in fairy tale is perhaps best seen in "The Combat," in the *Squire's Tale*; a huge monster with raised club pushes out of a whirlwind toward a small knight and lady tipped back as the horse rears in apprehension (223).

A compilation of the subjects represented shows greater emphasis upon story (twelve full-page, one half-page, eleven headings with capitals, two headings only, two capitals only, for a total of twenty-eight) than upon pilgrims (fourteen full-page [including the title page], one half-page, three headings with capitals, four headings only, for a total of twenty-two). The interlacing of sizes and positions makes for diversity; turning the pages of the book leads to another surprise. Nevertheless, there is less variety than the numbers immediately suggest, since more than half of the full-page illustrations are for three tales: three for the *Clerk's*, two each for the *Knight's* and *Nun's Priest's*. These are, of course, the most popular tales retold for children.

Thomson's first images define Chaucer. The title page shows him on his horse, his head turned to look at Canterbury Cathedral. Tiny cowled figures suggest devotion, while Chaucer sits very straight and tall, his gaze fixed on a reached destination. In contrast, opposite is an engaging frontispiece that is filled with excitement and humor, the chase scene from the *Nun's Priest's Tale*, which includes many animals—three dogs, a pig, a cow and a calf, ducks on the ground and geese flying in the air—and villagers. The large heading for the Introduction shows Chaucer seated and writing, with books on shelves in front of him. An adolescent girl opens the door for a youth who enters the room carrying a book (iii). The suggestion of a domestic scene is fully developed in the heading of The First Day. Here Chaucer sits on a chair, holding a young boy who sits on his right leg and a girl on this left; opposite another girl sits on a chair, while two boys sit on the floor, one on a box. By varying the ages of the children Thomson suggests that the stories can be read over a period of years. This Chaucer bears a striking resemblance to Edward Burne-Jones's drawing of himself and William Morris, embraced by Chaucer on their completion of the Kelmscott *Chaucer*, with the caption "Bless Ye My Children" (1896). The role of Chaucer as Father of English Poetry could hardly be more explicit. Thomson reiterates the point in the heading for the list of illustrations that also features four young children—three of whom are kneeling—with a dog peering intently into the grass as if seeking treasure; the figures lead the eye toward the captions. Thomson's final illustration, a heading for the Merchant's Second Tale of *Beryn*—one of the "others" retold by Darton—shows four lovely maidens looking after a baby with the caption "Beryn had four nurses" (320).

Tales of the Canterbury Pilgrims is a very inviting book; like many others published by Wells Gardner, Darton & Company, it is an example of the best of Edwardian traditional literature for children, a worthy Reward or Prize volume. (This author's personal copy has a plate for a Latin Prize, Modern Third Form, at St. Paul's Preparatory School, Michaelmas Term 1908.)

The volume's inclusiveness is salient, and Darton's text is close to the original. The introduction is by F.J. Furnivall, who is widely recognized as an "enthusiast" and one who did not ignore the importance of children's reading, for he also contributed an introduction to Shakespeare.[8] Furnivall prepares the reader for a scholarly treatment and makes a patriotic statement.[9] Great poets are "brought forth by great stirs in the nation's life" (iii). Furnivall gives a useful account of fourteenth-century England, quotes Macaulay about the amalgamation of races and the splendid artistic achievements of the period, and cites chivalric victories. His detailed biographical sketch includes brief comments about all of the works. *Troilus*, "though full of beauty, dwells too long on the course and miseries of thwarted love" (xvii), and Furnivall praises Chaucer for getting past "his first love bother" (xviii). Thus his Chaucer is free of the sexuality that children's literature ignored—until very recently. Furnivall's peroration marks Chaucer as a second rank of poet, behind Dante and Shakespeare, but with many praiseworthy qualities. Most esteemed is the "happiness of his nature," "his sunshine" in spite of his troubles. This view of a genial Chaucer is typically Edwardian, a sustaining of the Victorian approbation promoted by Haweis and Seymour and rarely evident among late twentieth-century critics. A corollary is Furnivall's recognition of Chaucer's crucial role in establishing England's heritage and language, "which we have to put and keep in the forefront of the world" (xviii).

An earlier gloss on Chaucer's place as a major author for children was made by John W. Hales, whose praise of Chaucer dominates his introduction to *Stories from the Faerie Queene*, retold for children by Mary Macleod and published by Wells Darton in 1897. Hales, citing Macaulay especially, identified *The Faerie Queene* as a largely unread poem and offered the retelling as helpful for the young who lack sophisticated under-

standing and for the old who "shrink from a little effort."[10] Edmund
Spenser—who had been included as a possible subject in the competition
to decorate the Palace at Westminster and Houses of Parliament, when
Chaucer was not—was thus earlier presented to children by the publisher
Gardner, Darton, and Company; however, Hales argues that Chaucer is
the superior author. Specifically, he contrasts their arts in Spenser's completion of the *Squire's Tale*. Having noted "the very opulence of Spenser's
genius [that] stands in the way of his due appraisement," and acknowledged Spenser's "most generous admiration" of Chaucer, Hales deplored
Spenser's comparative lack of "self-restraint":

> Chaucer is a masterly tale-teller: no one in all English poetry equals
> him in this faculty; he is as supreme in it as Shakespeare in the
> department of the drama. In his tales Chaucer is, "without
> o'erflowing, full." ...[Spenser] wanted some gifts and habits that are
> necessary for the perfect story-teller—gifts and habits which Chaucer,
> by nature or by discipline, possessed in a high degree, such as humor,
> concentration, realism.[11]

This paean is a prelude to Darton's own retelling of Chaucer stories with
patriotic enthusiasm and a chivalric emphasis in a context of high sentiment.

He not only includes the full sweep of *The Canterbury Tales* but also
provides a return journey with a conclusion that notes that Chaucer left
the work incomplete, so that he invites the audience to guess the winner
of the tale-telling competition and to attend the victory dinner at the
Tabard, the last of several attempts to involve young readers. Darton shifts
portions of the *General Prologue*, usually into combination with parts of
the individual prologues to introduce each tale, to create a simple narrative line that he makes even clearer by dividing the stories into five days
of pilgrimage. The order of tales is that used by the Chaucer Society and
Skeat's edition with the "Bradshaw shift," and references to places on the
pilgrimage route are sequential—Rochester, Sittingbourne, Ospringe,
Boughton-under Blean, Bob-up-and-Down, and Canterbury.

Perhaps the most fascinating dimension of *Tales of the Canterbury Pilgrims* is the introduction of five tales by "Others": *Sir Gamelyn*, Spenser's
conclusion of the *Squire's Tale*, *The Chequer of the Hoop*, *Beryn*, and
Lydgate's *Destruction of Thebes*. "At Canterbury: The Chequer of the
Hoop" draws upon the *Prologue to the Tale of Beryn* to develop the character of the Pardoner, who becomes involved with Kit, the wife of a tap-
ster at the well-known inn, the Chequer of the Hoop—an early revision
that removed the sexual difficulty of Chaucer's Pardoner. Darton next
recounts some of the activities of the pilgrims at Canterbury. The Knight

and several others go to the Cathedral to the shrine, while the Pardoner, Miller, and "some others of the more disorderly pilgrims clearly had not learnt the way to conduct themselves in church"—a relevant reminder to the young. As in the *Prologue to Beryn,* the pilgrims look at stained glass images and quarrel, then buy tokens, some of which the Miller steals, until he sees the Summoner, who demands a share. Back at their inn, they meet the Host, who invites a newcomer, John Lydgate, to join them on the return journey. Thus with some shifting of the non–Chaucerian material Darton prepares for the *Destruction of Thebes,* told by Lydgate, a fifty-year-old monk who had gone to Canterbury to seek health (283), and by the Merchant, who recounts *Beryn* as his second tale. The presence of these two tales, one the most famous supplement and the other obscure, signs Furnivall's involvement in the book; in 1887, with W.G. Stone, he had edited *Beryn,* which the Early English Text Society (EETS) reprinted in 1907. The text of the *Destruction of Thebes,* edited by Axel Erdmann, was issued by the EETS in 1911. Darton's prose versions for children, available in 1906, were earlier than these modern editions for adults.[12] A sketch by Hugh Thomson on the flyleaf of a copy signs easy collaboration and also echoes his first drawing of Chaucer as storyteller to children. Here Chaucer sits between Furnivall and Darton, both relaxed men, smoking; all three signed and dated the sketch in October 1904.[13]

The First Day, "At the Tabard; the Beginning of the Pilgrimage," supplies a context. Darton describes the time of King Richard II as more primitive and dangerous than the present. Persons who traveled about may seem to belong to legend, even to fairyland, but they were the ordinary people of the day, albeit with major differences. In Chaucer's day, "People were much more friendly, much gayer, and much more outspoken and unrestrained" (3)—a view of Merrie England both rueful and nostalgic. Despite sharp distinctions between rich and poor and very harsh circumstances—"much more discomfort, more violence, more oppression then than now"—there were advantages:

> But in spite of all hardships, men really loved gaiety—gay clothes of every kind of bright color, gay trappings to their horses, gay songs and dances (for everyone then was musical). They loved also the open air and spring and the sun and flowers, so that often young knights and ladies would spend their afternoon in the pleasant walled gardens of great castles, weaving garlands of blossoms and singing and dancing merely for the joy in the fine day. Fighting, too, was an amusement; a man went lightheartedly to his death in a tourney, as if to a joyful feast, and ladies looked on gladly at a fight, and encouraged their faithful knights to acts of prowess [3–4].

This idealistic view seems designed to excite young readers and to inspire chivalric aspirations. Nevertheless, Darton adds a caution, "Knights might be courteous and debonair in their manners, but they could be brutal and harsh as well" (4). Then he introduces the most crucial distinction, the freedom with which men talked: "But above all they were outspoken in regard to sacred things.... But though they talked lightly and freely of these matters [the clergy and religion], as it seems to us now, they did not think at all lightly of them but deeply and seriously" (4). Again Darton shows an Edwardian uneasiness with modern restraints and lack of conviction, in contrast to an age perceived as one with greater faith and order, when pilgrims and pilgrimages were commonplace. His fairly close rendering of the *General Prologue* interlaces explanations of social circumstances of many descriptive details and the Host's plan of telling tales.

The Second Day begins the tales, and Darton here most fully shows his devotion to chivalry, later expanded in his retellings in *The Wonder Book of Old Romance*, where the stories match the sentiment of the title. He retells the *Knight's Tale* fairly closely and keeps its division into four parts: I. Palamon and Arcita Fall Out, II. The Meeting in the Wood, III. The Answer of the Gods, IV. The Tournament. But, as these titles indicate, there is a different emphasis; the tournament is the climax, the most memorable part of Darton's version. Story is more significant than emotion, and chivalry is more important than philosophy. When Theseus heard the grieving women, "He swore a great oath, on his knighthood, to take such vengeance upon the tyrant Creon that all Greece should ring with it," and he arrives at Thebes "with all the flower of his chivalry in his train." However, the young reader is also told that Theseus assaults and sacks the city and that he stays "ravaging the country and doing with it as he pleased," while his soldiers pillage and strip the dead (21). Thus Darton keeps the toughness of Chaucer's account and a medieval juxtaposition of honor and violence. Theseus's decree that there be no killing at the tournament (47, cf. I.2537–2560) allows a full experience of the sport of knighthood that prevails over the initial violence of battle and siege. Several illustrations show a range of interest: Theseus meeting the women, Emily gathering flowers, a fierce duel on foot between the two young lovers, and some of the pilgrims riding with the caption, "'Tell me,' said the Knight, "which do you think is the better off?' (29), a direct appeal for reader response. This marks the end of Part I and effectively reminds the reader that storytelling is taking place; it is a skillful translation of the question of Chaucer's Knight to lovers (I.1347–54), who are not the audience of the children's book.

The remainder of the First Day sustains the Knight's upholding of chivalry. Darton summarizes the *Miller's Tale* in a single paragraph that contains nothing about sexuality but only a carpenter's being duped by a clerk into thinking that there would be another flood. The pilgrim audience is uncertain about whether to be angry because of the Miller's rudeness or to laugh. There is further sanitizing; the *Reeve's Tale* takes a single sentence: "the story of Simkin, the miller of Trumpington, who was cheated and laughed at, in spite of all his cunning, by two students from Cambridge" (55–6). In a startling rewriting the Cook completes the avoidance of the *fabliaux*; he begins an account of Perkyn the Reveller, but stops himself: "'Plague on it! I will tell no further,' he said. 'The tale is a bad one, not fit to be heard by you. But I will give you instead a story of a knight's three sons'" (57). This is *Gamelyn*, best known through Shakespeare's adaptation, via Thomas Lodge's *Rosalynde*, in *As You Like It*. Many gave this story to the Cook, and Darton uses it well to round out the First Day with another chivalric story. Gamelyn is the youngest son who perseveres through hardship and sibling oppression—a male Cinderella that is always appealing to children. With strength, determination, a sense of justice, and the aid of a faithful servant Adam the Butler (surely an amusing detail for middle-class Edwardians), he rightfully gains his inheritance and frees the country from his elder brother's tyranny.

Many of Chaucer's tales, and Darton's versions of them, exemplify chivalry, but this First Day shows principles of selection and emphasis. The *Shipman's Tale*, like the *Miller's Tale*, is a paragraph with no reference to sex but an added moral for women: the cunning monk teaches the wife "that it was best not to hide anything from her husband" (97). The Host's attack on the Pardoner's sexuality is changed into the offense of selling relics, "'You would swear a rag of your old clothes had belonged to some saint, and make me kiss it'" (147). Dame Alison of Bath speaks in a "loud voice," and the "burden of her talk was the way to rule a husband," but Darton reduces her prologue to a single page that refers only to husband number five. Thomson's illustration shows her as an elegant young woman, rather Edwardian in appearance, but with doubled fists that have just struck a man who tumbles from his stool as an open book falls. The caption is "Caught him such a buffet" (149). *Old Woman and the Knight* is a neutral title for the *Wife's Tale*. Edwardian children's versions did not refer to rape, but Darton suggests it:

> It happened that there was at King Arthur's Court a young knight, in the full vigor and pride of his strength, who one day, as he was riding out, came upon a maiden walking all alone. She was very beautiful, and the sight of her made him forget his knighthood. He went up to

her, and tried to carry her off with him by force. But before he could
succeed help came, and he was seized and taken before the King
[153].

A hint of the male point of view and female responsibility in being unpro-
tected suggests Edwardian stereotyping, which is in turn reinforced by
the illustration. It successfully represents ideal chivalry—a mounted knight
in plate armor with plumed helmet, sitting straight and bold, looking off
to the old hag seated on the grass (155). Moreover, the knight replies with
"manly voice" when he declares, "I have kept my word faithfully." His
answer is that women desire "Power best, whether it be over husband or
lover," but he accepts his fate, if this is not correct: "I am here ready to
die, if you so will it" (157). He repeats "truly I gave my word" but tries to
avoid the old hag as wife and laments his dishonor. The bride's teaching
centers on class distinction, an argument that there is nothing wrong with
poverty and that a "true gentleman" is he "who leads the best life both in
secret and in the open, who strives always to do gentle and honorable
deeds" (158). This moral is encouraging for the schoolboy, close in attitude to the code of scouting soon to be established by Sir Robert Baden-
Powell and advanced by the imagery of chivalry; for example, on the cover
of his *The Young Knights of the Empire*.[14] A final suggestion about gender
comes when the hag is transformed into "the most beautiful wife that
could be imagined," and the knight is no longer ashamed of her, an expression suitable to Edwardian society. Further, Darton's explanation of her
behavior places the *Wife's Tale* in the realm of folk and fairy lore. In his
history of children's literature, he observed that "the admission of our
authentic folk-lore into the nursery is a very curious piece of social history." Then he identified Chaucer, like Aesop printed by William Caxton, as "the true literary starting-point of the English fairy-tale, mainly
because of what he made the Wife of Bath say on the subject."[15] Darton's
explanation is that "the old woman was a fairy, and had wished to give
him a lesson before he knew her as she really was" (159). A corollary is
that the knight's initial offense is forgotten, while the mysterious and
potentially dangerous female, popular in Romantic poetry, and in Pre-
Raphaelite and early Symbolist painting, is enjoyed.

The fascination of the exotic is even more fully realized by the *Squire's
Tale,* which Darton richly expanded with Spenser's extension and an eighteenth-century conclusion by Stirling that provides wonderful Gothic
adventures. Spenser's continuation adds many chivalric details: another great
tournament to select a suitor for Canace, with magical renewing of strength
of the champions and a dramatic entrance of Cambina, a "daughter of a

fay" (Agape) in a chariot to stop the combat between her brother Triamond and Camballo, whom she has loved. The section concludes with a
double marriage, "and never were such lovers anywhere as these two
knights and their brides" (219).

The third section, much less well known, introduces more marvels
of the East. The two young couples "roam over the world in quest of
adventures" (219), leaving only Algarsif with his father Cambuscan. Algarsif also desires to see the world and rides off on the Brazen Horse. He
sets down in the midst of a battle and rescues Theodora, daughter of the
Sultan with whom he immediately falls in love, and they fly away. Another
adventure is an encounter with a fierce genie, a black monster. Thomson's
already mentioned vivid illustration, "The Combat," shows the young
couple on the horse galloping toward a swirling tornado that encloses a
huge creature that menaces them with a flashing club (223). Next they
find themselves trapped on the Dismal Mountain of an enchanter. Mean-
while Cambuscan begins a pilgrimage to Mecca only to have his pilgrim
group attacked by Arabs in the desert. Princesses and knights who set out
to aid Cambuscan are joined by Algarsif, who has been aided by Chos-
roës, who brought a warning of the threat to Cambuscan's kingdom. Chos-
roës was assisted by Alzobah, a fairy who gave him an apple that broke
open to reveal a silken ladder which allowed them to escape the valley.
The besieged pilgrims are saved, all return home to defend attacking enemies; Cambuscan reigns "in peace and prosperity," and after his death his
kingdom is "divided between Camballo, Algarif, and Triamond, who lived
long and happily with the ladies they had won in such strange fashion"
(230). The length and complexity of this expanded *Squire's Tale* play to
current Orientalism and fulfill Darton's wish to extend the chivalric content of *The Canterbury Tales* by significantly increasing the number of
fast-paced adventures.

He both adds chivalric material and mitigates lapses from chivalric
behavior. Aurelius in the *Franklin's Tale* begins as one who "ever kept his
love hidden, like an honorable knight," (234), Dorigen's rash vow is
"impossible" and "only in jest," and a question to the audience follows
Arveragus's decision with reminders about the need to keep one's word
(241). In a link preceding the *Manciple's Tale*, "A Quarrel and a Mishap,"
Darton renders the drunkenness of the Cook as his falling asleep on his
horse and having to be helped. When the Manciple chides about "tilting
at the quintain," Darton adds a paragraph of description and explanation
of this pastime of Chaucer's day, noting that a quintain can still be seen
at Offham, in Kent, near the pilgrims' route (268).

After the pilgrims reach Canterbury, the Knight again plays a

"The Combat" is Hugh Thomson's full-page illustration for Chaucer's *Squire's Tale*, a splendid example of orientalism. The menacing "terrible winged genie" in a whirl-wind raises his "flaming knotted mace" against the hero Algarsif who is trying to ride away with the lady Theodora. Chaucer's unfinished tale inspired several completions that Darton retold. Edmund Spenser's in *The Faerie Queene* (IV.2) is the best known, but not so spectacular as this monster episode "taken from an inferior writer of the eighteenth-century named Stirling." F.J. Harvey Darton's *Tales of the Canterbury Pilgrims: Retold from Chaucer and Others* (1906) acknowledges his followers.

prominent role. At the Cathedral door he puts the Parson forward as the person entitled to enter first. This recognition follows a brief but positive statement of the *Parson's Prologue and Tale*: "He gave them a noble sermon to remind them to repent of their sins, and remember the purpose for which they had come on this pilgrimage; and this was a fit ending to their journey, for they saw the spires and battlements and city walls of Canterbury itself before them as he was finishing it" (277). The Knight and "the better disposed of the company went at once to the shrine to do that for which they had come" (281). Thus there is an explicit connection between knighthood and piety. Darton's description of the pilgrims, some devout and others gawking and still quarreling, shows the diversity of medieval devotion, collection of relics, and tourist activity. Later, as they follow their other interests, the Knight takes his son, the Squire, around the fortifications of the city, carefully explaining and pointing out "the loopholes and points of vantage in the wall" (287). Before the return journey the Host reminds the pilgrims of their agreement, and the Knight's response — "Well said, Host! ... I am satisfied" (287) — signals accord. In the evening the Host appoints him "marshall of the hall, and it was his duty to see that the pilgrims sat down at table in their proper rank, without undue noise and brawling" (288). Knights upheld order in medieval society, and Edwardians admired a corollary maintaining of social hierarchy and decorum by gentlemen and ladies.

Earlier, in the introduction to the *Second Nun's Tale* of Cecilie and Valerian, Darton characterized the pilgrims as liking tales in which "some one single virtue" is dwelt upon. Such pointing of the moral increases the pedagogical role of Chaucer for children. In the *Franklin's Tale* this is truth-keeping; in the *Clerk's Tale*, patience and obedience; in the *Man of Law's Tale*, constancy and endurance (244). Darton admires unambiguous moral values, and he treats chivalry as a single virtue through revisions, deleting or changing the faults of knights to increase nobility and piety.

On "The Journey Home" the Host first turns to the newly joined pilgrim John Lydgate, who also acknowledges the priority of chivalry with his tale, *The Destruction of Thebes*. This is the most famous addition to Chaucer's *Canterbury Tales* and also a major contribution to the chivalric interest of Darton's volume. He divides Lydgate's medieval account of the great classic story into three parts: I. Edippus the Parricide, II. The Treachery of Ethiocles, and III. The Doom of Thebes. In the first section Edippus wins a tournament as "a stranger-knight" and thus delivers the people from the monster; but the most stirring part is the second, the scene of Tideus's valor. He is ambushed but leads the pursuing knights into a narrow pass so that he can defeat them one after another until he finishes off the last ten with a rockfall. Like a questing knight he wanders to a castle for rest and treatment of his wounds. The third portion of Lydgate's tale contains a fine account of a siege. Lycurgus is identified as he who later fought for Palamon against Arcita (314), an explicit reference to the *Knight's Tale*. This recurs after the end of the royal house of Thebes when the Thebans chose a tyrant Creon, "who, as you heard in the Knight's tale (so I am told), would not suffer the dead kings to be buried" (317).

Lydgate's presence as a pilgrim makes explicit the influence of Chaucer's tales, his role as the Father (begetter) of English Poetry; the tale is also another compelling example of medieval adaptation of classical literature. Perhaps Darton's subtlest use of the inspiring quality of such tales of chivalry comes in the final link. The Host celebrates the beauty of a May morning and accepts that the pilgrims may now be unable to think of another tale, so he does not specifically call upon an individual. The Merchant volunteers, and his second tale is of *Beryn*, another story set in classical times and suitable to the teller because it is an account of merchants and sailing. Moreover, the tale combines many episodes of trickery and lies and a final clever extrication with strong didactic purpose. Beryn is a profligate youth who ignores his dying mother and selfishly insists upon his own interests before he repents and tries to become independent. When his father, prodded by his step-mother, calls a halt to the young man's extravagance and stops merely indulging his every whim, the spoiled youth begins to think of reasons for his situation and at last acknowledges that he has obligations to something more than his own pleasure. This young man's moral growth is a model for behavior for youthful readers across social classes, but especially for the middle class, the defining market for Edwardian children's books. Beryn renounces his inheritance as a nobleman to become a merchant with five ships (328). He is constantly duped by the burgesses and citizens of Falsetown because, for all his faults, he assumes that people are telling the truth. Further, Beryn does not try to escape because, like a knight, he respects the law. The Master-Rogue Geoffrey, who pretends to be a cripple, lives pragmatically; he saves Beryn and his wealth through clever turning of the lies of Falsetown against those who sought to exploit Beryn. This story shows that a simple reliance on truth is inadequate in the world of commerce and wealth-seeking, and Beryn reforms both the country and himself. Acquitted, he goes to the King, Isope, a man whose extreme sense of honor led his people into deceitful ways lest they be punished for small lies, and Beryn is immediately liked. The tale has a romance ending: the hero marries the king's daughter and stays on to rule with the King and Geoffrey, "and by their wise government led the citizens away from their lying customs and evil habits" (364). Beryn's tale is a paradigm of acceptance for the newly rich merchant/industrial class of Victorian Britain that was the basis of Edwardian society and fostered its extravagance.

A review of publication shows wide promotion of F.J. Harvey Darton's Chaucer. His own house issued an abridged *Pilgrims' Tales from Chaucer* (1908) in the Children's Bookshelf Series. It included such titles as Mary Macleod's *The Red Cross Knight and Sir Guyon from Spenser's "Faerie Queene"* (1908) and *Honor & Arms: Tales from Froissart* (1910), which Henry Newbolt retold in the larger volume. In appearance the series is very like Jack's Told to the Children nursery books, even to the typeface. The paper cover is less expensive but adds a small picture in color, "The cart is free again" from the *Friar's Tale,* which is also reproduced inside.[16] This small book does not include Furnivall's Introduction or connecting material from the prologues, and there are only nine tales, reprinted without alterations in this order: *Nun's Priest, Prioress, Clerk, Wife of Bath, Pardoner, Friar, Franklin, Manciple,* and *Man of Law.* The selection indicates that chivalric romance is no longer the primary interest; there is an obvious reason for not including the non–Chaucerian tales, but the absence of the tales of the Knight and Squire suggests an alternative emphasis. Beast fables and magical transformations are traditionally the most immediately appealing children's literature, subsequently explored by Darton in *A Wonder Book of Beasts* (1909).[17] The tales of noble women reiterate a Victorian and Edwardian favoring of this kind of story; moral lessons and piety are dominant in this particular grouping of tales, which includes those with explicit Christian subject matter. Nevertheless, strong images of chivalry linger in the seven illustrations, three black-and-white and four in pastel colors. All are Hugh Thomson's pictures for the complete *Tales of the Canterbury Pilgrims* but reduced in size and some now colored in delicate pastels. The frontispiece shows Walter riding to the hunt, and in a second picture his courtly figure leads forth his bride (24); both are in color. The world of domestic knighthood is a scene of singing and dancing in the *Franklin's Tale,* also in color, while a black-and-white illustration, "They brought her back into the banqueting hall," shows a crowned lady attended by two ladies (43). All three pictures are for *Griselda.* Thomson's finest illustration of chivalry, the questing knight in the *Wife's Tale,* is an icon of idealism (51) and a sharp contrast to the black-and-white picture of the three rioters (all avaricious and sinister in appearance, one Falstaffian in figure) when they find the gold (63). This small book is attractive, if less impressive than the full, expensive *Tales.* It encourages a modest beginning knowledge of Chaucer, simply as storyteller, a favorite way to introduce children to his poetry.

There are two notable American editions of *The Story of the Canterbury Pilgrims*. Frederick Stokes issued the English edition with Thomson's illustrations for $1.50; a study of reading praised its qualities for American children: "English vigorous. Spirited illustrations by Hugh Thomson. Stories retain much of Chaucer's optimism, humor, and gentle courtesy."[18] J.B. Lippincott printed Darton's text but changed the illustrator, replacing Hugh Thomson with M(aria) L(ouise) Kirk (b.1860), an American. The Lippincot edition (1914) is not a luxury item; the paper is much cheaper, and the cover an austere gray cloth with blue lettering and a simple rose device.[19] Only the brief note that identifies the non–Chaucerian tales, not Furnivall's introduction, is included. This edition uses four of Kirk's pictures from J. Walker McSpadden's *The Canterbury Pilgrims*, which had eleven color illustrations (discussed later in this chapter). Three show young women: Emelie in the rose garden (17), Griselda spinning with her sheep grazing nearby (147), an Oriental Princess Canace listening to the bleeding-heart falcon (169). The fourth, which comes first, is of the Miller playing his bagpipe and leading the pilgrims on their way (12), a conventional procession picture that goes back to Blake and Stothard and to Haweis, while the other choices emphasize women. Kirk's illustrations were favored in the Untied States, perhaps because of publishing restraints or as an example of "the feminization of American culture" in the late nineteenth century. Kirk, born in Philadelphia, educated at the Philadelphia School of Design for Women, winner of the 1894 prize from the Philadelphia Academy of Fine Arts for the best painting by a woman, was a painter of portraits. She illustrated, in color, more than fifty books for children, including classic titles like *Heidi, Pinocchio, Hiawatha, The Secret Garden,* and *Shakespeare's Tales* (1911).

Darton reached another readership in the United States in a popular encyclopedia, *The Junior Classics,* issued by Collier in 1912. Volume 4, an anthology of favorites, is titled *Heroes and Heroines of Chivalry* and includes three tales from Darton's Chaucer: *The Old Woman and the Knight, Death and the Three Revellers,* and *Patient Griselda.* The only illustration is for *Patient Griselda,* that of Thomson with the caption "'This is my bride,' he cried to all the people." There are no identifications of pilgrim tellers or prologues; indeed nothing is said about a pilgrimage. A brief note names Chaucer as the first great English poet albeit difficult to read. The placement of Chaucer's stories in this volume puts them among the famous heroes—Arthur and his knights, Robin Hood, El Cid,

Roland and other peers, Don Quixote, Horn, and Havelock—whose exciting stories were a staple of Edwardian children's literature.

J(oseph) Walker McSpadden

Darton's closest rival was J. Walker McSpadden (1874–1960), who contributed the Chaucer volume to Harrap's Told through the Ages Series, for which he had already written *Stories from Wagner* and *Stories of Robin Hood* as well as *Waverley Synopses*. There are three distinct versions: *Stories from Chaucer* (1907) with black-and-white illustrations of the Ellesmere pilgrims, a Victorian painting and sculpture of Chaucer, and original pictures by Victor Prout; *Tales from Chaucer* (1909), a shortened version in the All Time Tales Series, often used as a school text, includes only Prout's pictures; and *The Canterbury Pilgrims Retold from Chaucer* (1917), a deluxe edition of *Stories from Chaucer* in a larger format with M.L. Kirk's lovely colored illustrations. As previously noted, some of these were used for Kelman's nursery *Stories from Chaucer.*

Harrap, who specialized in books for children, aimed their Told Through the Ages Series at children older than the nursery audience of Jack's Told to the Children Series, but it included many of the same titles.[20] Early advertisements identified "a new series of prize books" and used a subtitle "Truth and Myth from Song & Story." The professed intention was "to include those epics and stories of the past which have survived the chances of time, reflecting as they do, the genius of the nations which gave them birth." In short, children were to gain detailed knowledge of national/racial identity through literature. The standard large crown octavo volumes, measuring five-and-a-half by seven-and-a-half inches, are elegantly bound with brown half-leather spine and green cloth with elaborate decorative gold designs. They sold for two shillings and six pence. Harrap also offered "a superior edition of these books printed upon pure rag paper and bound in full and half-leather in various styles.... Full particulars upon applications." These, like the deluxe *The Canterbury Pilgrims,* were presumably for special prizes or gifts, a line that Harrap fostered longer than other Edwardian publishers. Alternatively, there were cheaper versions, of blue or gray cloth, with titles and author's name and an illustrative picture stamped in black. To own this series was to have a substantial library of canonical literature, a matched collection of well-written and very-well-produced books, each with at least sixteen full-page illustrations. In the United States Thomas Y. Crowell published McSpadden's many children's books, ranging from ghost stories to opera

18   Stories from Chaucer

Now I have told you in brief the array and number of this company of pilgrims who were

CHAUCER

assembled at Tabard Inn, and so it is time to tell you what happened with us that night, and afterward of the journey itself.

Opposite and above: The Ellesmere Chaucer portrait above, opposite Victor Prout's "We Rode away to St. Thomas's Well," juxtaposes medieval illumination and modern illustration in J. Walker McSpadden's *Stories from Chaucer* (1907) in the Told through the Ages Series. The fifteenth-century figures were often reproduced and Chaucer is easily recognizable. Alternatively, processions of pilgrims were inspired by modern paintings, notably Thomas Stothard's *The Pilgrimage to Canterbury* (1806–07) and William Blake's Chaucer's *Canterbury Pilgrims* (1810).

"After Him! The Fox! The Fox!" is the chase scene in the *Nun's Priest's Tale*. M.L. Kirk's busy rendering for J. Walker McSpadden's *The Canterbury Pilgrims: Retold from Chaucer* (1917) includes many human and animal pursuers of the fox that has captured proud Chaunticleer, a much-loved tale that for children becomes a simple beast fable. The thatched roofs on the cottages and glass windows put Chaucer's poor widow in a somewhat modern and prosperous situation.

to paintings to baseball. *Stories from Chaucer* was in a series Children's Favorite Classics that sold for fifty cents. The 124-page book was praised as "One of the best prose renderings of Chaucer. Parts of the original poems are woven in the narratives. Inexpensive."[21]

In Harrap's *Stories from Chaucer* the frontispiece is a photograph of sculptor George Frampton's bust of Chaucer in the Guildhall Library, London.[22] A reproduction of Ford Madox Brown's *Chaucer Reading to Edward III* appears later (28) as well as a reduced facsimile page from Harley MS. 1758 of the *Canterbury Tales* (190). Woodcut copies of fourteen Ellesmere pilgrims decorate the Prologue; but the major illustrations, twelve full-page, black-and-white original pictures, are the work of Victor Prout (1842–1912), a French watercolorist. He also drew his own equestrian groups, notably a processional scene that features Chaucer (18–19), but emphasizes narrative with twelve pictures from the stories. Many images are traditional: knights in armor (Arcite in the lists, 44; the Knight with the hag, 96) and pensive and grieving women (Constance adrift, 78; the old woman protesting her innocence to the Summoner, 112; Dorigen in despair, 152; humble Griselda in her shift, 134). There are two pictures of Gamelyn, the tested and vindicated youth (challenging with club in hand, 164, and bound while many in hall mock him, 172). Prout emphasized chivalry in images both of strong males and of women in need.

In contrast to Prout Kirk's images of feminine beauty decorate the larger format of *The Canterbury Pilgrims*.[23] Although she did draw a vivid scene of knights in combat, "For Two Hours More They Fought" in *The Story of Idylls of the King* (1912)[24] that could be used for the *Knight's Tale*, her illustrations of Chaucer tales feature women and stress gentleness. Of twelve, six focus on women exclusively, three on larger groups, while only four show men, none chivalric. The cover picture is of the pilgrims riding toward Canterbury and directs attention to the Cathedral in the distance, while in a *Prologue* illustration, "The Miller plays the Company out of Town" (16); both are stops below trees on the Pilgrims' Way. A third, a crowd scene, is dominated by women, as the widow and daughters, calling, "After him! The fox! The fox!" (63), rush past thatched cottages in the *Priest's Tale*. Peasant Griselda appears in a peaceful pastoral setting, "tending her flocks and spinning busily at the same time" (137). Dressed in blue with a white cap, she sits on the ground, while sheep graze near her or sleep peacefully under the trees. The aristocratic ladies are Emily, shown picking roses in the garden (26), and "Constance in the Boat" (86), holding her baby son. Both wear pink, an emblem of femininity; Emily is blonde and Constance has light-brown hair, and their heads are uncovered. A sense of quiet pervades. In contrast, the other lady, "Canace and

"Emily in the Garden" echoes an archetypal medieval scene of the enclosed garden, here in profuse bloom. The very young and beautiful maiden attracts the male gaze and innocently provokes the rivalry of the two imprisoned cousins who behold her from the tower and cease to be friends when they compete for her love. M.L. Kirk's color illustrations for the *Knight's Tale* in J. Walker McSpadden's *The Canterbury Pilgrims: Retold from Chaucer* (1917) are very feminine.

the Falcon," is a black-haired woman, exotically dressed in an Oriental costume patterned in red; pointed shoes and turban are also red, and she lifts her overskirt to catch the red blood that spills from the bird's breast (168). Only the Wife has two illustrations, and one is not apt. The frontispiece, "The Wife of Bath walks in Spring," shows her in an English garden with the Prioress, both very young. This pretty and charming scene is similar to one by Thomson in Darton's *Tales* and taken from the *Prologue of Beryn*—which McSpadden does not include. The other, the Wife's equestrian figure, marks her Tale (104). The Wife's costume is the same in both, a muted yellow dress with darker yoke decoration, and a broad white hat with blue ribbons over her long plaited hair.[25] Kirk's costumes, in comparison with Haweis's copying of authentic details derived from medieval images, are romantic imaginings and more softly colored.

Compared to these illustrations, those of men are less compelling, although a picture of the Squire that accompanies the *Prologue*, "Singing he was, or flute-playing, all day long" (10) is an appeal to adolescents. A young man stands against a wall, playing his flute, while other pilgrims rest or attend their horses. Like the aristocratic ladies, he wears pink, albeit patterned with white. The Friar is also shown as a musician: he sits on a bench, singing and accompanying himself on a stringed instrument before an audience of three young people (118). This portrait recalls the closing lines, "and when he played and sang his eyes twinkled like stars on a frosty night" (12) of McSpadden's softened description in the *General Prologue*. The Miller with his bagpipe is at the center of the scene of departure. The only other picture is "The Pardoner refreshes himself" (68). Seated at a table, with a relic cross set to the side, he bites hungrily into a cake and clutches a tankard of ale in his left hand; a maid bearing another tankard of ale is poised to come outside the inn, a hint at the Pardoner's excessive drink.

Although Kirk's images show some worldliness, like the edited passages in the *Prologue*, they do not portray licentious living. The absence of chivalric action, such as questing knight or tournament, underscores how this volume sustains the emphasis upon women in the nursery books of the Stories Told to the Children Series. The interests recall those in idealized paintings by Edward Burne-Jones, *Dorigen of Bretaigne Longing for the Safe Return of Her Husband* (1871) and several treatments of *Chaucer's Dream of Good Women* (1865), not to mention his early decoration of a cabinet for William Morris with scenes from *The Prioress' Tale* (1858–59). Edwardian versions of Chaucer for children similarly upheld much to emulate in women. Harrap's printing of McSpadden with Kirk's illustrations implies more than a shift to color, especially since other editions favored them. Darton's vigorous enthusiasm for male heroism and prowess and Thomson's illustrations are, of course, extraordinary. Kirk's illustrations accent feminine qualities, and their use as replacement for Thomson's vibrant male images possibly reflects an American publisher's urge to feminize Darton, in keeping with trends in nineteenth-century American culture. Ann Douglas has argued that a Victorian alliance between women and the clergy encouraged sentimentalism, especially in popular fiction and images of pure and beautiful females.[26] Nevertheless, McSpadden keeps high standards of moral virtue and knightly idealism by stressing nobility of spirit.

McSpadden renders Chaucer's stories fairly closely, but usually shortens them, especially by eliminating long passages of description and rhetoric. He sometimes modifies details to heighten the chivalric idealism and expunges or gives didactic explanation for unsavory vulgarity or immoral sexual actions. The book occasionally shifts from prose to modernized passages of Chaucer's poetry, usually to describe virtues of women and to intensify male idealism. Emily's description in the *Knight's Tale*, translated without shortening, illustrates such heightening. The concluding lines are:

> Her yellow hair was braided in a tress
> Behind her back—a yard in length, I guess;
> And in the garden as the sun uprose
> She wandered up and down where as she chose.
> She gathered flowers partly white and red
> To make a witching garland for her head,
> And as an angel heavenly she sang [24].

Like Darton, McSpadden attempts to maintain Chaucer's idea of a pilgrimage; he includes prologues but creates his own order for the tales and both cuts and adds to the dramatic framework. *The Canterbury Pilgrims* has an abbreviated *General Prologue*; ten tales, one of which is *Gamelyn*, here made Chaucer's Tale; and an *Epilogue*, which explains that Chaucer left the work incomplete and encourages imaginative speculation. The title of each tale identifies both the teller and subject matter, and tales are arranged to suggest connections among the pilgrims and to create a greater sense of drama. Those tales and characters included are, in order, *The Knight's Tale*, Palamon and Arcite; *The Priest's Tale*, The Cock and the Fox; *The Pardoner's Tale*, The Three Rioters; *The Man of Law's Tale*, Constance; *The Wife of Bath's Tale*, A Woman's Wish; *The Friar's Tale*, The Wicked Summoner; *The Clerk's Tale*, Patient Griselda; *The Squire's Tale*, Cambuscan and the Brazen Horse; *The Franklin's Tale*,

Dorigen; *Chaucer's Tale*, Gamelyn. There is one difference from *Stories from Chaucer*, which instead of the *Squire's Tale* provided a second version of the *Knight's Tale*, John Dryden's verse translation, after the Epilogue. Thus there is more chivalry and less magic and an example of Chaucer's place in the development of English literature. Prout's illustration that shows the confrontation between the two young men in the forest is the only example of figures in classical dress, a nice continuity with Dryden's neoclassical style. The simplest version of McSpadden's three retellings is *Tales from Chaucer*, with only seven tales, the Prologue and Epilogue, and Prout's illustrations. The cover picture, also the frontispiece, both in color, is "Constance." The six other illustrations are on ordinary paper, not glossy, and somewhat cruder versions of the same episodes in *Stories from Chaucer*. The only new illustration is an initial heading with small figures of mounted pilgrims, framed by the title and a bottom scroll carrying their names—Chaucer, Prioress, Squire, Friar, Knight, Pardoner. It is not a match: the Clerk is absent and the *Squire's Tale* is not in the book.

A few examples of McSpadden's revision in the *General Prologue* indicate something of his values. He leaves out entire portraits: the Merchant appears only as a name in a list with Guildsmen, along with the Shipman and Physician, and they have no tales. The omission, in contrast to Darton's introduction of *Beryn*, suggests a lack of interest in men in trade. Some other portraits, like the Prioress and Reeve, are preserved without tales to follow. McSpadden deletes physiological details that gloss the sexuality of the Wife and Pardoner, and the Friar's wantonness also disappears, since even his trinkets are "to give to people" (12). Instead of being "oure aller cock" (I.823), McSpadden's "clever Host gathered us together as a hen gathers her chicks" (19), a feminine and gentler image. This has a later resonance in the *Priest's Tale*, where the sexual relationship of Chaunticleer and Pertelotte consists of brief domestic talk with muted antagonism, and there is a quick shift to a description of seven hens pecking corn in the yard. Although all of the portraits are shortened, the general locations of campaigns for the Knight and Squire remain. Occasions of strife and vulgarity are cut completely or made nonthreatening. Thus the *Prologue to the Priest's Tale* explains that the Miller "began to spin out a droll yarn about a carpenter who was outwitted by two clerks" (55). The pilgrims recognize the danger of the Pardoner's "vulgar jests" (67), but the eschatological conclusion of his encounter with the Host when he attempts to sell relics is but "a wordy quarrel" (79) that the Knight stops. This is part of the *Prologue to the Man of Law's Tale*, where McSpadden introduces explicit verbal play: "The Landlord rolled these legal terms like sweet morsels under his tongue, and even the lawyer was forced to

"Arcite Spurred His Horse down the Lists" pictures the great tournament in the *Knight's Tale*, Chaucer's long chivalric romance. Victor Prout depicts the hero in plate armor with lance lowered, in J. Walker McSpadden's *Stories from Chaucer* (1907) in the Told through the Ages Series.

Victor Prout's "I am Palamon, Thy Mortal Foe!" shows the rival lovers in classical dress to illustrate John Dryden's *Palamon and Arcite*, or the *Knight's Tale*, printed at the end of J. Walker McSpadden's *Stories from Chaucer* (1907), in the Told through the Ages Series. The two versions allow comparison between Chaucer's original and a seventeenth-century neoclassical retelling, demonstrate Chaucer's place at the start of the English literary tradition, and increase the emphasis upon chivalry.

smile as he replied" (80). Thus geniality replaces many authorities, rhetoric, and high sentiment. The Landlord quickly cuts off the quarrel between the Friar and the Summoner (117), but at the end the Friar specifically identifies his fellow pilgrim as the object of attack. The self-revealing prologue that Chaucer gave to the Wife becomes a brief paragraph noting that "she launched into her entire history and that of her five husbands" (103).

Similarly, McSpadden reduces the Pardoner's long opening sermon about sins to a parenthetical paragraph and adds a reader/listener response: "The company were fain to yawn and gape before he was through his diatribe and ready to resume the thread of his tale" (69). Avoidance of the grim and heavily didactic suggests why McSpadden did not include saints' legends but relied upon moral warnings in much simplified versions of the *Priest's Tale, Pardoner's Tale,* and *Friar's Tale. The Cock and the Fox* is here a simple beast fable with almost none of Chaucer's philosophical and scientific elaboration and without rhetoric; *The Three Rioters* tells of the seeking of Death, a bare swift narrative, as is the devil's taking away of *The Wicked Summoner.*

The length of *Palamon and Arcite* is admittedly difficult, but McSpadden favored it in a way that Kirk's illustrations deny. He succeeds in emphasizing both that Theseus is "the flower of chivalry" and that Emily is very beautiful and inspires rival love from the cousins who are imprisoned and graciously acquiesces, "for women always follow the favor of fortune" (47). His finest descriptions of martial combat come in the *Knight's Tale*; several evocative passages are as powerful as any in countless Edwardian children's stories of chivalry. For example

> Such noise and clattering of horse and armor as was heard in all public places! Such an array of horsemen! Lords in rich steel gleaming with gold; knights with embroidered helmets; squires nailing heads to spears and buckling visors; armorers busy with file and hammer; yeoman on foot lacing the armor-plates; common soldiers hastening about armed only with staves—all was bustle and commotion while the foamy steeds champed upon their golden bits. Pipes, trumpets, clarinets, and drums resounded on every hand [43]. ...[T]hen the gates were shut and the herald cried aloud: "Sir knights, now do your duty!" The trumpets rang the charge loud and clear, and at the same instant the two companies sprang forward into shock of battle. Now might one see who could joust and who could ride! The spears shiver like straws upon the thick shields. Swords flash like fire and descend mightily upon helmets. Maces go crashing through breastplates.... Blood flows freely on every side, despite the first orders of Duke Theseus [45–46].

Comparison with Chaucer's text (I.2492–2515 and 2597–2635) shows that McSpadden preserves the excitement of the tournament and the ferocity of combat. He gives similar attention to the pageantry of Arcite's funeral and to Emily's marriage "with all bliss and melody" to Palamon. At the happy conclusion, McSpadden introduces a rhetorical question to add a hint of fairy tale: "Need I say that they lived happily ever after?" (52) before concluding with the last eight lines of Chaucer's poem. Since he cuts much philosophical commentary and speculation, McSpadden intensifies Chaucer's chivalry. "The good Duke Theseus, always mindful of the right thing," survives as a source of order and calm but with abbreviated speeches and appearances. In this child's version the concern is with the three young people.

Such readers like stories of magic, which the *Squire's Tale* generously supplies. Here again there are fine scenes with knights, like the entry into the hall where Cambuscan is holding a splendid feast, but greatest attention is given to magical items. The brazen horse, remarkable for its capacity to fly, is especially memorable, while mirror, sword, and ring are the kinds of things that children playing at knights would find helpful in their games. McSpadden chooses to keep the tale unfinished, indicating in a footnote that conclusions written by others, notably Spenser, are not "sufficiently near to the spirit of the original tale to justify inclusion in this volume" (170). This is antithetical to Darton's enrichment with Chaucerian apocrypha. The unfinished quality, the possibilities inherent in magic items, carry some of the excitement of chivalric romance and appeal to imaginative speculation, and study questions can ask for an ending.

While Palamon and Arcite are easily rendered attractive and worthy for the admiration of young readers, the Knight in Chaucer's *Wife's Tale* had to be drastically changed. Again the rapist's offense is simply unnamed; McSpadden indicates the young man's failure and situation without being specific: "He was in sore trouble, for he was in disgrace and banishment. He had sinned grievously against the laws of chivalry of the Round Table, and King Arthur had condemned him to die" (105). The Queen intervenes to save his life, but his year's experience is made sympathetic, since women appear not as victims but as oppressors. The Knight's answer is unqualified: "the thing that woman wishes for most of all, is to have the headship of the house, and make her husband obey her will" (109). This is more domestic and assertive than Chaucer's "sovereynetee" and "maistrie" (III.1038, 1040), which mean rule and dominion but do not specify obedience to another's will that suggests Edwardian views of sexual roles.

The Knight's indignation at being forced to marry evokes great sympathy. First, when the hag demands the man she has saved by giving the answer to the riddle, she is "turning to him with a horrid leer upon her wrinkled face." Second, authorial interpretation justifies his dismay: "Indeed it must be said that the Knight was more blunt than courteous in this speech; but he had sore provocation as he stood there in sight of all the court faced by this ancient crone" (110). This passage, especially for a youthful male reader, appeals for empathy with embarrassment in a public situation and provocation exonerates discourtesy, a kind of male energy. McSpadden even adds female sympathy for the unwilling bridegroom: "the Queen and her ladies were greatly amused by this scene, though they could not help being sorry for the Knight" (110).

Denigration of the Hag continues. Her teasing about the lack of male enthusiasm on a wedding night becomes a case of an Arthurian knight's not keeping his word in spirit. McSpadden retains the essential argument that he who deals most gently with others is gentlest born, but he changes the emphasis. The old woman's long exposition of "gentillesse" (III.1109–1219) becomes no more than this statement, without any authorities or reference to poverty. Instead, there is further analysis of the Knight's feelings: "Thereupon she took him quietly to task for his rudeness, and withal talked so wisely and so well that the Knight was amazed. He began to feel more kindly toward her, and to feel ashamed of himself" (111). Thus when the Hag describes alternatives and offers a choice, his response becomes the point of interest: "The nobler nature of the Knight was struck with this appeal. The winning charm of her wisdom drew him to her irresistibly." And when she asks whether she has the mastery, she is "laughing," and the question is called a riddle (112). This mitigates serious concern, while the conclusion alters the nature of the story. The Hag's transformation into a beautiful maiden is explained: "For she was a fairy who had taken this means of trying his knightly honor" (113). Thus the tale fits into a familiar genre for children and suggests a Victorian fantasyland of make-believe rather than a primitive folktale. A final paragraph describes a "model wife," and the well-matched couple live peacefully. The ambiguity of the last sentence—"But whether she continued to rule the house, or left the lordship to him, the chronicle does not say" (113)—makes possible a return to control by the male, at risk for a year, embarrassed and constrained, but regaining a position of strength.

The title *A Woman's Wish* signals McSpadden's change in argument; the action stems not from male violence but from some unidentified disgrace that is soon displaced by a testing set by a supernatural female, who is described as ugly and provocative, even "leering." The old hag is thus an inversion of *la belle dame sans merci*; instead of a pretty young temptress who leads a knight astray and to destruction, she is an old hag who reawakens his inherent nobility, restores his honor, and rewards him with an advantageous marriage. As a chivalric story, this *Wife of Bath's Tale* presents a hero who is discourteous, not violent, who briefly fails to realize his nobility but is amenable to kindness and gentleness of instruction, and whose positive response to conciliatory female behavior produces a magic and happy solution.

The married knight's situation is not always so simple as this fairy tale ending suggests. In the *Franklin's Tale* the quandary comes a year and more after the marriage:

> But the Knight had always been a man of war, and even this blissful wedded life could not keep him from restlessness. He wished to go to England to seek service in arms, and perchance win fame and honor. Dorigen thought he had fought enough, but would not say him nay, when she saw how his heart was set on the journey [176].

Here is comforting reassurance that male chivalry—and colonial service in the Empire—will not be deterred by marriage; wives support what their husbands want. Dorigen's plight, like Griselda's, suggests an inadequacy that male forbearance will set right. She is naive: "the pure-hearted Dorigen did not suspect him" [Aurelius]; although clear in her refusal ("This is my final word, and I pray you never to speak thus again"), she responds to his grief and "added as if in play" the promise to love him upon removal of the rocks. Finally, Aurelius explains to the magician that the lady "had given her promise only in jest and never dreaming such a miracle could happen" (189). Again McSpadden relies upon jest as a rationalization for dubious speech.

Aurelius's betrayal of a knightly code by seeking another man's wife is a temporary lapse, offset by his recognition of this failing when the couple's behavior inspires him:

> He began to ponder over it, and his heart was filled with great compassion. He saw how selfish he had been, and his true nobleness of nature overcame the evil which had been in his heart so long. Never, he thought, could he consent to deal so wretchedly and churlishly against knightly courtesy and honor [187].

Arveragus's nobility is specially marked because McSpadden gives the exchange between husband and wife in verse (186). He then simplifies the situation to terms easily accessible to children: "You have made a foolish promise, but it *is* a promise all the same, and must be kept" (187). Here the knight is both chivalrous in his own behavior and the inspiration for others to behave nobly.

Both the Clerk's Tale of *Patient Griselda* and the Man of Law's Tale of *Constance* contain incidental modifications to strengthen claims for the chivalry of male heroes. Walter's acquiescence to the demands of his people that he accept the "blissful yoke" of marriage (134) is described as "good-naturedly agreed" (135), and his persecution of his wife with cruel testing is finally identified as "a cruel jest" (157) and given value as a way of proving Griselda's glorious womanhood. Again the rationalization is somewhat extraordinary, but the Clerk explains in the Prologue to the next tale that "the moral is that every wight should be constant in adversity" (161).

That theme could be seen as apt for Chaucer's Tale, *Gamelyn*. The Prologue refers to an interruption of the *Tale of Sir Thopas*, but McSpadden, in keeping with his evasion of religion, makes Chaucer's second tale not the sermon *Melibeus* but another chivalric story. The issue is not love but the achievement of manhood and inheritance, a compelling subject for young readers, as previously noted. Brothers dispute and fight each other before the hero receives both his own rightful estate and the land of his elder brother. Instead of knightly jousts and sophisticated banter there are fights with cudgels and a wrestling bout that would remind a child of the merry adventures of Robin Hood, whether in ballads or prose retellings. The setting in a wood and outlaw band are favorite topics, often evoked by the phrase "under the greenwood." Further, the tale addresses a question of social justice; both sheriff and judge are hanged because they are corrupt. Such a triumph and the satisfaction of the winning underdog, the younger child who succeeds, are popular motifs in fairy tales. The Chaucer books of both Darton and McSpadden were widely disseminated and influential, but others took different approaches.

Emily Underdown

Like Darton and McSpadden, Emily Underdown is a major writer of canonical stories for children. Her *The Gateway to Chaucer* (1912) is probably the most thoughtful presentation to children and a luxurious example of printing. She had already contributed two other books to the Gateway Series, published by Thomas Nelson. Under the pseudonym "Norley Chester," she wrote *Stories from Dante* (1898) and *Knights of the*

Grail: Lohengrin: Galahad (1907), and with Richard Wilson retold *Three Northern Romances: Siegfried—Lohengrin—Undine* (1925). These classics are indicative of her long-lasting interest in medieval stories, including their prolongation with *The Adventures of Don Quixote* (1910). The thoughtfulness of Underdown's treatment of Chaucer begins with the endpapers that have framed lines from the lyric "Soothfastnesse" that urges "Flee from the press.... Suffice thee of thy good though it be small." The cover is a brilliant blue, stamped in gold with floral decoration; there are sixteen full-page colored illustrations on glossy paper, five of pilgrims, ten with incidents from the stories; Brown's great Victorian painting of Chaucer is the frontispiece. Most unusual are delightful marginal drawings, as in a medieval manuscript, black-and-white, 118 in all, plus four headings and nine endings.

The artist Anne Anderson (1874–1930), skilled in both watercolor and in black-and-white line artwork, contributed to more than a hundred books, annuals, and treasuries. She followed the tradition of Charles Robinson and Jessie M. King, Jessie Wilcox Smith, and Mabel Lucie Atwell. Like them, she was able to continue working after World War I, which—with a few notable exceptions—marked the end of Edwardian extravagance in children's publishing. Anderson's early art was part of the decorative style that flourished with the Arts and Crafts and Art Nouveau movements; her illustrations are exquisite examples of a romantic use of period costume, slim elegant figures, swirling flourishes, and flowing curves. Subjects of her line drawings are remarkably varied—castles and town scenes, weapons, warriors, ships, a treasure chest and banquet table, flowers, animals—but the dominant image is an Art Nouveau lovely lady, beautifully attired and often alone, central to the chivalric emphasis of the stories.[27]

The *Gateway to Chaucer*[28] is one of several imposing volumes designed to introduce major authors; Underdown also wrote *The Gateway to Romance: Tales Retold from "The Earthly Paradise" of William Morris* (1909) and *The Gateway to Spenser* (1911); other volumes were gateways to Shakespeare and Tennyson. These books were expensive, priced at five shillings. Nelson issued a selection the following year as *Stories from Chaucer* in their extensive Golden River Series of literary classics in small format (five by six-and-a-half inches) that was suitable for school use and sold for one shilling.[29] The text and color illustrations are the same, but there are no Interlude sections about the pilgrims or marginal drawings; the purpose is simply to offer the stories. The Gateway Series is in a large format that allows Underdown to include extensive supporting materials; she also creates a theme of "Soothfastnesse," announced in the end papers that quote lines from Chaucer's lyric. The frontispiece is again Ford Madox Brown's

Anne Anderson's marginal drawings in *The Gateway to Chaucer* (1912).

Chaucer Reading to King Edward III, and an introductory essay about Chaucer quotes Tennyson's praise of him as "the morning-star of song … the first warbler, whose sweet breath" was prelude to Elizabethan "melodius bursts" (10). Thus Underdown sustains respect for the Father of English poetry and Victorian appreciation. A brief biography includes several of Chaucer's comments about himself in his poems and attempts something of a character study: bookish, a confessed scholar and recluse whose work shows great knowledge of humanity in characterizations that are not matched until Shakespeare. Underdown singles out Chaucer's love of nature, again citing his poems. She shares the Edwardian reading of the genial Chaucer and sums him up as

> [T]he most cheerful of poets. Never throughout his works is there trace of the self-pity or of the complaints which often mar the work of even great poets; and more unusual still, among the twenty-four stories which he tells in the Canterbury Tales, there is hardly one which does not end happily [19–20].

In contrast, she turns to the political situation of the fourteenth century, citing the early promise and courage of the boy King Richard II and the later need for Chaucer's urging him to "steadfastness." Finally, Underdown indicates that *The Gateway to Chaucer* is, as the title of the series announces, only a beginning that relies on modern English prose with the hope that Chaucer's original language and poetry will be read in subsequent years.

The layout of *The Gateway to Chaucer* is clear: The Prologue or Introduction followed by six numbered parts, divided into Interlude and Story, and then an Epilogue or Conclusion. Small pictures for Contents and Illustrations give a nice balance of gender, a knight on horseback and a lady seated under trees. The *Prologue* is brief, describing the meeting of the pilgrims and explaining the plan for a storytelling contest. Individual portraits are kept as matter for the Interludes, reinforced by a picture for each small group; for example, Knight, Squire, and Yeoman, to introduce Story I the *Knight's Tale*. The images of chivalry are many: Creon's "unknightly and unchivalrous conduct" brings grief to the ladies and "a burning indignation" to noble Theseus (38). The Queen and Emily feel pity for the two young knights who quarrel and plead for mercy, and the tournament is described in some detail and colorfully pictured in "At once the fight began," in which the ladies are a large foreground and the mounted knights are drawn with swirls of banner and cloak, rather like scenes of the nineteenth-century Eglinton tournament. The theme of steadfastness emerges fully in the comment of Egeus, who rarely survives in children's versions, and Underdown's change to verse highlights it:

> This world is but a thoroughfare of woe,
> And we but pilgrims passing to and fro;
> Death is an end of every earthly pain [89].

"At once the Fight Began" shows the tournament, the set-piece in the *Knight's Tale*, featured in many versions for children. Chaucer's description reveals expert knowledge; as clerk of the king's works he oversaw the building of the seating for royal and noble spectators and the lists at Smithfield in 1390. The artist Anne Anderson, in Emily Underdown's *The Gateway to Chaucer* (1912), foregrounds the scene with ladies who look toward the knights ready to joust. Their sumptuously draped costumes like the banners contribute to the swirling lines of her Art Nouveau style.

Interlude II includes portraits of the Miller, Reeve, and Cook, but no quarrel. The illustration foregrounds the Man of Law as the largest figure, and Story II is his. Again there are notable pictures, like the rudderless boat, a tiny marginalia of a Viking-style vessel (107), and then a full color page "Once more she was adrift" with Constance in blue to evoke Mary, and White Cliffs to indicate Britain. This image, favored in Chaucer retellings, is the cover picture used for Underdown's *Stories from Chaucer.*

Interlude III puts together the portraits of five pilgrims in church offices—Friar, Pardoner, Summoner, Parson, Prioress—who are in the illustration captioned "The Prioress had a simple, innocent smile" (136). But the Host chooses the Priest, who is not described or shown, since Story III is of the *Cock and the Fox.* Underdown preserves much of Chaucer's flavor; for example, she concludes the domestic discourse about dreams with, "Chanticleer having thus as he thought asserted his dignity, turned to more cheerful topics, and began to flatter Pertelote, and tell her how much he admired her beauty" (143–44), and she devotes a paragraph to the laments after the Fox seizes the Cock. Her theme echoes in the Fox's wish that he "thrive badly who has so little self-command as to speak, as I did, when he ought to have held his peace" (152).

Interlude and Story IV belong to the Wife, though there is a bit about the quarrel of the Friar and Summoner. Underdown reduces the Wife's challenging Prologue to one sentence: "No sooner was she called upon than she set forth on a long rambling story of her own life, with a description of her five husbands, and an account of why she had married each in turn, and what worldly goods each had left her" (154–55). Anderson's illustration shows a youthful "lively lady from Bath" (168). In this fairy tale the young Knight is guilty of "a serious offense against the rules of true knightliness. So grave, indeed, was his misbehaviour that the great king felt compelled to pass sentence of death upon him" (158). The finest illustration is in Art Nouveau style with deep rich colors and graceful swirling curves. The Queen with many attendant ladies, says to the kneeling Knight, who wears plate armor, gorgeous red surcoat, and rich blue cloak, "I give you a year and a day" (160). Underdown significantly revises the wedding night scene to reaffirm her theme of steadfastness. The Knight does not leave the choice to the Hag, but makes a bold decision: "There is much wisdom in what you say. You are my wife and my love, and it were better to have such as you for wife than a younger and less virtuous bride" (166–67). He has certainly achieved maturity.

Although Interlude V continues the dispute between the Friar and the Summoner, and includes a paragraph summary of the former's tale,

Two facing pages, one with text and a small ship marginalia and the other a full-page color illustration, "The Bride Entered the City," show the sophistication of Anne Anderson's work in Emily Underdown's *The Gateway to Chaucer* (1912). Constance's entry into a Syrian city is an extraordinarily rich image for the *Man of Law's Tale*. The mosque in the upper portion is set off by the curve of the panoply under which she rides. Large feather fans frame the main figures, and exotic costumes—veils, turban, jewels—appeal to Western fascination with Oriental difference.

interest is on the Clerk of Oxenford, who met Petrarch in Padua and thus heard his tale, which the Clerk retells in its six parts. Griselda, who is "very fair to look upon, was even more fair if we speak of beauty of the mind, for then it would be hard to find her equal under the sun" (177). Her exemplary life of filial piety is a sound basis for obedience to her husband and a life of grace: "Her judgments were so just and her words so wise that every one said that she might have been sent direct from Heaven to help mankind and right all wrongs" (188). The narrator does not admire the ingenuity and subtlety of Walter's testing, but holds it "no merit in him, but the reverse, to tempt his wife to disobey him, and to cause her all the anguish and fear which now came upon her" (190), and he repeats these objections (200–01). At the happy ending, Walter praises Griselda in the terms of Underdown's theme: "Now in truth, dear wife, I am convinced of your steadfastness" (215). Underdown sustains her sophisticated level of retelling with comments about patience and humility (210) and a conclusion that "everyone in his degree should be as firm and patient under adversity as she was" and a progression from mortal man to the "Almighty Power" (218).

The final sequence centers on the Merchant and the Franklin, shown as alert and poised riders (225). There are further comments about wives, including the Landlord's shrew, but Dorigen's story is ultimately a happy one. An authorial comment reiterates the Clerk's point about the virtue of patience and universalizes the need for it in terms easily understood by a child reader: "Every one is sometimes hasty or bad-tempered, and says or does things that are wrong. But these small difficulties should be borne patiently, and people should not be constantly chiding each other for their faults" (227). The happiness of the marriage of Dorigen and Arveragus comes from such understanding. Yet the melancholy of separation is palpable and well illustrated. Again the lady has black hair, but this time wears pink and sits above the shore looking out to an approaching ship (232). Dorigen acquiesces to urgings for "a little change of scene" and "a little diversion" in company; she responds to Aurelius "playfully" (235), thinks the removal of the cruel rocks "can never happen," and urges "put your foolish notions out of your head, and remember that I am a faithful and loving wife of Arveragus, and that I cannot therefore give my heart to any one else" (236). Underdown qualifies the magic demonstrations as only an appearance; she stresses Arveragus's urging, "Truth is the highest thing that man can keep" (245), albeit he grieves over the circumstances. The conclusion is fully "in the chivalry of your action" (251).

The question about who was most generous in the *Franklin's Tale* leads to an Epilogue that explains the similar difficulty to decide which tale is worthy of the prize. Underdown considers divergent points of view among pilgrims and resolves uncertainty with Chaucer's intervention. He reminds the company that "the whole affair is but a pastime" and that he would make the conclusion (256). This he did in his study in Westminster, where he wrote down all of the stories, and his worth is shown in their being read today. The final section of *The Gateway to Chaucer* is another rich introduction to language for the young reader; there are several Middle English passages (with pronounced final-*e* marked)—the opening of the *General Prologue*, portraits of the Knight, Squire, Prioress, Clerk of Oxenford, Poor Parson (all ideal characters to Edwardians), and the Host. The final item, which reaffirms the thesis of *The Gateway to Chaucer*, is "Chaucer's Counsel": "Flee from the press, and dwell with soothfastness."

Thus Emily Underdown, an experienced children's author, wrote one of the most thoughtful collections with great philosophical and historical interest. The distinction of the large *Gateway to Chaucer* sharply contrasts with her *Stories from Chaucer*, which has only three tales—*Knight's, Man of Law's, Clerk's*—and no introductory interludes. The texts of the stories are the same but poorer in *Stories from Chaucer* without the contexts created in *The Gateway to Chaucer*. Underdown continued her advocacy of the Father of English Poetry. In 1925 Nelson published *The Approach to Chaucer*, which reprinted her six prose tales along with some verse renderings by R.H. Horne, Leigh Hunt, and Thomas Povell. "Some of the Canterbury Pilgrims" is an Introduction with portraits from the *General Prologue* in verse; and after the *Knight's Tale* there is "More of the General Prologue," pilgrims with church offices. Since this is a school text, the Epilogue consists of study questions. Such double use of the same retellings in deluxe and school books argues some continuity of expectations. There were, of course, stories from Chaucer written directly for the schoolroom, which are considered in chapter 6.

In Mixed Collections

Another type of extravagant Edwardian collection was of stories from several authors. The Raphael House Library of Gift Books Series resembles Nelson's Gateway Series in elegance but features nineteenth-century authors (Scott, Tennyson, Dickens, Longfellow) and collections of fairy tales and legends, so that it does not devote a volume to Chaucer. But his obvious beast fable, *The Cock and the Fox*, is in *Children's Stories from the Poets: Tales of Romance and Adventure Told in Prose* (1915).[30] M. Dorothy

Belgrave and Hilda Hart also wrote *Children's Stories from Old British Legends* (1921), and *Children's Stories from the Northern Legends* (1916) for the same series. Again mostly nineteenth-century poets are retold, but the book begins with another medieval story, *Havelok the Dane,* which has a miraculous element and includes Pigwiggin's adventure from Drayton's *Nymphidia,* a story rarely retold but highly suitable for the fairy tale emphasis. Belgrave reduces Chaucer's tale to the essential beast fable, which heightens the excitement, and she adds details to suit her audience. Thus the most marvelous thing about Chanticleer is "that he could tell the time of day without a watch to help him," and he crows "Cock-a-doodle-do" (26). Belgrave makes a few didactic points to advise the young: nearly nine o'clock is "much too late for well brought up birds to be still resting on their perches" (29–30); the moral of the tale, though it "is only about a hen, a cock, and a fox," is "that we should keep our eyes open when there is anything about worth looking at, and our mouths shut when there is nothing sensible to say" (33).

Notably, Belgrave retains something of Chaucer's consideration of gender roles, within demure Edwardian language. Partlet first calls Chanticleer "dear heart," but names him "coward" because of his fearful dreams, caused by "eating too much" and remedied by "some medicine." His indignant response is a telling moment for male pride and stretches the audience's sophistication:

> "Thank you," replied Chanticleer, with a sneering sort of chuck—if you can imagine what that is like. "Thank you, Madame, for your very, very, *very* clever advice." He meant this for a scoff, because, although he loved Partlet dearly, he despised her brain, and thought himself much wiser than she was [27].

Like an Edwardian gentleman, Chanticleer fears that he has given offense, "so being a very tactful cock, he decided to smooth things over with a little delicate flattery." However, her "pleasure at her husband's compliment" must have put a "twinkle in Chanticleer's eye," for she knew no Latin to understand the sentence, for which Belgrave gives both a false and real translation (28). Later, when all the hens are happily outside, "their lord was singing away as merrily as a mermaid" (30).

Illustrations by Frank Adams greatly contribute to the effectiveness of *Children's Stories from the Poets*; as in Nelson's Gateway Series they are vivid, numerous, and placed to add variety. In eight pages of text are one full-page and five smaller black-and-white illustrations and one full-page illustration in color. The tale's heading shows Chanticleer on his perch with hens to either side (26), while in a larger closing picture he perches tall with only Partlet; open beaks sign their talking (33). Such detail gives charm to the illustrations, but there is also clever placement. One opening has a wily fox peering from foliage, while opposite is the full-page "What a noise and scrimmage there was!" (28–29), the familiar busy scene in which a crowd of people—bearing spoon, stick, and ax—rush forward; two dogs, a pig, and a goose are at the center. In the next opening Chanticleer has taken refuge on a tree branch at the top of the left page, while Dan Russell looks longingly from the bottom of the right page (30–31). But the full-page "Chanticleer and Dan Russell" is the gem. The cock, rich blue-black feathers with light red neck and head and a bright red comb, crows with his eyes closed while standing on tiptoe on a rock that serves as a stage; opposite, the fox stands on his hind legs with his front legs in position ready to spring and seize him. The fox's mouth is slightly open in anticipation, as its eyes glance warily. He is a magnificent animal, red fur with white front and sweeping long tail tipped in white. The figures emerge from a lush background of green trees with a spot of blue sky and white cloud; yellow flowers in the foreground center Chanticleer's podium. The image is archetypal since Aesop, but Frank Adams has gone back to Chaucer's text for the exact details.

A second mixed collection, *My Book of Stories from the Poets Told in Prose* (1919) by Christine Chaundler (1887–1972), also favors the nineteenth-century, all English Romantics and Victorians except Longfellow.[31] Medieval texts are Chaucer's *Knight's Tale*, Spenser's *The Red Cross Knight*, five poems from *Percy Reliques*, and the old ballad *Valentine and Ursine;* they underpin the chivalry well represented in the modern poems chosen for retelling. Illustrations by A.C. Michael (Exh. 1905–09), including page decorations in black and white (a bishop crowning a king, a knight slaying a dragon, and jousting) and several full pages in color present familiar images of medievalism. Since there is no mention of literary history, this emphasis suggests why Chaucer's *Knight's Tale,* second in length to *Evangeline,* and Spenser's *Red Cross Knight,* were selected. Chaundler retells straightforwardly, in simple language, a series of main events; her objective is to make a story accessible where poetry is not:

> They used long words that only the people who write dictionaries have ever heard of, and they wrote sentences that were so tangled up that even the very cleverest folk found them hard to understand.... [M]any of these poems are so long and so difficult to understand that young people do not care to read them, but all the same the stories they tell are beautiful and interesting, so that it seems a pity that you should miss hearing them altogether [xi].

This ressurance assumes a dislike of poetry, a sign of unusually low expectations about children's skill and imagination, albeit Chaundler concludes her apology with a hope that later on, when they understand more, children will read the originals. Like other retellings for children this *Knight's Tale* features the three young people and stresses friendship, romantic love, and reconciliation. Some details are adjusted: "lights" not "fires" burn on the altar where Emilia prays (I.2331, 32); where "a furie infernal" starts from the ground to startle Arcite's horse (I.2684–87), here "a miracle happened. The ground opened at his feet, and a flame of fire, sent by Pluto from the underground regions at Saturn's request, sprang upward" (36). Arcite's dying speech (I.2765–97) is much simplified, but the reconciliation after his enmity and fighting Palamon is crisply put: "'now that I am dying I have forgotten all else save the great love I once bore him. I pray that you will wed with him when I am gone'" (37). One vivid color illustration, "The Duke rode in between the fighters." (28) concentrates on youthful tension. In the top center of the picture a forceful ruler, his flowing red cloak blown behind him, rides his white horse toward the two energetic youths who wear classical armor to fight with shield and sword. *My Book of Stories from the Poets* is just what the title promises, a good read with adventure, heroism, sentiment, and nobility.

The extraordinary beauty of extravagant Edwardian children's books should not obscure the fact that there were also modest offerings of Chaucer, a recognition of his broad appeal. The key place of the child reader is signed by R. Brimley Johnson (1867–1932), who identifies his *Tales from Chaucer* (1909) as "neither a literal translation nor a free paraphrase" and "not designed exclusively for children."[32] The same text, then, can serve and was presented to both child and adult. Johnson was a prolific editor of letters (Hannah More, Jane Austen, Shelley, Robert Burns) and wrote for a popular audience, as with *A Book of British Ballads* (1912) for Everyman's Library. His *Tales* is of average scale, with notes on the Canterbury Pilgrims (paragraphs from the *General Prologue*), the suggestion of a competition, and six tales: *Knight's, Man of Law's, Nun's Priest's, Pardoner's, Wife's,* and *Clerk's,* or as Johnson titles them: *The Story of Palamon and Arcite, The Story of Constance, The Story of Chanticleer, The Story of Death, The Story of King Arthur's Knight, The Story of Griselda.* One distinctive quality is that Johnson casts Chaucer's stories in a realm of long ago or fairy tale with formulaic openings such as "Once, as the old stories tell us, there lived," "Once upon a time," and "There once lived." He also includes the kind of censoring typical for children, as in the *Wife's Tale,* when "a rude and cruel knight" was seized with a "desire for gold and, without heeding her cries, he roughly attacked her and robbed her of all that she had" (85). And there is a muting of expectation when wives "could not, if they would" follow Griselda in her humility (112). These qualities suggest a child audience, but an absence of extravagant publishing values—handsome covers, engaging illustrations, additional materials for a child's amusement—does not. American publishers often matched their extravagant Edwardian counterparts, as several retellings by American writers show.

᧒ 5 ᧓

American Retellings

The close relationship between American and English literature in general, and children's literature in particular, is obvious in American editions of British books. As shown in chapters 3 and 4, American encyclopedias and collections of medieval stories included Chaucer tales taken from Kelman or Darton, while a British series featured McSpadden. Several other Americans wrote Chaucer stories in the United States during the first decade of the twentieth century. Three collections, two rather comprehensive and one smaller, indicate a wide range of engagement. The popular writer Percy Wallace MacKaye, a man of the theatre, furthered Chaucer's reputation with a play and an opera as well as translations for both adults and children. The books of Calvin Dill Wilson, a reteller of several canonical texts, and of Eva March Tappan, a leading educator and prolific author for children, are very different in the number of tales and complexity of treatment. George Philip Krapp, a literary scholar and editor, wrote versions of four Chaucer tales for his medieval collection, as had the American Abby Sage Richardson and British authors David Murray Smith and Ascott R. Hope in the nineteenth century. Both many similarities and some differences in attitude and ways of presenting him to children indicate distinctions between English and American views of Chaucer, also evident in schoolbooks of Chaucer, which are discussed in chapter 6.

Percy W. MacKaye

While Darton, McSpadden, and Underdown usually wrote children's literature, the work of Percy MacKaye (1875–1956) was more varied, and he achieved greater fame. He was the son of a dramatist and actor and himself became a poet and dramatist as well as a teacher and lecturer. Some of his writing popularized medieval subjects; among his dramatic pieces are *Jeanne d'Arc* (1906), *Saint Louis* (1914), and *Kinfolk of Robin Hood* (1926), but his treatment of Chaucer is a more sustained effort. MacKaye wrote two books of retellings, a play, and an opera. He began with *The Canterbury Tales: A Modern Rendering into Prose* (1904), in collaboration with the academic scholar J.S.P. Tatlock, with whom he subsequently published *The Complete Poetical Works of Geoffrey Chaucer* (1912), with the claim, "Chaucer's entire poetic works have never before been put into modern English."[1] As *The Modern Reader's Chaucer* this volume was reprinted in 1938 and 1940 and was the most widely used translation in the first part of the twentieth century. From the initial edition came MacKaye's children's book *The Canterbury Tales of Geoffrey Chaucer* (1907), which included the *General Prologue* and nine tales, all somewhat revised for easier reading. *The Canterbury Pilgrims: A Comedy* (1903) is an original four-act play, a minor success, reprinted at least twice and subsequently developed.[2] It became an opera with music by Reginald de Koven. MacKaye's text and de Koven's score were published in 1916; the Metropolitan Opera House, New York, accepted it for performance in the 1916–17 season.[3] The impetus for *The Canterbury Pilgrims* was both a love of Chaucer and a wish to balance current dominance of realism on the American stage, which might parallel European efforts of the plays of Yeats. Moreover, MacKaye's early dramatic treatment of Chaucer prepared for his work in pageant drama and community theatre, which were regarded as his greatest contribution.[4] He was one of the most prolific and varied popularizers of Chaucer, and this continued with the publication of a recent facsimile of the children's *The Canterbury Tales*.

From the outset, with Clarke, Haweis, Seymour, and Storr and Turner, there have been two critical issues for retellings of Chaucer for children: the difficulty of his language and abridgments to maintain propriety of subject matter and manageability. Whether for adults or children, any translation differs from and is always lesser than the original. Nevertheless, a translation is better than total ignorance. As MacKaye and Tatlock explain in the Preface of *The Complete Poetical Works*, Chaucer can be read only "by dint of somewhat thorough study ... and undoubtedly such study at first may form a mist between the reader and a sympathetic comprehension of the poet" (vii). Thus they

> have striven always to paraphrase as little and to be as faithful to the
> original as they could; certainly never to misrepresent it. They have

departed from it only to save their version from one or another of four possible stumbling blocks: rhyme and excessive rhythm, obscurity, extreme verbosity, and excessive coarseness. Their rare omission of words or short passages for the last reason has not been indicated; in the still fewer cases where a whole episode is incurably gross or voluptuous (yet Chaucer is never merely vicious), its omission is shown by asterisks [vii].

This is a valuable statement because it makes clear an affinity between Chaucer for adults and for children at the start of the twentieth century, an affinity shaped by an aesthetic and moral code that avoided coarseness. Asterisks and unacknowledged omissions are, predictably, in the *fabliaux.* What some critics decry as Edwardian misrepresentations in children's stories from Chaucer are, in fact, what their parents and teachers accepted with probity. In short, the Edwardian apologias in adult and children's translations are markedly similar.

In a Preface to *The Canterbury Tales of Geoffrey Chaucer* MacKaye begins, "The barrier of obsolete speech is the occasion and the apology for this rendering of the Canterbury Tales in English easily intelligible," and he puts aside whether the barrier is real or imagined. The wish is to present Chaucer to "the educated public" in a translation that "shall best preserve for a modern reader the substance and style of the original."[5] Comparison of the language in the two versions shows that MacKaye made it less archaic in a translation not quite so literal as that initially published. Criteria for aesthetic and moral adjustments are, as we shall see, also quite close. At first glance this is obviously not the case with illustrations, which are not the same in the child and adult volumes—perhaps because of publishing issues. Nevertheless, there are striking correspondences between Warwick Goble (1862–1943) and Walter Appleton Clark (1876–1906), not in style but in choice of subjects and spirit evoked.

Goble, whose career in the 1890s included work for magazines, *Pall Mall Gazette* and *Westminster Gazette*, became noted both for his Orientalism and imaginative strangeness when he illustrated H.G. Wells's *The War of the Worlds.* Extremely talented as a watercolor painter, he became in 1909 the resident illustrator for Macmillan, with offices in London and New York. Much of Goble's work was for deluxe children's classics, notably Kingsley's *The Water Babies* and Grace James's *Green Willow* and *Other Japanese Fairy Tales* (1910). The assignment of this British artist, who worked only occasionally after World War I, to *The Modern Reader's Chaucer* indicates the book's importance to the publisher and an expected affinity between Chaucer and children's literature.

The cover is an example of "Edwardian extravagance" that resembles

"'In the Name of Christ,' Cried This Blind Briton. 'Give Me Back My Sight,'"
marks Constance's arrival in Britain, a Christian in a then pagan land. Warwick
Goble's style is Art Nouveau; here he also shows contemporary interest in Viking
ships, following from discoveries in Scandinavia, and ancient costume. This illustration is for the *Man of Law's Tale* in Percy MacKaye and J.S.P. Tatlock's *The Modern Reader's Chaucer* (1912).

the finest Reward books. Its dark navy cloth, extensively stamped in gold,
has a principal device of a large ship in sail and smaller ships in the background. The endpapers show Blake's traditional procession of pilgrims,
but Goble's pictures make the book memorable. Eighteen of his thirty-
two illustrations are for *The Canterbury Tales*. The pictures are astonishingly beautiful, in Art Nouveau style with some similarities to works by
Edmund Dulac, René Bull, and Kay Nielsen. The number of illustrations
for each tale echoes the favored items in children's stories from Chaucer:
three for the *Knight's Tale*, two each for the *Man of Law's*, *Wife's*, and
Clerk's Tale; and only three for tales not usually found in collections for
children. Two scenes for the *Knight's Tale* focus on men: an initial "Theseus Returning in Triumph," a processional scene in woods below an
acropolis (17), and the "The Meeting in the Wood," when Palamon and
Arcite in delicate Greek robes and not wearing armor first see each other
amidst flowers (even a wreath on Palamon's head, 27). The third is "Emily
in the Garden" of a classical villa with red, white, and pink roses and a
similarly laden bush of oranges (18); it is the first example of Goble's

"An Elf Queen Will I Verily Love" shows magical fantasy for *Chaucer's Tale of Sir Thopas* in Percy MacKaye and J.S.P. Tatlock's *The Modern Reader's Chaucer* (1912). Warwick Goble's delineation of Chaucer's knight of metrical romance riding through a dark forest looks somewhat Quixotic, white bearded and richly clothed, in contrast to a youthful elf queen swathed in and surrounded by swirling drapery.

favored image, slender elegant young females in gorgeous clothing. In the *Man of Law's Tale* there is a different historical interest. "'In the name of Christ,' cried this blind Briton, 'Give me back my sight'" (84) and "Constance and her child leaving Northumberland" (88) show a barren landscape with Viking ships; the costumes express the Edwardian view of what early Northern peoples wore, familiar from countless children's books and public, civic pageants. The *Wife's Tale* emphasizes youth and beauty: in "The Knight and the Old Woman," a bevy of maidens, behind the Hag, look in rapt fascination at the young hero on his white horse (172); and she is almost lost in "The Knight and the Old Woman at the Court"— which is exclusively female, apart from one youth at the shore where there are two Viking ships against a background of cliffs (174). The hero is not the Romantic medieval figure in armor but a Viking warrior (horned helmet and horse's decorated bridle) more suitable to King Arthur's time. The illustration for *Sir Thopas* is "An elf queen will I verily love" (108); here a Quixotic knight, albeit he holds a lance aloft, wears a broad brimmed high hat, a colorful long sleeved coat, and a yellow cloak, as he rides a white horse toward a fair-haired maiden in floating blue gossamer. The figures are set against bare trees that could be found in a picture of Arthur Rackham. "Dorigen Pledging Aurelius" has two figures, dressed in vivid dark colors, standing on a promontory at the center of a scene dominated by gray-blue rocks and sea; discreetly visible just to the side are three ladies to preserve propriety (256).

Attractive and winsome images of women, whether alone or with others dominate the volume: Emilia, mentioned above; "Zenobia," an Oriental lovely out hunting (bow and arrows) with her two leopards (122); "Griselda robed in Cloth of gold," with an extraordinarily long train (rather like those of Gustav Klimt), held by two of the three attendant ladies who are dressing her (204); an Oriental "Canacee and the Falcon," again with a featured patterned cloak with lovely swirls and small flowers, in a setting with both bare trees and exotic flowers (246); and an "Alison" (54), wearing a dark blue dress with long patterned over sleeves and long black ribbons swirling down from her hair against a plain background, and smiling barely to hint at the action in the *Miller's Tale*. Goble is bolder for the *Merchant's Tale* with "January Helping May into the Tree" (236). Here Damien is a youthful fair-haired squire to match pretty May. However, the real interest of the picture is not so much the action (chosen at an innocent moment) as the clothing—exquisite, colorful, patterned—and the tree, hugged by January, with its convenient stepped branches and a canopy of leaves and pears; daffodils and Japanese tulips delicately fill the lower space.

In "Griselda Robed in Cloth of Gold," Warwick Goble pictures extraordinary preparations for the marriage in the *Clerk's Tale*, in Percy MacKaye and J.S.P. Tatlock's *The Modern Reader's Chaucer* (1912). Her cloak dominates the picture, its size and golden color similar to ones in Gustav Klimt's Secessionist work, *Art Nouveau in Vienna*.

A few illustrations, in addition to the meeting of Palamon and Arcite, emphasize men. In "Virginius and Virginia" the lovely maiden in swirling pink drapery is fainter than her father, a Roman in dark robe and shoulder armor, who holds her as he prepares to thrust his short sword (144). In the first meeting of "Griselda and the Duke," his rich blue-bordered cloak and the jewels about his neck as well as his arms thrown back in supplication are more compelling than her ragged dress and bare feet—albeit this female image is one often presented by the successful nineteenth-century French painter William Adolphe Bougereau (1825–1905), for whom children were a favorite subject. An exclusively male picture, "The Three Rioters and the Gold" (154), shows plotting but, like that of Palamon and Arcite, stresses costume and a setting under massive trees. The last image, "The Angel presenting the crowns to Cecily and Valerian" (272) in the *Second Nun's Tale*, is a renunciation of sexuality. This unusual pictorial ending is a strong didactic finish; a splendid angel in the center, whose arched wings are reiterated by a swirling drapery, signs a worthy conclusion of Christian sanctity. The Art Nouveau style is more

"January Helping May into the Tree," is a scene from the *Merchant's Tale*, a *fabliau* and thus usually ignored in Chaucer books for children. However, Percy MacKaye and J.S.P. Tatlock's *The Modern Reader's Chaucer* (1912) is a complete works. It was often favored for high school students with Warwick Goble's illustrations specially recommended. This picture is one of the most engaging, again emphasizing gloriously decorative and colorful costume but also a dramatic situation shown at a crucial moment that avoids indecency.

developed than in W. Heath Robinson's illustrations for Kelman's nursery *Stories from Chaucer*, but nothing in Goble's pictures would be out of place in a book for children. A reviewer in Chicago decribed *The Modern Reader's Chaucer* as "extremely attractive" because of Goble's illustrations, albeit they are in black and white. This less expensive edition ($3.75) was recommended for high school libraries, although another reviewer cautioned, "very desirable if it can be afforded."[6]

MacKaye's selection from *The Canterbury Tales* resembles those of many Edwardians, since his choices reiterate the privileging of certain tales, typically ones with high sentiment, of religion and chivalry, and some humor. Like their British counterparts, Americans found in classic texts from the Middle Ages much that could inspire and reassure: adults choose the values that they want children to encounter. MacKaye's adaptation of his translation for adults to a book more suitable for children may express an American's less-conscious need to build a national literature, but he sustained his dedication to Chaucer more than to other medieval subjects. Very telling is the fact that in an ethos consistent for child and adult, the favorite stories from the *Canterbury Tales* are remarkably consistent.

MacKaye's chosen and somewhat modified tales are those of the Knight, Nun's Priest, Physician, Pardoner, Wife of Bath, Clerk, Squire, Franklin, Canon's Yeoman. The order is, as in most Edwardian collections, that of Skeat's edition, praised as the best commentary. Aesopian stories, such as the *Cock and the Fox*, as earlier noted, are especially popular for children, and in a collection without *fabliaux*, its comic qualities contrast effectively with the seriousness of the *Knight's Tale* in both subject matter and style. Thus MacKaye sustains Chaucer's principle of alternation. Each of the nine tales is preceded by its prologue, but with this order and omissions the connection is often missing. A footnote to the *Canon's Yeoman's Prologue*, for example, must explain that Saint Cecilia was the subject of the *Second Nun's Tale*, which MacKaye did not include. More revealingly he did not include the *Prioress's Tale*, often favored because of its child protagonist. Instead the *Physician's Tale*, rare in children's collections, and the *Pardoner's Tale* provide didactic argument, as does the *Canon's Yeoman's Tale*, which is especially pointed. This story of alchemy rounds out the exploration of magic in the *Squire's Tale* and in the *Franklin's Tale*, and the three form a discussion of science, appealing to the enthusiasm for technology in the United States. The central section of the volume contains the so-called Marriage Group—less the *Merchant's Tale* (a *fabliau*)—and the *Squire's Tale* enhances the interest in chivalric elements in the tales told by the Wife, Clerk, and Franklin.

Six colored illustrations, made especially for this edition, heighten this emphasis, since there are no pictures for the *Physician's Tale*, *Franklin's Tale*, or *Canon's Yeoman's Tale*. Walter Appleton Clark, who had won a medal at the Paris Exposition of 1900, created extraordinarily beautiful images, as had Warwick Goble. But they are strikingly different, with Clark's illustrations evoking the Middle Ages with vivid colors and the quality of stained glass rather than expressing a contemporary Art Nouveau aesthetic as had Goble. Three, reminiscent of several windows at Canterbury Cathedral, show the pilgrims riding in small groups (Frontispiece, 16, 144). If placed side by side they form about half of the long paintings of pilgrims by William Blake and Thomas Stothard. More startling is "The three Rogues search in the woods for Death" (80); they stalk through trees made somewhat less intimidating by the flowers blooming

Walter Appleton Clark's "Palamon Desireth to Slay His Foe Arcite" is a close-up of the hit in a joust. This version of a tournament scene for the *Knight's Tale* in Percy MacKaye's *The Canterbury Tales of Geoffrey Chaucer* (1904) has the quality of stained glass with its bold lines and color and of manuscript illumination in details of armor and heraldic devices as well as a border of flowers.

In "There Came a Knight upon a Steed of Brass," Walter Appleton Clark uses the patterned background, red and gold diamonds, of a medieval illumination and static figures to suggest a moment of awe when a strange knight enters in the *Squire's Tale*, Percy MacKaye's *The Canterbury Tales of Geoffrey Chaucer* (1904). The King of Araby and Ind have sent gifts: the magic horse that he rides, a ring, and a mirror that he holds in his hand; all allow extensions beyond human capacity—in movement, insight into truth, and understanding the language of birds.

beside the path, but the commanding detail is the skeleton Death, encased but for face and extremities in a black cloak and facing the viewer. The other two illustrations, Clark's brightest and most compelling, are of chivalry: a battle clash with two knights in the foreground, "Palamon desireth to slay his foe Arcite" (48)[7] and a court scene showing king, lords, and lady gathered at table, with a young musician on bended knee, when "There came a Knight upon a Steed of Brass" (176). This image, for the *Squire's Tale*, inspires adventure and quest and has a zestful youthful appeal.

In his preface MacKaye places himself in a long tradition of modernizers of Chaucer's tales, beginning with Dryden. Like other retellers for children, he aimed at "promoting study of the original" (xxii), describing his work as "a modified form" that differs because it is in prose. The exception is *Chaucer's Epilogue to the Clerk's Tale*, identified as a song and in verse (171–72). Because MacKaye's prose paragraphs follow those in Chaucer's verse, a comparison with the original text is straightforward. Changes are of several kinds. First, "omissions on the score of propriety, of intelligibility ... of redundancy" indicate a turn-of-the-century aesthetic, and putting propriety first suits a youthful audience. The *General Prologue* is an example: MacKaye, like Victorian Charles Cowden Clarke, softens details about the sexuality of the Pardoner and Wife. There is no hint that the Pardoner is "a geldyng or a mare," and the Host silences him with a charge that he would make him "kiss thine old hosen, and swear that they were relics of a saint, were they never so filthy" (115). Though MacKaye includes the *Wife's Prologue*, he expurgates it (III.444–50, for example). He often mutes Chaucer's explicitness, albeit the antifeminine arguments survive largely intact—including prolix examples. Unusually, MacKaye does not finesse the rape:

> It so befell that this King Arthur had in his house a knight, lusty and young, that on a day came riding from the river, and it happened that he saw, walking before him, a maid, alone as she was born, whom anon, despite her utmost, he bereft of her maidenhood, for which oppression there was such outcry and such complaint unto King Arthur [134].

This is a challenging reminder of how difficult it is to choose appropriate subjects for children. In fact, a concern for propriety governs MacKaye's principles of selecting only "from among those which are neither too broad (as the Summoner's), nor too prolix (as the Parson's)." His other objective of "clearness" includes both rearrangements and "the necessities of prose-style" (xxii). His critical perspective is explicit when he explains that he included the unfinished *Squire's Tale* for "its own romantic charm" and because Milton immortalized it as a piece to summon up Chaucer, a nice recognition of the canon.

In addition to principles of selection that make chivalry the major theme in *The Canterbury Tales of Geoffrey Chaucer*, occasional translations underline this point. Agreeing to meet Palamon to fight for Emily's love, Arcite says, "I swear by my chivalry" (41), MacKaye's rendering of "Have heer my trouthe" (I.1610). Generally, the text is very close to the original but understandable to a reader who does not know Middle English.

MacKaye has a tendency to emphasize fancy; in the *Squire's Tale* Chaucer's "fantasies ... old poetries" (V.206) becomes "fancies ... old poetic fables" (177). However, he is usually so close to the original—except for deletions—that there is nothing to remark except a change to accessible language. A lessening of medieval piety is MacKaye's most striking adaptation.[8] Of pilgrims with religious affiliations, only the Nun's Priest and the Pardoner tell their tales, which are among the most highly esteemed and universal stories. Similarly, MacKaye's ending avoids Chaucer's didacticism, iteration of sin and urge to repentance and confession, and praise of the good Parson. Instead, the *Canon's Yeoman's Tale* offers a picture of a corrupt priest with a very worldly interest in acquiring gold, to precede the last paragraph with its pious conclusion through its recognition of God's power and fitting *explicit*: "And here an end; for my story is done" (230).

Part of MacKaye's audience, "the educated public" would have been classes in school, a group that also performed *The Canterbury Pilgrims: A Comedy.*[9] MacKaye thanks two American scholars, J.S.P. Tatlock for his assistance and validation of the treatment of Chaucer's language in the translation and George Lyman Kittredge for assistance with an original hymn of St. Thomas. In the United States as in England there is, then, a direct connection between the academic and popular as well as between the adult and children's versions. A notable example is a production of the English Club at the University of California, Berkeley, on April 28, 1917, in the Greek Theatre, which seats crowds and suits pageant drama. A poster challenged the undergraduate audience: "GIRLS: Are you trying to catch a Man? See how the Wife of Bath does it. MEN: Are you Women Haters? If so beware of Alisoun, she has caught forty already."[10] MacKaye's play has many scenes that deploy information from Chaucer's poem and life, and it is enriched by the introduction of other characters from history, perhaps most forcefully John Wycliffe.

MacKaye's seeming secularism, better identified as Protestant revisionism, informs *The Canterbury Pilgrims*, as is evident in the choice of scenes. Three of the four acts are at taverns, Act I begins at the Tabard on April 16, 1387, while Acts II and III occur on the afternoon and evening of April 19 at the One Nine-pin Inn at Bob-up-and-down. Act IV takes place the next day before the west front of the Cathedral. There is a great deal of merriment, song and dance, drinking, and enactment of descriptive details from the prologues. Thus in the opening scene the Miller breaks down a door with his head (11); the Pardoner sells relics; the Prioress has a little hound called Jacquette, and she sends a note written in bad French; Alisoun of Bath flirts, both singing and drinking with the Pardoner, Summoner, and Manciple and competing with the Prioress for the attentions of Geoffrey. MacKaye redeploys some points: Chaucer reads from a book about the "wickedness of women," and the Wife tears it. Chaucer's apparent antifeminism is later offset when he recognizes the extraordinary "incongruities" of action, "Alis, I drink to thee and woman's wit" (175). MacKaye invents other actions; for example, the dicing and fighting of the Guildsmen. At the opening of Act IV, in which vendors of souvenirs and guides try to engage the pilgrims, is an extraordinary spectacle; Chaucer enters with a singing *"bevy of Canterbury brooch-girls, who have wreathed him with flowers and long ribbons, by which they pull him"* (182).

Amidst all this color of Merrie England two lines of plot develop. The Wife, who is indeed looking for husband number six, sets her cap for Geoffrey. She identifies the Prioress as a rival for his attention—a provocative denial of the nun's vow of chastity—and thus the second action becomes intertwined. According to MacKaye the Prioress expects to meet her brother, a knight just returned from a Crusade in the Holy Land, and his son at the inn in Bob-up-and-down. They have not seen each other for years, but an identifying token will be his ring with a letter A, and the same inscription that is on her brooch: "Amor vincit omnia." Many actions, largely farcical, occur before the pilgrim Knight is identified as the Prioress's brother, and the Squire can call her "Aunt." Most outrageous is a sequence in which Alisoun of Bath is dressed as the Knight, after much going and coming to the cellar for disguises, when she tries to show that the Prioress is really meeting a knight lover. Similarly farcical is the Wife's appearance in the last act, as a bride who claims that Chaucer has promised to wed her—a quasi enactment of her tale. Having consulted the Man of Law, the poet has a legal loophole because she already had five husbands; however, he gets the King to agree to an exception, and the Wife weds the Miller! The role of women is, then, prominent; their wishes motivate the action. Only the Wife tells her tale, in a brief summary: the Knight simply rides in with an answer "Women desire to do their own sweet wills," and King Arthur says "that's the best I've heard / Since I was first henpecked by Guinevere" (66). The old wife claims her husband, and the "grizzly bride" is soon revealed as "the Fairy Queen," called "Queen Mab" by the Friar. Enthusiasm for fairy tales may explain these details; however, MacKaye's aims are to create new bold situations for the pilgrims and to sustain comedy. Other rollicking events fill the stage: the Friar manages to fall into a fireplace (147), and there is a helpful chimney sweep; the Canon's Yeoman reports that Wycliffe flattened the Pope (151); Chaucer and the Prioress dance together (70), and he draws sword against Alisoun as pseudo-knight. Act I ends as the poet takes the Prioress on one arm and the Wife on the other.

Indeed much of the play's interest centers on Chaucer himself. His girth is noted, as well as his devotion to reading, developed in a sharing of books with the Clerk. The Squire identifies Chaucer as "King Richard's royal poet" and asks that he write a love poem for his suit. In Act II MacKaye shows Chaucer as a working poet; he recites the opening lines of the General Prologue and develops the description of the Prioress, who is a bit miffed when she hears his observations. Further, the poet's reputation is publicly acknowledged: Johanna, Marchioness of Kent, whose love is sought by the Squire, is trying to meet the poet, having just returned from Italy. Most interestingly, she is traveling in the company of John Wycliffe, which adds a Protestant interest. As previously noted, Ford Madox Brown, the great Victorian historical painter of the well-known *Chaucer at the Court of Edward III*, also pictured Chaucer and Gower in *John Wycliffe Reading His Translation of the Bible to John of Gaunt*, and again linked them with the Reformer in *The Trial of Wycliffe*. In Edwardian literary histories written for children, which are discussed in chapter 7, Wycliffe was regarded as a major author because he translated the Bible into English prose. In Act III the pilgrims hear Wycliffe preach, discuss his impact, and express a variety of responses to Lollardy. Thus Protestantism is one focus of attention.

However, the play is a comedy. One of the bigger jokes is that Johanna does not identify the blundering pilgrim Geoffrey as Chaucer, so that she offers to help him become a "court fool" (143). In the final scene King Richard arrives at the Cathedral, accompanied by John of Gaunt, Johanna and Wycliffe, and De Vere. The King calls upon his poet, who reminds him of his chivalric heroism when as a boy he stopped the rebelling peasants led by Wat Tyler, and quotes the famous "When Adam delved" (204–05). The argument for the people, "singing hearts of Englishmen," inspires cheers from the pilgrims, and the poet receives more cheers than the King. MacKaye rewrites Shakespeare's deposition scene in *Richard II*: his Richard seizes his mirror from a supercilious De Vere and smashes it. Political overtones of American reaction against royalty and privilege recall Grace Greenwood.

Chaucer's benediction, when he calls all together, argues that his poem will last:

> Yet they who drink the vintage I will brew
> Shall wake, and see a vision, in their wine,
> Of Canterbury and our pilgrimage:

These very faces, with the blood in them,
Laughter and love and tang of life in them,
These moving limbs, this rout, this majesty!
For by that resurrection of the Muse,
Shall you, sweet friends, re-met in timeless Spring,
Pace on through time upon eternal lines
And ride with Chaucer in his pilgrimage [207].

This is a grander and more public statement of the poet's self-portrait, epitomized in the line "Life, in whatever cup, / To me is a love-potion" (129). Thus MacKaye's Chaucer both responds to the peal of cathedral bells and the laughter of an ale-wife.

John Dryden's famous seventeenth century description of the *Canterbury Tales* as "God's plenty" has rarely received richer amplification than MacKaye's efforts in his extraordinary comedy *The Canterbury Pilgrims*. He casts almost all of the characters in absurd situations. A notable exception is the Knight, who plays a very minor role in the hurly-burly of this pilgrimage. The Wife's scheme means that the Knight must not be on stage while she is Knight-pretender. When the Knight is present, high sentiment governs the action, although there is little of it in Mac-Kaye's comedy. The Knight first speaks to Chaucer as a fellow soldier, albeit not realizing that Chaucer could not have fought at Cressy (5–6). As a father, he is firm with his son when he faults courtesy because of his love sighs. His response to the scheming Alison is an epitome of knighthood. She distracts the Knight's attention from her companions who plan to bind him by claiming prior association with him in Granada or Algezir. He gently thinks her "ill" and asks for a leech to help her. Next he prays to the Virgin, and as the Wife becomes more importunate, he cries out, "By St. George, I know you not," and then, "Off me, thou wife of Satan!" before finally exclaiming, "Sorcery!" (90). The Knight's firm judgment and clear evaluation are unusual amidst the incongruities and confusions of this pilgrimage. When he returns at the end of Act III, Chaucer, who sees a way to extricate himself from Alison's wild claims, takes control of the action.

There is, then, some ambivalence in MacKaye's estimate of the poet; the translation of *The Canterbury Tales of Geoffrey Chaucer* is a close one, and the role of knighthood and ideals of chivalry predominate. In contrast, the play about *The Canterbury Pilgrims* challenges these sentiments through farcical laughter, which is innocent but produces riotous effects analogous to the *fabliaux* that were not included in the translation. The interlacing of historical matter, which centers on the claims of the populace and a challenge to the medieval ideals of ordered society, and the significance of Wycliffe are part of this transformation. The role of Chaucer the poet and claims that his work will last recognize that the time has passed when knighthood and monarchy were in flower. Nevertheless, Chaucer's concern for others, giving each just deserts with generosity and playfulness, his courtesy and his humility, sustain an ideal of geniality that was regarded as his salient quality and much admired at this time.

Percy MacKaye's introduction of Chaucer's *Canterbury Tales* to American audiences, as a play in 1909 and as opera in 1916–17, is a significant analog to English pageants of history and literature in the period before World War I, such as those at Warwick (1906), Oxford (1907), Bury St. Edmund's (1907), Winchester (1908), and Bath (1909). Performances of MacKaye's play took place in theatres in the Midwest and New York, but were outside in the Greek theatre in Berkeley, California. Another close parallel of open air public performance occurred in the South, at Mardi Gras in New Orleans in 1912.[11] The Crewe of Comus chose "Tales from Chaucer" as the theme for its pageant floats, an annual offering of a parade to the public by the oldest and socially most élite Carnival organization. The twenty-three floats showed *Canterbury Tales* (*Squire's*, *Clerk's*, *Wife's*, and *Nun's Priest's*) and other poems ("Truth" and *Anelida and Arcite*). Carnival pageantry delights large audiences, and the level of recognition from those who lined the streets is a subject of great interest, a modern reenactment of the suggested variety in Chaucer's audience who were given tales derived from major writers such as Boccaccio and Petrarch but also had many details from familiar folktales. Recognition of *The Canterbury Tales*, if not of some of the lesser known poems, was no doubt partially dependent upon the many ways in which Chaucer's stories were told to the children in beautiful Reward books, school texts, and encyclopedias. Percy MacKaye had moved easily from adult to child audiences and demonstrated that Chaucer is performable. Many who lined the streets could have recognized Griselda as a model of loyalty and identified the Orientalism of the *Squire's Tale* from similar representations in book illustrations. The luxurious richness of the decoration of costumes and pageant wagons, including sweeping curves and flowers, resemble the fashionable Art Nouveau designs favored in several Edwardian children's books already discussed.

Calvin Dill Wilson

A small book, four-and-a-half by seven inches, published by A.C. McClurg & Company in Chicago, deserves to be cited as an American

t night there came to that
hostelry a company of
nine and twenty folk,
all pilgrims that would
ride toward Canterbury

Opposite and above: The decorated frontispiece and title page of Calvin Dill Wilson's *Canterbury Tales: Prologue and Selections* (1906) shows how children's books sometimes imitated the printing efforts of William Morris' Kelmscott *Chaucer*. Ralph Fletcher Seymour created an opening scene of the pilgrims gathering as a woodcut from an early printed book. Borders frame every page of text, with different devices for each tale. A.C. McClurg published a number of books for children with similar decorations, a fine example of American medievalism at the start of the twentieth century.

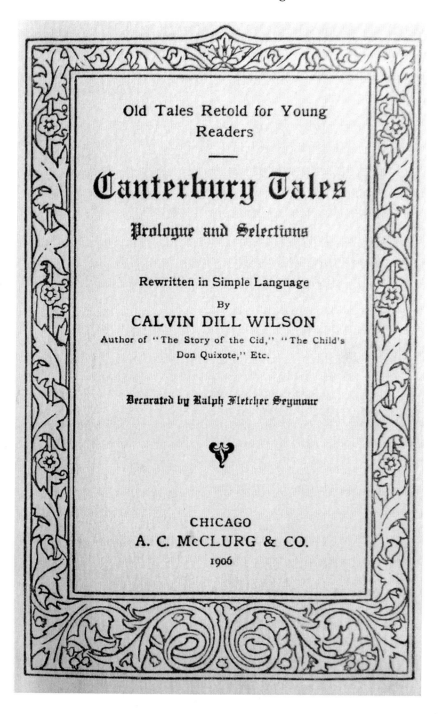

Old Tales Retold for Young
Readers

—

Canterbury Tales

Prologue and Selections

Rewritten in Simple Language

By

CALVIN DILL WILSON

Author of "The Story of the Cid," "The Child's
Don Quixote," Etc.

Decorated by Ralph Fletcher Seymour

CHICAGO
A. C. McCLURG & CO.
1906

example of Edwardian extravagance, for it resembles the Kelmscott *Chaucer* in design. *Canterbury Tales: Prologue and Selections* (1906) by Calvin Dill Wilson (1857–1946) is in a series Old Tales Retold for Young Readers, to which he had earlier contributed *The Faery Queen* (*First Book*), priced at $1.00. The book was "Decorated by Ralph Fletcher Seymour" (1876–1966); decoration more than storytelling pictures makes it distinctive. Like other McClurg books, this one has a cover of linen weave, here a pale green, but instead of a picture there is a decoration of a stained-glass window in dark red and green. At the top of an heraldic shield in an enlarged round panel is *Canterbury Tales*, while a scroll above carries the name of the series on two lines. This cover design anticipates the framed pages, which imitate a medieval manuscript as had Morris and Burne-Jones. The frontispiece and title page set a pattern of all-enclosing leaf and flower borders printed in green. The frontispiece is a wood-cut, as in an early printed book, that shows the pilgrims gathering, some standing and others still on horseback, on a pavement before a Gothic building. A large red capital begins the caption "At night there came to that hostelry a company of nine and twenty folk, all pilgrims that would ride to Canterbury." This is an inviting and compelling first image; its precise detail contrasts with the simplicity of the opposite page that has the title in red and other words in black. The first page of each tale has a heading, a wider upper border of a frame with appropriate woodcut figures. Every page carries a red running title and the same frame of leaves and flowers, with black woodcuts on every lower bar. These are of small figures appropriate to the tale and teller; opposite pages in each opening reverse the figures. The result is an extraordinary richness with just enough variety since there are only four items, the *Prologue* and the three tales— *Knight, Man-of-Law,* and *Clerk of Oxford*—those most frequently retold for children. What distinguishes Wilson's retelling is its exactness, more translation than paraphrase, with relatively few omissions, albeit occasional mistranslations from Middle English.

A brief Foreword explains that "Men in former days were accustomed to think that the going upon pilgrimages to shrines of saints or to places made sacred by the deeds of heroic men and women was one of the best actions they could perform."[12] He cites both journeys to Palestine and Mahometan and Hindu analogs. Then very briefly he places the custom of pilgrimage in Chaucer's day and explains the plan for storytelling on the journey to Canterbury, before concluding that he has retold only a few stories but hopes to "tell for you other famous stories from other great books." Wilson is, then, not making a case for the development of the English language and a literary tradition but telling important stories.

McClurg had earlier published his *The Story of the Cid* (1901) and *The Child's Don Quixote* (1901), both examples of chivalry and the high sentiment that mark his choices from the *Canterbury Tales,* and his advice to the young, *Making the Most of Ourselves* (1909) and *Working One's Way through College* (1912).

These ideals explain Wilson's only large deletion from *The Prologue,* Chaucer's apologia (I.725–46) that he will repeat each person's tale truly, however crude, since language should fit the action. There is little in the three chosen tales to give offense, so that adjustments are minor. Like other retellers for children, Wilson omits Chaucer's reference to the Summoner's control of young girls (I.663–65) and the line about the Pardoner's sexuality (I.691, 37). His portraits are usually simpler and kinder, or he misunderstands the Middle English; this Prioress, "did not like to counterfeit the cheer of the court, and to be stately in her manners and to be held worthy of reverence" (19–20), while Chaucer's "peyned hire to countrefete" (took pains, I.139). The Miller, "a janglere and a goliardeys" (teller of dirty stories and buffoon, I.560) is for Wilson "a babbler and a low fellow" (33). However, in severer renderings the Cook's "mormal" becomes "gangrene" (I.386, 28), and the "gat-tothed" Wife is "goat-toothed" (I.468, 30). Sometimes a translation offers a familiar connection, as when the Friar's "rote" is identified as a "guitar" (I.236, 23), and "William" is "the Conqueror" (I.324, 26). Most disconcerting is a mistranslation of "hy sentence" as "elevated sentences" (I.306, 25), reiterated when the Host's plan for "Tales of best sentence and most solaas" (I.797) becomes "tell the best story, that is to say best in sentences and in mirth" (40). Fortunately, Wilson understands fully the high sentiment of the three tales he chose, so that this short collection is one with a consistent and inspiring theme.

The *Tale of the Knight* is the longest and most complex; thus Wilson alters it more, but still offers a very close translation. Cuts, usually reiterated details, come from elaborations: Theseus's fight against "Femenye," May celebrations, love complaints, descriptions of the temples and fine points of classical mythology, and several philosophical passages such as reflections on destiny (I.1663–72) and the afterlife (I.2810–16). However, unusually, Wilson translates Egeus's wise advice to Theseus and follows it with a shortened First Mover speech (I.2987–3074) :

> He declared that the Creator had made all things subject to change; that the oak lasts a long time, but finally wastes away; that the hard stone under our feet wears out; the broad river becomes dry; and all things have an end. Of men and women the same is true; in youth or in age each one must die whether he be a page or a king; and there is no help for it. All things shall die; this is the will of Jupiter; and it

avails not to strive against his wish. It is wisdom to make a virtue of necessity, and to take that which we cannot refuse. And certainly a man has most honor to die when he is sure of a good name; it is best for a worthy man to die, when his fame is at the best. Why do we murmur? Why have we sorrow, that good Arcite has departed with honor? [99–100]

Although this lacks Chaucer's sophistication, it preserves, as other retellings for children do not, a quality of philosophical romance that shows a special dedication to the original.

Wilson twice adds brief explanations, set in brackets, to help the child reader understand ancient circumstances. First, he attributes Theseus's life sentences for Arcite and Palamon to a conqueror's wish to avoid rival claims to the throne of Thebes (49); second, he explains Theseus's anger when he finds the two fighting as a violation of an old law that forbade fighting in the presence of the king "except in regular battle, or at a tournament of knights; for it was considered unseemly to brawl and quarrel before a king" (66). As always in Chaucer for children, the tournament is a major focus; here in full details not only the thrilling description of the combat but also complex physical arrangements, rules of combat, and care of the wounded. Young readers had a rich introduction to chivalry's pageantry and gallantry, as all respond to the injunction, "Proud young knights, now do your devoir" (I.2598, 88). This balances the visual messages. The heading shows Palamon and Arcite in prison and looking toward the bars, while opposite them Emily reaches toward a flower in a walled garden (45). The border woodcuts reiterate the conflict of love and war with heads of a named Mars and Venus. She is crowned but has one bare breast and holds up an apple, an obvious icon of seduction, while a bearded Mars, wearing a classical helmet, holds his sword. The corner figure is a knight, an older man in plate armor with sheathed sword, who stands and holds a stick across his left shoulder.

In the *Tale of the Man of Law* most of the cutting is again of classical examples and repeated rhetorical exhortations, as when two stanzas are reduced to "O Sultaness, root of iniquity!" (II.358–71, 111). Wilson translates Constance's prayers but eliminates a stanza on miracles (II.477–83) and some biblical examples. To maintain turn-of-the-century propriety there is some eliding of sexual material, both about Constance's conceiving Alla's child on the wedding night and rhetorical exclamations against the would-be rapist. Chaucer's tale of "piteous joy" (133), centered on a "noble creature" with "tenderness in her blithe heart" and "virtue and holy deeds of charity" (134), is faithfully rendered. The two images of the heading promise adventure; on the left Constance follows the Sultan (signed by a large turban), while on the right she grasps a rope of the billowing sail as the boat surges forward (105). The image of the boat is the decoration of the woodcuts in the lower borders where Constance kneels and holds wide her arms in prayer. Since the images are reversed, the boats sail toward each other. In the corners stands an elegant professional who holds a parchment in his right hand.

Wilson's close translation extends to his keeping the marked division into six parts in the *Tale of the Clerk of Oxford*. Walter tests Griselda's "steadfastness," and "constancy" is cited with "pacience" as her virtue. Some translations express modern decorum: Griselda's bringing to Walter "feith, and nakednesse, and maydenhede" (IV.866) becomes "To you I brought nothing else but faith" (166), while Chaucer's "sturdy markys" (harsh, cruel, IV.1049) becomes "this obstinate marquis" (172). Like Haweis, Wilson eliminates the concluding remarks about wives and the Lenvoy to avoid the challenge of their interpretation. The woodcuts leave no doubt about the emphasis of the story. An older, bearded clerk stands in the lower outer corners, while a modest wife kneels in supplication before her husband seated on a throne. This contrasts with the heading's two sets of figures: a chivalric crowned knight in plate armor rides out with attendants below his castle; opposite, a laborer cuts grain while a maiden carrying a jug walks away from their hut toward the linear interlace that separates the two images (137). The combination of close translation and late medieval woodcuts and decoration make Wilson's *Canterbury Tales* a very sophisticated rendering.

Eva March Tappan

Like Wilson, Eva March Tappan (1854–1930) wrote primarily for children. She was an educator, one of the best established in the United States, with wide influence in Britain because Harrap published several of her books in its Told through the Ages Series. The daughter of the pastor of the Free Baptist Church and a teacher, she graduated from Vassar in 1875, taught at Wheaton College in Illinois and in private schools in Massachusetts and New Jersey, received a Master's degree in 1895 and a Ph.D. in 1896 from the University of Pennsylvania. She then returned to high school teaching, where she was particularly helpful to students with immigrant and poor backgrounds. After her writing, especially folk and historical stories, increased, she devoted herself to it full-time. Tappan, who was an assistant editor for the United States Food Administration during World War I, is thus an early example of the successful professional woman.

Her most comprehensive effort was the selection and arrangement of the texts in Houghton Mifflin's ten-volume *The Children's Hour* (1907), a mark of her skill and versatility, extended to pedagogy in Robert Newton Linscott's *A Guide to Good Reading* (1912). Here she identifies her objectives as an editor, with stories

> ... intended to stimulate imaginations, to arouse ambition, to inculcate admiration for moral and physical courage, or to give information regarding the facts of history, biography, or science. Whatever the immediate purpose, the ultimate aim has always been to develop character.... The intention of the editor of The Children's Hour has been to make the selections of such a character that the reading of them will naturally tend to develop a taste for the literature to be found in the writings of the world's greatest authors.[13]

Included are stories from classical writers, legendary heroes (Beowulf, King Arthur, and Robin Hood, along with Havelok, Frithiof, Charlemagne, Roland, Siegfried, the Cid, Rustem), myths from many lands, and poems. American education often put English into a world literary tradition. In a volume of *Seven Old Favorites* Tappan includes three of Lamb's *Tales from Shakespeare*, but neither Chaucer nor Spenser.[14]

However, Tappan subsequently published *The Chaucer Story Book* (1908), which may indicate an awareness of Chaucer's growing significance as a teller of stories for children or perhaps a desire to give special attention to the poet. Several of Tappan's earlier books concentrate on a single figure: *Robin Hood, His Book* (1903), novels such as *In the Days of King Alfred* (1905) and *In the Days of William the Conqueror* (1901). *When Knights Were Bold* (1911), issued by Harrap as *In Feudal Times: Social Life in the Middle Ages* (1913), most obviously shows Tappan as a social historian. She recommends these books in *A Guide to Good Reading*, which assigns stories to the appropriate age levels and explains something of child development in literary taste and skill. In the same year that Storr and Turner described the significance and extent of the study of the canon of English writers, Tappan published *A Brief History of English Literature* (1914), which is considered in chapter 7. Now it is appropriate to review her treatment of Chaucer's tales.

Tappan's *Chaucer Story Book* both resembles and differs from MacKaye's selection for children. Her Preface, in contrast to Haweis's confident expectation, makes a similarly aggressive statement about the difficulty of reading Middle English, unless one "knows a little French, a little German, and a little Latin, ... has a shadowy recollection of Grimm's Law, a good memory for obsolete and half obsolete expressions, and a natural talent for discovering the gist of a word, no matter how it is spelled."[15] Without these qualifications no one reads Chaucer for pleasure: "that is why the Chaucer Story Book has been written." Tappan shows herself a university academic with this short list for doctoral study, but she makes no comment about children's subsequent reading of the original. However, like other Edwardian retellers of Chaucer for children, she explains that she chose the twelve stories "requiring fewest omissions to adapt them to the taste of the present day" (vi). This count includes "At the Tabard Inn," her rendering of the *General Prologue*. The tales are those of the Man of Law, the Friar, and the Prioress, but not the Doctor, MacKaye's choice for the homiletic. These two American retellers share enthusiasm for the magical (Wife, Squire, Franklin, Canon's Yeoman), but Tappan more strongly favors high sentiment and piety. Subtitles (names of characters or brief statements of subject) facilitate easy recognition.

Although Tappan's interest lies in stories, illustrations are of the pilgrim tellers. Eleven portraits reproduced from the Ellesmere manuscript, black stamped, decorate the red cloth cover with the title in gold; they also introduce each tale. The only other picture in the text is John Urry's 1722 engraving of pilgrims riding out from the Tabard (3); the frontispiece, a double page, is an engraving of Stothard's *The Pilgrimage to Canterbury*, with numbered pilgrims identified below. There is no separate picture of Chaucer, but Tappan features him in her adaptation of the *General Prologue*, which has little detail about pilgrimage and includes only the portraits of her storytellers. She attributes to the observant "quiet traveler" evaluations of his companions, such as an explicit contrast between the greedy Summoner and dainty Prioress. Generally the prologues and links are very short; Tappan's is not a dramatic rendering.

The *Knight's Tale* begins "Once upon a time," and tells the story simply, without minor characters such as Theseus's father Egeus. Tappan retains a division into four parts and shows her enthusiasm for chivalry by making the tournament the longest part. She adjusts the introduction to the *Man of Law's Tale* to have Harry Bailey directly call upon the lawyer and thus neatly eliminates the three *fabliaux* that follow Chaucer's first tale. Unlike MacKaye, whose Protestantism is often evident, Tappan keeps medieval religious elements: the conflict of the Sultan's mother, details of conversion, the Gospels, miracles, and piety, as in Constance's prayer when Alla orders her into "the rudderless boat":

> "Lord, whatever thou dost send is always welcome to me," and she said to the sorrowing folk around, "He who cleared me from a false charge when I first came to this land can also care for me on the wide

ocean, even though I see not how. He is no less strong than he was before. I trust in him and his mother, and that trust is for me both rudder and sail." Her little son lay in her arms weeping. "Peace, little son," she murmured; and then she cast her eyes upward to the heavens. "Mother Mary," she cried, "thy Child was tortured on a cross, and thou didst see all his torment. No suffering can compare with thine; for thy Child was slain before thine eyes—and my child lives" [69].

A plea for the child's innocence follows, and then Constance walks to the boat, "hushing her child as she went" (70), an appealing figure of a loving mother for young readers.

Marian devotion is the main element in the *Prioress's Tale*, in which Tappan lessens the emphasis upon the Jews. After these three stories, the Host's need for something merry seems more authentic than formulaic; the *Nun's Priest's Tale*, "without prelude or introduction," is a welcome change. It is much abbreviated, as when laments are but a line, but something of two dreams remains; the action is lively, especially the chase. There is less marital conflict, but Tappan keeps Pertelote's speech that no woman can love a coward. She has fewer subtle reminders of the beast fable, but universalizes the didactic, when she adds, "Some folk behave better when they are in trouble than when all goes smoothly with them, and Chanticleer was one of these people" (98); she concludes with the two morals of the original.

Didactic concerns continue with the *Pardoner's Tale*. The link admits his drinking, when the pilgrims insist "we do not want any barroom stories. Tell us a tale with a good moral" (103). The elimination of the Pardoner's long sermon and self-revelation both heightens the immediacy of a fine story and avoids some unsuitable topics among the sins described, even though the story of the three revelers includes reference to behaving "tipsily." The figure of Death, introduced with mystery and menace, dominates.

The *Wife of Bath's Tale*, subtitled "The Unknown Bride," begins after a two-sentence introduction. Again there is no analysis of character; the interest is the fairy tale, not complex interactions of pilgrims. Tappan treats the knight's offense delicately; he "forgot his vow to guard all women and treated one despitefully" (116). She retains only one exemplum, King Midas, which appeals as magical transformation and parallels the change from old crone to beautiful wife. There is no ambiguity about the solution to the riddle: "The thing that women most desire is to rule their husbands" (120). The wedding night scene puts the essential arguments of *gentilesse*: "I am of gentle blood if I live virtuously and do not sin ... sometimes poverty teaches a man to know both his God and himself.... Often it happens that with age comes wisdom" (122). These maxims, particularly in an American society assumed to be classless, were designed to encourage children to behave properly. The knight's capitulation is absolute: "I believe that you are wise and good, and I take you for my true and faithful wife" (123). Thus the issue is a matter of trust not rule.

Tappan's *Friar's Tale* is comparably simple. The link explains what a summoner was in the Middle Ages and introduces a swiftly told story of the Yeoman, who admits: "I am a fiend, and my dwelling place is hell" (130). There is some discussion about the form taken by fiends in and out of hell—part of the fascination with nonhuman experience typical of *The Chaucer Story Book*. The two bailiffs—who extort others for money—join company and swear to share proceeds. They have only two encounters: the Carter who does not mean his curses on his horses and cart, and the Old Woman who refuses the Summoner's demand for money. He declares, "May the fiend take me if I let you off," and that happens quickly, once the fiend has confirmed that the Old Woman's curse is genuine.

The *Clerk's Tale* is another long narrative, again not divided into sections. Tappan's retelling of this most-favored story emphasizes obedience and religion but without an allegorical interpretation. "God gives such grace" to the Marchioness (146), she makes the sign of the cross over her daughter (149); she gently warns against the presumed bride's tenderness and inexperience of adversity, and her only response to the return of her children is joy (158). The letters from the Pope agreeing to Walter's putting aside his wife are "forgeries" (152). Although religion is always present, the human nature of the story is paramount, as indicated by the last line. Their son and heir: "wedded a wife who loved him truly and was ever faithful to him; but he was wiser and more tender than his father, and never put her to such a sad and cruel test" (159).

After these didactic stories, *The Chaucer Story Book* finishes with three tales in which magic plays a crucial role. In the *Squire's Tale* horse, mirror, and ring have wondrous properties, exactly the subject matter that appeals to children. Tappan eliminates the adult issue of false love; she describes the falcon's distress but does not let her speak, and Canacee cares for her. A bracketed statement explains that Chaucer left the story unfinished, and then Tappan gives Spenser's completion in *The Faerie Queene* (IV.2–3; 176–77). This signs Chaucer's role as the Father of English poetry, but the increment also heightens the chivalric content by adding another tournament, with a happy ending when a fairy stops the strife through "the magic power that she had learned from her mother, wise in Faerie lore" (180). Canacee rides home with her new "sister," while Camballo has a wife and a new brother—a celebration of family.

Tappan adjusts the *Franklin's Tale* and introduces a few moral statements, after abandoning most of the elaborate examples and laments. Dorigen hardly seems to make a "rash vow," because she urges: "Thrust this folly from your heart. What pleasure can it be to a man to love another man's wife?" (191); and Aurelius's claim, "you promised that when every rock on the coast should have disappeared, you would leave Arviragus and come to me as my wife?" (196), is more respectable than claiming "love." Finally, Aurelius's explanation to the magician is cogent. He did not insist upon Dorigen's promise because her husband honors truth, but also "Dorigen had never heard of magical appearances when she gave her promise, and she sorrowed so sadly that I sent her back to him" (200). Naive innocence can be excused, a generous example for children.

Just how fascinating and corrupting "magical appearances" can be is reiterated in the *Canon's Yeoman's Tale*, with which the book concludes, as does MacKaye's. Details in the use of quicksilver, the trickery of sleight of hand, a hollow stick, and substitution of metals are as exciting as technical books and how-to books of magic that appeal to children. But the last line warns that "the magical recipe" does not work when the duped priest tries it. No selection captures "God's plenty" in the *Canterbury Tales*, but Tappan demonstrates that he tells compelling stories, and by her selections within the Chaucer Society's order of the tales she gains the coherence of thematic groups.

Tappan's *The Chaucer Story Book* is more elementary than those of Darton, McSpadden, and Underdown, previously cited as prime examples of Edwardian extravagance, beautifully illustrated and conceptually sophisticated. Her preface candidly admits that most American readers have not studied the languages needed to understand Middle English. Chaucer's absence from *The Children's Hour* may also reflect this uneasiness. An even more prolific American writer, Hamilton Wright Mabie, edited several volumes in the Every Child Should Know Series (*Heroes, Heroines, Fairies, Legends*) but found no place for Chaucer, although Kelman's stories were in two encyclopedias for which he was an editor, *The Young Folks' Treasury* and *The Bookshelf for Boys and Girls*. Moreover, as previously discussed, Collier's *The Junior Classics* reprinted three parts of Darton's *Tales of the Canterbury Pilgrims*.

In Mixed Collections

While Tappan was a very successful teacher and writer for children, George Philip Krapp (1872–1934) was a distinguished Professor of English at Columbia University best known as coeditor of *The Anglo-*

Saxon Poetic Records (1931–42), but he also wrote *Tales of True Knights* (1921) for children.[16] This wide-ranging collection includes four of Chaucer's tales among its fifteen items. Collections of medieval narratives are generally by British writers, part of a long tradition of chivalric stories, usually non–Chaucerian, told to the children. As noted in chapter 2, there were early precedents, David Murray Smith's *Tales of Chivalry and Romance* (1869) that combines two Chaucer tales (Knight and Squire) with retellings from Shakespeare, Froissart, Malory, and Ascott R. Hope's *Stories of Old Renown* (1883) that includes *Patient Griselda* along with *Robert of Sicily, Guy of Warwick, Ogier the Dane* and several others.[17] Krapp's tales are in prose and somewhat abbreviated. Along with *King Horn, Havelok the Dane, Sir Gawain and the Green Knight*, and *Sir Orfeo*, are four favorites from the *Canterbury Tales*. *The Rival Friends* is the *Knight's Tale*, never better told than by Chaucer, according to Krapp's introduction. *The Three Revelers* has many versions, one very long ago in India. Krapp notes that "Chaucer makes a kind of sermon out of the story, and certainly after we have enjoyed it merely as a story, if one wishes to go farther, there is a very good lesson to be learned from it" (xv). The other Chaucerian tales are the religious romances about noble women, *Patient Griselda* and *Constance*, which Krapp relates to *Eustace* because "all tell about the experiences of people who were very patient in bearing the misfortunes of their life" (xii). After raising critical objections to the extreme nature of the *Clerk's Tale*, he concludes, "we must acknowledge that if Griselda had too much patience, most of us make up for it by not having enough" (xiii). The high moral tone in this rich and comprehensive selection of medieval narratives appropriately, albeit unusually, places Chaucer with other romances, lais, saints' legends, and allegories—at the center of medieval literature.

Having reviewed the variety and richness of many Chaucer stories for children prepared mostly for reading at home, often given as prizes or presents, the next chapter turns to those available to the greatest number of children. In addition to school versions of extravagant editions of Haweis, Darton, McSpadden, and Underdown already discussed, there were others, both British and American. Works produced more directly for the schoolroom, an immediate and sure market, were essential to the success, even survival of many publishers.

6

Chaucer in Schoolbooks

Chaucer stories simply told in schoolbooks were widely required reading and thus were known to children who neither were given books by parents and relatives nor earned fine copies as rewards. In addition to redeployed texts in smaller collections—Haweis's *Chaucer for Children*, Darton's *Pilgrims' Tales from Chaucer*, McSpadden's *Tales from Chaucer*, Underdown's *Stories from Chaucer*—several versions of *The Canterbury Tales* were originally designed for school use. These usually have a modest appearance and contain more educational matter than do the other editions. Both British and American schools used children's texts of canonical books that helped to strengthen the study of English, and in diverse ways Chaucer stories explicitly make the case for the importance of the Father of English Poetry, who is to be read early so that students have a sense of tradition and an appreciation of literature, learn something of social and historical contexts, develop their imaginations, and experience the pleasure of fine storytelling.

Clara L. Thomson

Like Eva March Tappan, Clara L. Thomson was greatly interested in medieval narratives. She wrote one of the more-sophisticated collections of *Tales from Chaucer* (1903), illustrated by Marion Thomson, who had exhibited at Liverpool, 1895–97.[1] Her earliest translation was *The Adventures of Beowulf* (1899) for a New English Series. She followed this with selections from *Morte Darthur*, entitled *King Arthur of Britain* (1902), and later edited a version of *Pilgrim's Progress* (1913). Her preface to *Tales from Chaucer*, like those of Storr and Turner, contributes to our understanding of pedagogical development in English studies. She explains that the little book was published "at the request of several teachers who have felt the need of some reading-book by means of which they could revise the oral lessons that they had given to their classes" (v). Here medieval oral tradition and modern teaching methods meet. Thomson offers her simplified version only as a way of becoming acquainted with Chaucer and hopes that students will go beyond it.

In fact, the small book, modest in appearance with its green cloth cover stamped in black, is a remarkably rich combination of stories and academic information. The introduction gives a brief account of Chaucer's time and an overview of his life and poetic output. Thomson notes the recent discovery of two leaves of parchment that proved to be from an account book of Elizabeth, wife of Lionel, third son of King Edward III, that contained items about gifts to Chaucer. This early biographical information, now well known to Chaucerians, became available "a few years ago." Thomson uses Skeat's edition and usually follows the text closely— apart from a discreet elimination of material considered objectionable for children.

One attractive feature is a mini critical history through comments about Chaucer across the ages from Gower, Hoccleve, Caxton, Drayton, Sidney, Dryden, Spenser, Tennyson, Longfellow, and J.R. Lowell. This list confirms the current view that American writers are part of English literary tradition. Quotations from these authors are printed on seven decorative pages that modestly resemble a manuscript folio, with text surrounded by an elaborate border, a floral pattern on the left and right, and figures at the top and bottom. These figures vary—a castle and three kneeling knights, a sailing ship and three kneeling clerks, five walking monks, and a funeral effigy of a king and queen. Since one is the design stamped on the cover, the reader is alerted to the significance of literary tradition. Thomson's range of authorities anticipates recent surveys of critical attitudes toward Chaucer, and their judgments are consistently straightforward praise, reinforcing her description of "the fascination of Chaucer's verse—its mingled wit and pathos, its simplicity and its art, its satire and its loving sympathy with human nature in every aspect" (v). The Edwardian view of Chaucer, eloquently affirmed by G.K. Chesterton as late as 1932, is of a genial and pious man and poet, not the ironic figure discerned by most critics since the mid-twentieth century. Five of the twelve bordered pages contain quotations in Chaucer's Middle English, and all reinforce idealism: the description of Emily in the garden (69) and Aegeus's

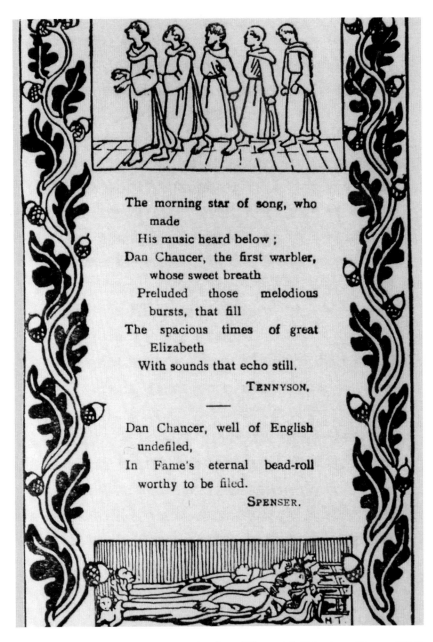

The morning star of song, who
made
His music heard below ;
Dan Chaucer, the first warbler,
whose sweet breath
Preluded those melodious
bursts, that fill
The spacious times of great
Elizabeth
With sounds that echo still.

TENNYSON.

———

Dan Chaucer, well of English
undefiled,
In Fame's eternal bead-roll
worthy to be filed.

SPENSER.

Marion Thomson's decorated pages for Clara Thomson's *Tales from Chaucer* (1903) resemble those in Calvin Dill Wilson's *Canterbury Tales*. They are interspersed to counterpoint the stories with an awareness of Chaucer's role in English literature. Lines from Tennyson and Spenser acknowledge Chaucer's greatness and indebtedness of others.

consoling words to his son Theseus (98), the description of Constance quieting her child and her prayer to Mary (141), the old wife's definition of a gentleman (201), and part of the "Balade of Bon Conseyl," as a gloss on the *Pardoner's Tale* (205). Each illustrates a virtue—beauty, good character, maternal devotion, piety—to strengthen the character of children.

Thomson's choice of tales is more comprehensive than many others. *Tales from Chaucer* begins with the *General Prologue*, somewhat abbreviated, but it includes none of the prologues or links to the tales, so there is no dramatic development. This puts the emphasis upon the tales, Chaucer's skill as a storyteller, and the virtues extolled in the tales. Thomson includes six tales, those of the Knight, Nun's Priest, Man of Law, Clerk, Wife, and Pardoner. She begins with a chivalric adventure and beast fable, two of the most popular kinds of children's fiction. Then come two tales of noble women, Constance and Griselda, who are models of humility, constancy, patience, and obedience. *The Wife's Tale* also focuses on women, but it is primarily an argument about the nature of a gentle person, the education of a young man; it is also a chivalric adventure with a fairy tale quality. Indeed, as earlier noted, F.J. Harvey Darton identified it as the first English fairy tale in his seminal history of children's literature.[2] The final tale of the three rioters is a fast-paced adventure, one with mystery and murders, that warns against greed and deception and includes the figure of Death, always a useful holder of attention. Thomson's selection includes tales that remain favorites, but it is representative not comprehensive. The dominant tone is serious, and a moral is always clear.

Thomson deletes Chaucer's apologia from the *Prologue*, and indeed there is nothing to defend. She does not include the *fabliaux* and alters or cuts sexually suggestive or obscene details in other tales. The description of the Prioress does not suggest ironic comment, the Friar is described as having "arranged many marriages between young people of his acquaintance" (29), the Pardoner is a deceiver and beardless but his homosexual nature is not indicated, and the description of the Parson is expansive (42–44). Pilgrim portraits of the Knight, Squire, Prioress, Friar, Merchant, Cook, Doctor of Physic, Wife of Bath, Miller, and Pardoner attractively decorate the *Prologue*. Marion Thomson acknowledged that these equestrian figures, positioned to fill the center half of the page, were based on the illuminations of the Ellesmere MS, an example of the scholarly content of *Tales from Chaucer*. Further enrichment comes from several other smaller designs—a knight's head, narrow bars with a row of shields with heraldic devices, heads of youth, birds, and a lady's head—for short pages of text, and decorative capitals begin tales or parts of tales. As in a manuscript or chapbook, frequent and well-placed pictures offer variety and maintain interest.

The editing of the *Wife of Bath's Tale* indicates how Clara Thomson adjusted Chaucer's tales for child readers. The occasion for the quest is not a rape: "Now, it happened that in the court of King Arthur there was a gallant knight, who nevertheless had sinned against the laws of the Round Table" (192). As the reluctant bridegroom listens to the argument of his wife, he is "struck by her wisdom and eloquence ... and repent[s] of his harshness towards her" (199). An explanation of the transformation scene enhances the element of fairy tale, "For she was indeed a fairy, who had pity on him in his trouble, and had taken this means of testing his honor" (200), as does the conclusion that "they lived together in peace and happiness, and in all Arthur's court there was no more loving couple than these two" (203). Increased high sentiment comes from a mitigation of failure in knighthood at the start and greater happiness at the end.

In other tales chivalric figures become similarly more praiseworthy, either by an indication that loss of knightly virtue is a temporary lapse or an occasion for teaching. Walter in the *Clerk's Tale* is "a little blameworthy" because he thinks not of his future (152), but he becomes the "wicked marquis" (179). He apologizes for testing his wife Griselda: "God knows that it is very distasteful to me, and I will do nothing without your knowledge; but now the time is come for you to show that patience and obedience which you promised to me on our marriage day" (166). Griselda's behavior is characterized by "sweet humility," and the concluding general moral is "to show how every one should be as patient in adversity as she was" (190). The *Man of Law's Tale*, which precedes the *Clerk's Tale*, makes a point about woman's place. When Constance is ready to depart for Syria, she accepts her father's will and prays for help from the Lord, but also observes woefully: "For what matter is it though I, a wretched woman, should die? Women are born to service and sorrow, and to be under the command of men" (125). The lines are Chaucer's (II.285–87), but Thomson does not retain many other rhetorical passages and details. To confront negative roles of women she shortens the account of King Alla's love and adds a note about the similarity of the two wicked mothers-in-law (137). However, she does not forego a desire to increase the happy ending; the single year that Constance and Alla have together and Chaucer's emphasis upon the brevity of earthly happiness (II.1139–46) is harmlessly rendered: "After some time Alla and Constance returned to England, where they lived in peace and happiness till Alla died" (151).

Some changes clearly suggest adaptation for didactic purposes; others are designed to shorten and simplify a story to make it attractive and accessible for a child reader. Massive cutting includes the dream lore, laments, and barnyard sexuality in the *Nun's Priest's Tale*, the entire preliminary sermon of the *Pardoner's Tale*, rhetorical flourishes in the *Man of Law's Tale*, part of the description of fighting and much of the philosophy in the *Knight's Tale*. Full-page illustrations reinforce the simplified tales and indicate points of emphasis. All are black-and-white line drawings, many very detailed but some rather spare. The *Knight's Tale* has two: Emily in the garden with a good view of the castle (61) and two young squires picking flowers to welcome May (75); there is nothing of combat or tournament. For the *Nun's Priest's Tale* "All the Neighbors joined in the pursuit" (112), but we do not see the beasts. Exotic scenes illustrate the *Man of Law's Tale*: two seated figures in Oriental dress hear of the Emperor's daughter from two elegantly dressed young men (119), and Constance in her boat floats on high waves (145). The *Clerk's Tale* has more illustrations than any other, three scenes of women: Griselda as shepherdess, barefoot and in simple shift, holding a crook in one hand and wild flowers in the other looking toward the reader as the sheep graze on the hill behind her (159); elegantly attired and attended by her maidens inside the palace (167); and returning to her father's cottage barefoot and in her shift, as she leaves behind several supercilious courtiers and ladies (181). A single illustration for the *Wife of Bath's Tale* shows the Queen, with many ladies behind her, looking at the Knight kneeling before her, while the Old Hag moves from behind a pillar, and the caption reassures boys, "The Knight spoke with a manly voice" (194). Finally, "The Three Rioters," who are elaborately dressed, walk down a path, arms locked together and smiling. In the background is the old man with his staff and a hand raised in admonition, and on the horizon the sun is setting (211). The image is a didactic warning to frivolous youth. Anyone looking at these illustrations, which are always engaging and drawn with sure and bold lines, would find an appreciation of the feminine and a deflection of interest in the masculine. This is a typical emphasis, and other school texts promoted it.

Margaret C. MacCaulay

Margaret C. MacCaulay's *Stories from Chaucer Re-told from The Canterbury Tales* was published by Cambridge University Press in 1911; it is quite academic, clearly not a Reward book, but still attractive.[3] The frontispiece is the illumination from Charles d'Orleans's manuscript of London Bridge and the Tower; other illustrations are drawings based on the

Luttrell Psalter, including several agricultural scenes, while a feast and jousting represent chivalry. The Ellesmere pilgrim figures decorate the *Prologue*.

Although the translation is not always exact, MacCaulay gives the general sense, albeit she omits much and rearranges lines to create a simple prose rendering. Her avowed objective is to preserve Chaucer's complete vision with interaction among pilgrims as well as selected fine tales. Thus she presents the *Prologue* and four days of storytelling, a scheme helped by some links that give a fuller sense of the pilgrims. MacCaulay's choice of tales shows the same attention to high sentiment displayed in other collections for children. The order of tales is Skeat's. The First Day has only the *Knight's Tale of Palamon and Arcite*. The Second Day includes: the *Man of Law's Tale of Constance*, *Prioress' Tale of the Boy Martyr*, an exchange between Chaucer and the Host, the *Monk's Tale of the Falls of Great Men* (very brief, but Ugolino in full), and the *Nun's Priest's Tale of Chanticleer*. A theme of fortune, loss and recovery, is common to these tales. The Third Day is mostly about women. It begins with the *Wife's Prologue* and her *Tale of What Women Love Best*; the occasion for the question is the Knight's "act of violence" against a woman (123). Another old woman's insistence upon justice is central to the *Friar's Tale of the Summoner and the Fiend*, followed by an exchange between the Friar and Summoner before the day concludes with the *Clerk of Oxford's Tale of Patient Griselda*, again the late Victorian and Edwardian ideal. The Fourth Day has tales of magic or the supernatural, and sermonizing about human responsibility: the *Squire's Tale of Cambuscan*, something of the *Pardoner's Prologue and his Tale of the Three Revellers*, an exchange of Manciple and Cook before the *Manciple's Tale*, and the *Parson's Tale*, summarized succinctly in a statement that gives MacCaulay's *Stories from Chaucer* a serious religious conclusion: "The Parson's discourse was a sermon on the Seven Deadly Sins, their causes, and their remedies, and upon the joys of Heaven which await true penitents who, by toil, humility, and death to sin in this world may purchase rest and glory and eternal life in the kingdom of bliss" (193). Because MacCaulay offered a direct retelling without glossing of the text or adjustment to create a thesis, her version is the one singled out as the closest translation by Storr and Turner, who were deeply concerned about academic issues. They express one dimension of social concern, the improved study of major English authors in school. The same concern dominated writers for children in the United States.

Katherine Lee Bates

The issue of academic study received much thoughtful attention. As noted earlier, Katherine Lee Bates (1859–1929), Professor of English at Wellesley College in Massachusetts, addresses it provocatively in her introduction to the Canterbury Series from Rand McNally, an American publishing house with many school texts:

> That childhood is poor which has not for friends Hector, Achilles, Roland, Sigurd, My Cid, Don Quixote, Lancelot, Robin Hood, Percy, the Douglas, Gulliver, Puck, Rip Van Winkle, and Alice in Wonderland. College classrooms, where Dante and Spenser, Goethe and Coleridge, are taught, speedily feel the difference between minds nourished, from babyhood up, on myths of Olympus and myths of Asgard, Hans Christian Andersen, old ballads, the "Pilgrim's Progress," the "Arabian Nights," the "Alhambra," and minds which are still strangers to fairyland and hero-land and all the dreamlands of the world's inheritance. Minds of this latter description come almost as barbarians to the study of poetry, deaf to its music and blind to its visions. They are in a foreign clime. In the larger college of life, no less, is felt the lack of early initiation into literature. A practical people in a practical age, we need the grace of fable to balance our fact, the joy of poetry to leaven our prose. Something of the sort we are bound to have, and if familiarity in childhood with the classic tone has not armed us against the cheap, the flimsy, the corrupt in fiction, we fall easy victims to the trash of the hour. We become the sport of those mocking elves who give us dry leaves for gold.
>
> This series ... [serves schools] but it aims also to help in arousing a desire for the more imaginative and inspiring legends of the Aryan race.[4]

Bates's prefatory material to *The Story of Chaucer's Canterbury Pilgrims Retold for Children* (1909) is a compendium of Edwardian ideas about the canon, educational and social values, development, and race. The heroes cited, and favorite children's books, are exclusively from the western tradition, predominantly European, of which American authors are an ancillary. Moreover, a quotation from Mrs. Browning's *Book of the Poets* faces the introduction to define Chaucer's role as the originator of the English tradition and to cite his pilgrims as a defense against the evils of modernity:

> And he sent us a train of pilgrims, each with a distinct individuality apart from the pilgrimage, all the way from Southwark and the Tabard Inn, to Canterbury and Becket's shrine: and their laughter

comes never to an end, and their talk goes on with the stars, and all the railroads which may intersect the spoilt earth forever, cannot hush the "tramp, tramp" of their horses' feet [8].

Victorian medievalism underlines this criticism, as does religious high sentiment, yet the emphasis is on medieval laughter, heard across the centuries.[5] What is needed, as Chaucer urged is, "And eek men shal nat maken ernest of game" (I.3186).

Bates supports Chaucer's place as a canonical author and, unusually, offers the poet to children in translations into modern English verse, her own and three earlier versions: Dryden's *Knight's Tale*, Wordsworth's *Prioress's Tale*, and Leigh Hunt's *Squire's Tale*. A reliance on previous literary adaptations of Chaucer reinforces the concept of a continuous and long English literary tradition. Bates is a female poet who assumes that her efforts, not least in innovative links, have a place with those of the male community in which Chaucerians envision themselves.[6] She is most famous for the patriotic lyric "American the Beautiful," first published in the *Congregationalist* in 1895 and subsequently as title to one of her six collections of poems. Her school text of Chaucer is limited to the *General Prologue* and six tales, assigned to four days; the others are *Tale of Sir John, the Priest, The Pardoner's Tale*, and *Tale of the Clerk of Oxenford*. The eloquence of Bates's description of "barbarians" in the college classroom who come with no knowledge of heroes or of poetry, probably evokes many painful memories of what it is like to deal with today's classes of similarly untrained students.

In "Beseeching Pardon," a poem that precedes the texts, Bates claims an affinity as a writer for children with Chaucer's own redressing of "the subtly-spun labors of old astrology ... in phrase befitting childhood's simpleness." The time between Chaucer's language and "the children of this new demesne over the western wave" is five centuries, so that they cannot read the "ryding rime." Bates's Chaucer is the genial poet, and her poem leaves no doubt about what she believes children can derive from reading him:

> Some glimmer of thy sunny soul might fall,
> Hint of the brave old days and figures quaint,
> When pilgrims sought the Canterbury saint
> Less for his saintship than the merry way.
> Grant us to follow after as we may,
> Fed on the fragments of thy gentle mirth,
> Loving with thee the beauty of the earth [15].

A useful appendix (300–16) includes detailed commentary on pilgrimages, St. Thomas of Canterbury, Geoffrey Chaucer, and authorities; the giving of sources is to encourage further reading. Bates's biographical sketch notes changes from the Norman dominance of Becket's time and stresses Chaucer's relation to the court and to John of Gaunt but also how busy and varied his life was and his love of reading and contribution to the forming of English speech. Like many others, her conclusion is his worthy character:

> For he had learned the sweetness of patience and of charity,—how to season life with laughter and make the most of human fellowship. His heart had its sorrows, his mind had its grave thoughts of truth and righteousness, but as the world went harder and harder with him, he entered more and more into the secret of joy, so that in after times one who loved him well, Edmund Spenser, found something holy in this wise, twinkling, tender mirth of the old poet and hailed him as "Most sacred happy spirit" [312].

The illustrations are by Angus MacDonall (1876–1927), a painter and illustrator, who produced a double spread for *Life* magazine for many years and was part of the artists' colony in Westport, Connecticut. Fifty-four pictures combine art and history to affirm scholarly breadth in the text, not least in an opening list of subjects with their origins: photographs for many buildings and locales, several manuscripts, an effigy of an English pilgrim, and prints. The pictures are both traditional and new: an engraving of Blake's *Chaucer's Canterbury Pilgrims* as a frontispiece, and then MacDonall's drawings of the individual pilgrims from the Ellesmere manuscript, several from photographs of Canterbury Cathedral, including Chaucer's tomb, Rochester Castle, Osprings hospice, a pilgrims' rest house and flasks, a tithe barn, and from a copy of a contemporary painting of St. Thomas's martyrdom. Three portraits of Chaucer sign the comprehensiveness of this schoolbook: as rider with the pilgrims in Blake's procession (frontispiece), the detail of his head after Hoccleve (16), and the Ellesmere equestrian figure (150). All are black-and-white, useful images of cultural history that are engaging and animate the text as precise glosses of fourteenth-century England.

Because of Bates's insight and role as an educator, her *Chaucer's Canterbury Pilgrims* is discussed in this chapter. However, an alternate edition places her among American retellings that share publishing values of Edwardian extravagance. Rand McNally issued this elegant edition the same year as the school text. Its cloth cover is a rich cream color decorated with a large Celtic cross with a central roundel. It has a cropped

picture of the Miller holding his bagpipes as he rides; he wears a blue
hood and shoes that match the sky. The figures are outlined in dark green,
and the title and author's name are stamped in gold. In short, the book's
appearance is very inviting.

Contents of the two editions are almost the same; both contain the
texts, black-and-white illustrations, and appendix with historical and biographical material; the deluxe version lacks the pedagogical introduction
to the series but is much enhanced by the addition of four color illustrations by Milo Winter (1888–1956). His style is somewhat like that of
Arthur Rackham, especially in the use of large bare tree trunks, while
delicate showings of buds and green sign the April springtime. Subjects
of the illustrations are the pilgrimage and pilgrims, not episodes from stories. Thus they reinforce the black-and-white pictures that offer such a
variety of medieval scenes and add vitality and freshness. A frontispiece
shows an inn with a thatched roof before which stand a servant who is
waving good bye and a boy restraining a dog that barks at the departing
pilgrims—an archetypal image to involve the audience. The Monk, Squire,
and Knight are riding off, while Chaucer has turned to wave farewell.
Their green, red, and yellow costumes are colorful; birds in the thatch and
sky are the kind of detail that fascinates children. Winter reiterates the
attraction of the chivalric pilgrims in a second illustration in which the
Knight is in the central foreground (his horse's pink saddlecloth marked
with a K in a circle, like a brand), with the Squire and Yeoman on either
side, riding along the Pilgrims' Way. In the distance is a castle and the
caption "Now let us ride and hearken what I say!" points to storytelling
(48).

In another scene on the route, with a house on the horizon and a
stone bridge at the center, there are four equestrian figures. The Prioress,
Yeoman, and Monk wear dark colors, but an expansive Host in red, blue,
and yellow gestures, "Come here, Sir Priest! ride in the midst with me!"
(160). Again the bold tree trunk and green grass evoke Chaucer as a poet
of nature. The final color illustration is an indoor scene, the main room
of an inn with a large table and a sideboard, both with plates and tankards;
the caption is "Trencher, tankard, pot, and cannikin / Appeased all ran-
cours of the road" (258). The Knight is again present, this time standing,
while seated are the Prioress, Squire, and Priest, whose chair has a carved
back. Other details are a Celtic cross and a glass window, but the picture
features much lovely grained wood—table, floor, ceiling—to create
warmth. Winter's fanciful and eclectic imagery contrasts with the many
historically accurate and severe pictures so that the deluxe edition fosters
more-colorful imagining and an aesthetic luxury.

Ada Hales

An alternate text for British schoolchildren is rather different. Ada
Matilda Mary Hales (1878–1957), daughter of a clergyman, read English
at St. Hugh's College, Oxford and wrote two children's books, though she
is best known as a novelist. Her *Stories from Chaucer* (1911)—not to be con-
fused with Emily Underdown's small selection that carries the same title
and was also a schoolbook—is part of Methuen's Stories of the Great
Writers Series, which included Dickens, Chaucer, Bunyan, and Morris's
The Earthly Paradise.[7] The editor was E.M. Wilmot-Buxton, another
prolific author of books for children, many about the Middle Ages, a
period favored by Methuen in three other volumes in a Stories from Old
Romance Series.[8] Hales's *Stories from Chaucer* has a very different thesis
from most collections since she focuses on the dramatic element of *The
Canterbury Tales.* Thus her concern is the appropriateness of tellers to
tales and work, so that characterization becomes a rival interest to storytelling. Nevertheless, the chosen stories are remarkably similar to those
in many of the collections already considered. Similarly, Hales's preface
introduces Chaucer with comparable enthusiasm and high sentiments,
although she presents an alternative way to appreciation. Some notable
Victorians and Edwardians viewed Chaucer as so resonant of their own
time that he did not seem a poet dead for centuries. Hales notes his variety and skill in creating scenes that are distant from present day life, yet
she too urges their universality:

> ... in all this world of fighting men and submissive, inactive women,
> of fairies and supernatural beings, of birds and beasts which can think
> and talk as we can, of glamour and magnificence such as we never see,
> we find so much after all that does come into our own lives—pity and
> pathos that bring the tears to our eyes, fun and mischief and humor
> that make us laugh, the joy that belongs to the long sweet days of
> spring, and the love that nothing can kill [vii].

With her unusual commitment to a dramatic interpretation, Hales chose
ten tales especially suited to the tellers, "For Chaucer knew well enough
how a person's character shows itself in the tales he likes and the books
he reads" (ix). She reiterates the pedagogical hope that her little book will
inspire students to read Chaucer's original but, adding a Romantic authority, hopes they may "one day say of 'Father Chaucer' as Southey did:—'At
whose well undefiled I drank in my youth and was strengthened'" (xi).

Hales rearranges the order of pilgrims in the *Prologue* to focus on
their estates and work; she also makes occasional summary comments.

Thus the Friar, Pardoner, and Apparitor (Summoner) follow the Prioress and Monk, and she evaluates:

> Very different from these four pilgrims, whose duties were all more or less connected with the Church, is Chaucer's description of the Parson, or Parish Priest.... But poor as he was in this world's goods, he was rich in learning and still more in godliness. He was wonderfully kind to his flock, teaching them the gospel patiently, and never finding any trouble too great to take for them.
>   And though he showed himself so long-suffering and compassionate towards sinners, yet there was nothing weak about this priest. There were times when he was most severe, and he knew how to scold those who showed themselves obstinate and disobedient [10].

The translation of "despitous" (scornful) as "weak" warns against bad behavior, a repeated lesson in an age when disciplined behavior was a part of civilized society.[9]

Hales next describes the professionals, again modifying the order (Oxford Scholar, Doctor, Lawyer, Franklin, followed by five Tradesmen) to emphasize the ideal pilgrims. She compares the Clerk to the Parson, "For though he was a pure philosopher and more entirely devoted to study than the parson, he had the same simple, unworldly character which would prevent his ever seeking his own advantage" (11). Her description of the Franklin caters to children's keen interest in food by highlighting, "It snowed in his house of meat and drink!" (13), and later she deletes negative details from the portrait of the Cook. Like Chaucer, Hales names the remaining pilgrims—Manciple, Steward, Miller, Merchant, Sailor, and Cook. The Wife followed the Prioress, "a charming and amusing companion" favored by "many of the more refined among the pilgrims" (4) who must have been relieved by her conversation after the Wife's unrestrained loud boldness. Finally, Hales offers her view of the Host or Landlord:

> no ordinary innkeeper; he was such a fine-looking fellow and so well educated that he seemed altogether fitted for a higher post than that of landlord of an inn. There was almost too much manliness about him, for he was so free in saying exactly what he thought that sometimes he was rather rude. His sense of humor was very strong [19].

This kind of elaboration shows how Hales overlays the medieval portraits with Edwardian judgments, and there are similar glosses in the tales, although her translations are fairly full and straightforward. In the *Knight's Tale*, for example, she stresses Theseus's setting up the tournament to avoid bloodshed, while she cuts the philosophical passages such as his Prime Mover speech. In the *Man of Law's Tale* there is a hint of Empire as Custance sets out ("from friends … to a strange nation"), sympathy about arranged marriage ("to be bound in subjection to one about whom she knew nothing") and women's distress ("Wives know well enough whether husbands have all been good in the past—that is all I can say in the matter!" 52). However, the primary emphasis is religion at a time when Wales was the home of British Christianity, whose followers "were never so exiled that there were not a few who worshipped Christ in secret" (57). Marian elements in the *Prioress's Tale* develop the religious interest.

Hales follows a principle of alternating seriousness and mirth, an extension of Chaucer's contrasting of tales in Fragment I and, to a lesser extent, in subsequent fragments. A short segment from the *Monk's Tale*—including the definition of tragedy and the tale of Ugolino, still the favorite—follows the interruption of *Chaucer's Tale of Sir Thopas*. Next the *Nun's Priest's Tale* is a merry change, heightened by abbreviating the laments. Quick narrative continues with the three rioters in the *Pardoner's Tale*, before the more earnest matter in the *Clerk's Tale*. Hales stresses that Grisild is a model for children: "a dutiful and loving daughter, prolonging his [Janicula's] life with every attention and care that a child can give a parent" (100). There is no stinting of objections to Walter's treatment of his wife (104, 109); unlike the Victorian Mrs. Haweis, Hales offers no justification for the tests and seeks a tear in the intensely moving reunion of mother and children: "In her swoon she kept such a firm hold of the boy and girl she was embracing that it was quite difficult to release them. Those who saw the sad sight were moved to tears and could hardly bear to stay in her presence" (117). The final two tales, of *Squire* and *Canon's Yeoman*, give something of young love, much magic and excitement, and a last warning that "all that glitters is not gold" (191).

Sturt and Oakden

Even though World War I is the great marker for the shift to modernity in the Western world, there was a strong continuity in the presentation of Chaucer to children, both through reprintings of Edwardian retellings and in the creation of new versions after 1918. Most notable is M(ary) Sturt (b. 1896) and E(llen) C. Oakden's *The Canterbury Pilgrims: Being Chaucer's Canterbury Tales Retold for Children* (1923), which is #94 of The Kings Treasuries of Literature.[10] They later contributed #115, a selection from Spenser, *The Knights of the Faerie Queene* (1924) and #159, a collection of *Minstrel Tales* (1928). Sir A.T. Quiller-Couch was the general editor of the series, and this marks it as Edwardian, as does the continued use of the order of the tales according to the Chaucer Society and Skeat's edition. But there are also innovations that sign the 1920s.

The inclusiveness of tales, initiated by Calder and Darton, reaches another high point in Sturt and Oakden, whose retelling in prose translation adheres to the bare narrative and deletes many details but at least mentions all of the tales. The title is a close echo of F.J. Harvey Darton's *Tales of the Canterbury Pilgrims* (1904), and the book is also a return to his comprehensiveness. The emphasis remains on story, with Chaucer making authorial comments. An introduction supplies biographical matter, including a statement that the poem is a record of an actual pilgrimage and stressing Chaucer's love of nature and the variety of pilgrims. Sturt and Oakden acknowledge differences in language and that translations "lose much of Chaucer's vivacity and spirit," so that they urge children to read the originals someday and "learn to love one who has been dear for his humanity, kindliness and humor to poets and ordinary folk alike, from 1370 to now" (8). This rendering, then, still presents the genial Chaucer, not the angst and ambiguity of modernity, and the editors reaffirm his canonical status for disparate levels of society.

Sturt and Oakden somewhat reorganize the *General Prologue*, keeping the essentials (but little of the ambiguity) and reserving most of the descriptions of pilgrims to introduce individual tales, and thus mitigate the dramatic quarrels. Atypically, they include the long prologues of the Wife and Pardoner, albeit reduced to essential points. Their cutting in tales is substantial; this is a book of 160 small pages. The *Knight's Tale*, for example, takes only twelve pages; but the tournament, popular chivalric action, is lively. The *Squire's Tale* is a romance with exotic details of banquet and magic items and the Falcon's description of the tercelet as "the very flower of chivalry" (128), but he taught her of "the faithlessness of men." Chaucer reports that he has heard others tell of how Cambalo fought for his sister against two knights, and "I would fain know the end of that fight." He offers a challenge: "The Squire's tale remains half told. Try, reader, if you can finish it!" (129). This call for audience response is bolder than the question about nobility and generosity that ends the *Franklin's Tale of Three Generous Souls*, a subtitle that adds to the emphasis upon religion in the collection.

The *Clerk's Tale of the Patient Wife* is about the same length as the *Knight's Tale* and includes the Clerk's "merry song" in verse, in which all joined and "felt much cheered by its merry tune." The *Man of Law's Tale* takes eight pages; its subtitle *The Miraculous Journeyings of Constance* points the stress upon Christian elements. There is a balance; each setting forth carries an explanation that pity moved some to stock well the ships, but "God's hand guided it, and God protected it, so that Constance and her child were fed and happy" (51). Thus child readers have both practical and spiritual explanations. Sturt and Oakden retain the strong Marian elements; Constance prays, "O Mary, Mother of God, help me now, a poor mother with her little child, alone, at sea" (51); and the concluding paragraph rejoices, "The ways of God are wonderful indeed!" and offers a prayer to Jesus Christ (52).

Religion is favored in this collection. The *Prioress's Tale* begins with a prayer, a stanza of verse, and concludes with a similar prayer, which adds blessed Hugh. The audience's response is to be "silent and wondrously solemn" (57). The *Nun's Tale of Saint Cecelia* is entirely in verse, the "Invocation to Mary" and the explanation from the *Golden Legend* as well as the tale and life. The contrast between verse and prose translations marks these religious tales. Similarly, the four examples from the *Monk's Tale of Diverse Men Who fell into Misfortune* (Lucifer, Adam, Hugelino, and Holofernes) are in a verse translation, though not in the Monk's stanza.

The only other use of verse in *The Canterbury Pilgrims* is *Chaucer's Rime of Sir Thopas*, stopped before the hero encounters anyone. Sturt and Oakden make this an occasion for characterizing Chaucer, who is accused of the worst "doggerel." He responds, "I must say I was offended by this remark," and goes on with a "very virtuous [tale] about Melibeus and his good wife Prudence. It was full of quotations from the classics, and I fear it was rather long, for I noticed that towards the end many of the company began to yawn…. So perhaps, as it was not exactly a success, I will not repeat it here" (61). Such self-effacing heightens an affinity with the *Parson's Homily on Penitence*, the other long prose tale, here given more space (three pages) but eliciting a parallel comment about "the Parson's droning voice" (157). Yet there is a very clear statement about the many spiritual paths and an explanation of the three species of penitence (solemn, common, and private) and its unfolding through Contrition, Confession, and Satisfaction to attain to blissful and eternal life. Then the pilgrims see the towers of Canterbury Cathedral, illustrated (158), and are "prepared to do penance on the morrow at the shrine we had come so far to seek" (159). Finally the *Author Takes Leave of His Readers*, with the Retraction, which is rarely found in Chaucer for children.

Even rarer in Edwardian collections is the inclusion of the *fabliaux*, yet the most imaginative efforts of Sturt and Oakden are their treatment of these tales, which adults suppressed in editions for children (and themselves) until well into the twentieth century. The *Miller's Tale of a Carpenter Outwitted* is best. Sturt and Oakden greatly expand the details about medieval plays, which become the center of the action. "Alisoun greatly wanted to go, but she knew it was no good asking her tyrannical husband" (34). Nicholas contrives his building of tubs to escape Noah's flood so that he can get Alisoun out of the house; they go to the fair, where they dance and are admired as the best couple. On the way home, he is

> quite forgetful of the lighted torch he was carrying until the flame blew aside in the wind and caught one of Alisoun's ribbons which began to burn. "Water, water!" cried the wife. "Water, water!" called Nicholas, and others near, thinking that a thatch must be afire, called loudly, "Water, water!" [37]

Thus the duped carpenter awakes and behaves foolishly and gets a broken arm; "and Nicholas and Alisoun had a jolly day at the plays" (38). The improvisation here is extensive and ingenious, an affront to a Chaucer purist but yet worthwhile and fine comedy. Child readers get a bit of literary history of the drama and a fast-paced tale of fairly innocuous deception and no disturbing sexuality.

Similar laundering occurs in the *Reeve's Tale*. Sturt and Oakden retain the deceptions of cheating in the measure of meal, the release of the horses, and an invitation for supper, at which the exhausted Miller falls asleep. Then Aleyn kisses Simpkin's daughter and provokes the wrath of her mother, who wakes her husband, and a fight ensues. The Miller is knocked out, and John helps the wife carry him to bed, so that Aleyn and the daughter are alone for an exchange: she tells him about the stolen meal, and he promises to marry her when he is rich. Unsavory qualities of the *Cook's Tale* are simply not heard: the pilgrims come to a bad stretch of muddy road; Chaucer, riding at the end of a straggling line, "heard no more of the Cook's story, nor of the tales that followed it that day" (44). The *Shipman's Tale* becomes a mere line about a merchant whose home was robbed because "his wife was not true to him and let false priests trick him. It was a coarse and vulgar tale, as sailors' stories often are. It amused some of the company, for indeed men's tastes are different and are pleased in different ways" (53). Sturt and Oakden repeat such critical distinction to dismiss the *Merchant's Tale* "of a wife who was the exact opposite of Griselda, and much more akin to the Wife of Bath. Many of the company enjoyed it, and of a truth it was a good contrast to the Clerk's tale." (107). Another discreet adjustment of sexuality is in the *Wife's Tale*; "a goodly knight once fell into sin through the charms of a lady" (85), while the physical grossness of the Host's rejection of the Pardoner's hard-sell becomes, "You would have me kiss your dirty old rags" (81). This *Summoner's Tale* has only the story of a friar taken by an angel to Hell, where he sees "thousands and thousands of friars all suffering the vilest torments" (94) before the Host interrupts him and stops the quarrel, "We want good temper in this party" (95). All the pilgrims agree to this statement that reiterates the authors' intention to produce a rich and engaging children's book at a time when high sentiment was still encouraged. Black-and-white illustrations, all traditional images, enrich the book. The frontispiece is a cropped portion of Urry's eighteenth-century engraving of the Tabard, while other full pages show the Cathedral (158) and an old map of the road from Southwark to Canterbury (160). However, the principal images are again Ellesmere portraits: a full page Chaucer (7) and nine other smaller pilgrims to mark tales. To compensate for alterations, and to emulate Edwardians like Darton, Sturt and Oakden include the *Tale of Gamelyn*, but unusually they assign it to the Yeoman. Thus a loyal servant to the Knight is aptly the teller of a tale of youth oppressed before triumph but helped by a faithful follower.

Bright Story Readers

The age level deemed appropriate to introduce Chaucer is explicit in a large series of schoolbooks for English schoolchildren from E.J. Arnold Educational Publishers in 1908–09. The "A.L." Bright Story Readers are "suitably graded" for six grades, three for the lower school (ages five to seven, six to eight, seven to nine, and eight to ten) and three for the upper classes (nine to eleven, ten to twelve, and eleven to fourteen). According to the advertisements on the green paper covers, Books for the Lower Classes were offered for use "as Additional or Continuous Readers throughout the School Year—one or more each term: they will be found excellent for Silent Reading," and Books for the Upper Classes "as Alternative Literary or Continuous Readers—one or more each term. The Notes at the end of each book make the Series unequalled for Silent Reading." *Stories from the Canterbury Tales* is #43, intended for grade 4 in a list that includes *The Seven Champions of Christendom, Stories from the Life of King Alfred, Stories from the Earthly Paradise,* and many novels—by Walter Scott (*Ivanhoe, The Talisman,* and *Quentin Durwood*), Charlotte Yonge (*The Little Duke, The Prince and the Page,* and *The Lances of Lynwood*), and R.M. Ballantyne (*Erling the Bold*). This list of adapted novels includes, of course, both those written originally for adults and for children. The Victorian appetite for historical novels continued for a long time, and although some of the books are not set in the Middle Ages, that period dominates this list. One possible explanation is to form a coherent group of alternative reading books, but an advocacy of medievalism is as likely a reason. In fact, some medieval stories are recommended for every grade level—beginning with *The Story of Beowulf* and *Havelok the Dane* as well as *The Knights of the Round Table* in grade P (preparatory, ages five to seven) and going on to grade 6 with *Brave Tales from Froissart, Stories from Barbour's "Bruce,"* and *Tales from Tennyson's "Idylls."* Thus the placing of *The Canterbury Tales* seems carefully gauged to come in the middle year of elementary school.

Small Selections

An alternative type of collection was the schoolbook with two or three tales. *In Golden Realms*, an English Reading Book for Junior Forms in Arnold's School Series (c.1902), price 1s 3d, offered an introduction to literature: fairy and folk tales, classic and Norse myths, *Song of Roland*, *Beowulf*, Bede, Dante, Malory, Spenser, Shakespeare, Scott, Froissart, and Longfellow. Black-and-white reproductions of famous paintings add an art lesson and sophistication. Stothard's *The Pilgrimage to Canterbury*, nicely placed across two facing pages, illustrates the Chaucer section. The first selection is an abbreviated *Prologue* that explains the pilgrimage and plan for storytelling, and gives shortened portraits of the pilgrims but only names the Reeve, Miller, Summoner, and Pardoner. The favored story is a short but clear *The Tale of the Clerk of Oxenford* in six parts.

Chaucer's poems are usually retold in collections of stories, but he was also featured in *Form-Room Plays: Junior Book* (1920), a collection "compiled from English Literature" by Evelyn Smith and published in "The King's Treasuries of Literature" by Dutton and Dent. The frontispiece, a portrait of Geoffrey Chaucer's head, indicates his role as Father of English Poetry; it includes a small sketch of Canterbury Cathedral in the lower left corner to sign his Englishness and most famous work, and in the upper left corner a heraldic shield with a daisy suggests his role as poet of nature. The page is elaborately bordered, as is the facing title page. The two Chaucer plays are *The Parlement of Foules* and *The Cock and the Fox* (*Nun's Priest's Tale*); the first is an unusual choice, but as a beast fable it offers the same rich opportunities for young performers as the more familiar story. There are helpful suggestions about costumes and flexibility in casting and staging. The action is direct, with the text much abbreviated, ten and six small pages, respectively. A headnote for *The Parlement* explains that Chaucer lived in the Middle Ages at the time of Edward III and Richard II, and wrote in an older language, Middle English, that pupils will probably learn to read when they are older. The other medieval text is *Robin Hood* from an old ballad. All thirteen plays are from stories that were popular in schoolbooks: two fairy tales from Hans Christian Andersen, two Norse myths and one Greek (based on Hawthorne's *Tanglewood Tales*), episodes from Alcott's *Little Women*, Dickens' *A Christmas Carol*, Lewis Carroll's *Alice in Wonderland*, and Scott's *The Lady of the Lake*. The last play is the child's favorite fairy tale in English literature, Shakespeare's *A Midsummer Night's Dream*, a version limited to the menials, their play, and Bottom's experience with Titania and her attendants. The combination of American and British authors shows how English literature was viewed as a whole, not separated by national identity.

In the United States Houghton Mifflin's Riverside Literature Series had a modern paraphrase of Chaucer, *The Canterbury Tales* that included *The Prologue, Knight's Tale*, and *Nun's Priest's Tale* in 124 pages and sold for forty cents. The combination of fourteenth-century portraits, a romance of chivalry, and a beast fable seems to have been considered a very effective introduction to Chaucer, as shown, for example, in several modern versions of Skeat for ordinary readers.

Rather more sophisticated was *The "Beeching" Chaucer Reader: An Introduction to Chaucer* (1925?), compiled by Arthur Bullard (1879–1918), who also modernized the *Prologue to the Canterbury Tales* (1926).[11] At the time of the Great War he wrote about Great Britain's sea policy and diplomacy. The title page explains that Chaucer's text is "with modern spelling and slight alterations, for use in schools, or for adults who have not the leisure to study the original" and signs the typical Edwardian style of providing for children and a popular adult audience. A quotation from L. Alma Tadema, a Victorian painter, identifies a high moral purpose: "It is a joy to place within the reach of one's fellows, what one believes to be admirable and good." Bullard's view of Chaucer resembles that of Haweis, albeit he is somewhat less confident about the reading of Middle English. He attempts to stay very close to the original poetry, and his "Hints to the Reader" are cogent: the sounding of final -*e* and *ö* marked in words like "lamentatiön" to indicate it should be five syllables, old-case endings in -*en*, and a retention of the original spellings ("fader, moder, suster," and "axe" [ask], and "owene" [own]. Each page carries numbered glosses to translate or explain significance.

Bullard's coverage is limited to the *General Prologue* and two tales (the *Knight's* and *Nun's Priest's*), and selected minor poems ("The Former

Age," "Truth A ballad of Good Advice," "Gentilness," "Lack of Stead-fastness," "L'Envoye to King Richard II" and "L'Envoye de Chaucer" to Henry IV, and "The Complaint of Chaucer to His Purse." The selections from *The Canterbury Tales* are the same choices made by Rev. Richard Morris for the Clarendon Press Series, published at Oxford in 1882 as an adult text. The short pieces included by Bullard reinforce a moral concern that is explicit in his dedication to Dean Beeching, whom he praises for "critical encouragement and Christian kindliness." Indeed this Chaucer makes a strong Christian argument. The *Nun's Priest's Tale* is both a notable example of Christian kindness and redemption and the delight of a beast fable, while the *Knight's Tale* shows the hold of chivalry upon late Victorian and Edwardian imagination. Both are very long and complex, and neither is an easy introduction, but their excellence and richness well answer the intent of the book. The only illustrations are brown drawings of five Ellesmere portraits. Chaucer is the frontispiece; the Squire, Prioress, and Wife decorate the *General Prologue*, which is broken with titles to introduce each pilgrim, and the Knight precedes his tale. Bullard's school text is fairly advanced but still suitable for older children.

Perhaps the most interesting material in *The "Beeching" Chaucer Reader* is a page of comments that support the book, for these show current critical judgments (117). The late Dean Beeching finds Bullard's version of the *Nun's Priest's Tale* "much more reverent than that of Dryden," and Professor Gilbert Murray, who is "much interested in your 'Chaucer' modernization," thinks "there is a much better chance of success in rendering him [Chaucer] into the present style of English than there was in the days of Dryden and Pope." Finally A.W. Pollard, editor of the "Globe" Chaucer, praises Bullard's sound pedagogy: "I should be glad to see 'Chaucer' in use in the Elementary Schools in any form that fairly represents him, and your version is quite close enough to the original to be a useful substitute." Two points are notable: that the level is still elementary school, Chaucer for the young child, and that distinguished scholars support the endeavor to make Chaucer a part of the curriculum. Thousands of copies were printed.[12]

Enthusiasm for the *Knight's Tale* is fascinating because, although it splendidly introduces Chaucer and his complex world, it is also very long and often difficult. An early collection, edited by Rossiter Johnson and published in the United States, *Works of the British Poets, from Chaucer to Morris* (1876) contains only the *Prologue*, but adds to this Dryden's *The Knight's Tale* and *The Wife of Bath's Tale*. Rossiter's brief biographical introduction situates Chaucer in the context of the "brilliant ... disastrous ... warlike and magnificent reign of Edward III" and quotes the

French literary historian Taine, whose highest accolade is that Chaucer, "romantic and gay like the rest," was able "to satisfy the chivalric world" and depict it even better than did Froissart. Chivalry, then, explains reasons for selection and praise of a man "of a cheerful and benignant disposition, fond of mirth and jollity, yet studious in the midst of a busy life."[13]

Reliance upon Dryden's poetic version of the *Knight's Tale* was one solution, as was seen in Bates's *The Story of Chaucer's Canterbury Pilgrims Retold for Children* and in McSpadden's *Stories from Chaucer* that gave both his prose retelling and Dryden's *Palamon and Arcite*, or the *Knight's Tale*. A volume in an American series, The Lake English Classics, includes May Estelle Cook's edition for high school use of *Palamon and Arcite, or the Knight's Tale from Chaucer by John Dryden* (1898). Here Chaucer seems to be the focus, but he has been relegated to the role of documentation for Dryden's tale. Her preface explains that "The unique feature of this edition, that of the footnotes from Chaucer's text, has been introduced in the hope that comparative study will not only add zest to the pupil's work, but will give him a basis for the forming of opinions of his own, and will consequently foster keenness of insight and power of enjoyment."[14] The pedagogical apparatus is extraordinary: biographical sketches of both poets, very detailed notes—many about meanings of words, and a glossary of proper names to provide for focused study as well as suggestions for short, well-defined essays and exercises, often designed to teach words and sentences. However, she stresses the importance of developing the students' imagination and understanding. Thus she asserts, "For any broad literary criticism the high school pupil is not ready. By attempting it he only befuddles himself, and takes away the pleasure of trained discrimination which awaits him in his college courses if he confines himself to the a b c's of criticism before entering" (35). Cook's expectation is further study, another step up from nursery and schoolbooks. She is among those who are reassuring about the ease of managing Chaucer's language, but even if the student cannot learn enough, "it would be better for him to mispronounce Chaucer's lines than to leave them unread" (33). That this schoolbook is overly ambitious seems to be acknowledged by a *Standard Catalog for High School Libraries* (1926), which instead recommends Haweis's *Chaucer for Schools* priced at $1.25; Darton's *Story of the Canterbury Pilgrims*, cost $2.50, and features Percy MacKaye's *Modern Reader's Chaucer*, for $3.75, reviewed as "very desirable if it can be afforded" and "Extremely attractive because of its black and white illustrations by Warwick Goble."[15] The black-and-white pictures are, of course, less expensive and not so compelling as those described in chapter 4, but the reviewer reiterates that illustration remains a significant part of a book's likelihood of engaging the student. Books of Chaucer in Middle English are not on the lists, an absence which signs that the interest is literary rather than linguistic.

Very popular in the United States were "Macmillan's Pocket American and English Classics: A Series of English Texts, edited for use in Elementary and Secondary Schools, with Critical Introductions, Notes, etc." Identified as sixteenmo, these little books are the same size and shape as the nursery Told to the Children Series published by Jack, but the pedagogical apparatus is substantial. They sold for twenty-five cents, were bound in brown cloth, and typically had no more illustration than a picture of the author. *Chaucer's Prologue and Knight's Tale* is on the list, where Malory's *Le Morte d'Arthur* is the only other medieval title. Apart from eighteen of Shakespeare's plays, the greatest number of titles are works by nineteenth-century writers.[16]

All of these schoolbooks are designed for classes in literature and language, part of the development of the study of English. More extraordinary is to find Chaucer in a history book prepared for the sixth grade, ages twelve or thirteen, under the auspices of the Committee of Eight, appointed by the American Historical Association in 1905 to design a course of study for elementary schools. Alice M. Atkinson wrote *The European Beginnings of American History* (1912) to satisfy the need for an introduction to the history of the United States, and she made English history the basis of her narrative.[17] Several facts justify this decision: the east coast was largely settled by the English, the first one-hundred-fifty years were under English rule, and customs and ways of thinking continued to form "the English-American manner of living," to which emigrants from other European countries adapted, not least by learning English. Indeed what is most familiar to the Englishman who comes to the United States is literature:

> [I]n town and country, he would find that the works of the great English writers, living and dead, were read and treasured here in the United States just as they are in England. And with the best of reasons, for do they not, most of them, belong to us, just as they do to the English? Shakespeare is ours, and Chaucer and Milton, for our forefathers were English people when these poets were writing their immortal plays and poems. Those English authors, too, who have lived and written since the time when our country became independent of England give us as much pleasure as our own American writers. When we read "Alice in Wonderland," or "Tom Brown at Rugby," or the "Jungle Book," we do not stop to think whether it was written

by an Englishman or an American. The books of each country belong to both, and they give us a pleasure that we cannot get from the writers of any other country [7].

The history ends with the death of Queen Elizabeth, when "the eyes of all Europe were turning toward America" (390). Thus there is no place for Milton, and only a brief reference to Shakespeare; Chaucer is the key poet, and Atkinson devotes a full chapter to him.

There are three sections; the first is biographical and ties the poet to his age. A small portrait elicits an archetypal analysis, reiterated by Victorians and Edwardians: "his face was thoughtful, humorous, and kindly, — the face of a man who saw every one's virtues and every one's faults and took the world as it came, getting the best out of it always" (258–59). Atkinson's general account of *The Canterbury Tales* closely resembles those in collections of stories: she gives a few examples of differences in spelling and meaning of words, an explanation of pilgrimages to Canterbury, a selection of portraits—including some Middle English descriptions and several Ellesmere pilgrims (Squire, Prioress, Wife, and Friar)—and the plan for storytelling. The final section is a simple retelling of the *Knight's Tale* (266–70). A concluding paragraph quotes "some lovely lines that he wrote of the daisy." This reiterates earlier praise of Chaucer as a poet of nature, one reason for the "delight and charm" of his work. A litany of praise defines other reasons for revering Chaucer:

> a wonderful power of making us feel that we can see and know the persons he is writing about ... almost hear them telling their tales ... full of humor and sometimes of pathos, so that he can make his reader merry or sad as he wills ... full of a love of all that is noble in men and beautiful in the world, and he can make us see it all as he did. And finally, all that he has written is in exquisite, poetic English [261].

In the study of history as in literature Chaucer has an honored and unmatched place. Several different kinds of adults devoted to the advancement of children's education and character have recorded just how they were enabled to be a part of the delight and nobility of the quintessential English/American author.

Pedagogy: Home, School, and Library

The extensive writing, illustrating, and publishing of books of Chaucer for children expressed a belief in the classic text, which educators and librarians eloquently made in studies of reading and book lists. The crucial role of Chaucer for the study of English in Britain has already been considered in chapter 1 in the discussion of the Newbolt Report of 1921. A corollary in the United States is the work of two librarians and a teacher supervisor whose books show the close relation between English and American ideas about the reading and study of Chaucer. The three precede the British government report, partially because of World War I but also because library resources for children were developed earlier in the United States and were the model and inspiration for parallel institutions in Britain, not least with the generosity of Andrew Carnegie.[18] As early as 1898 the Pratt Institute offered courses to study library work with the young, and A Children's Library Association was founded in 1905. Montrose J. Moses and Frances Jenkins Olcott approached children's reading through the library, while Mary L. Burt's main focus was the classroom, both in developing teaching plans and analyzing the results achieved. Their studies are a gloss on Chaucer in Schools, and the relation of school study to reading at home and in libraries.

Mary E. Burt (1850–1918) in *Literary Landmarks* (1889/1897) resembles Victorian retellers by urging that the study of Chaucer should begin at an early age but she differs by making him part of a study of world literature. She identified the fourth grade as the time "when a child can add two landmarks to his outline—the ages of Homer and Pericles being all one great Greek age, and the age of Dante and Chaucer all one great epoch."[19] Burt named several versions of Chaucer for children in her list of books. Mary Seymour's *Stories from Chaucer* appears twice, first designated as "Simple enough for third, fourth, and fifth grades" and then as "Simple enough for fourth grade" (118, 147). Another Victorian collection, Mrs. Haweis's *Chaucer's Stories*, is named as a "supplement to fifth and sixth grade work" in Burt's discussion of "works of the creative imagination" (70). Burt's book is remarkable for including exact details of how children responded to reading Chaucer in school; she both describes what happened in actual classrooms and prints sample essays written by children as part of their schoolwork.

A diagram "Literature plan for Fifth Grade" names "Chaucer's Griselda" (71), a story that Burt used as an example of how students react:

> Chaucer's Griselda calls forth various expressions; some children regard the heroine as an example of self-sacrifice, and others a specimen of stupidity. A child will take home the lesson of self-sacrifice, when he has discovered the beauty of it by looking at it from a scientific standpoint, when he will revolt against it if it is preached at him [31].

The worth of the *Clerk's Tale* is not ultimately challenged, and Burt reiterates her case for the advantages of classics over made-to-order didactic books for children. These observations show that Grace Greenwood's self revelation in her prose retelling of the ballad of "Patient Griselda" was not the only expression of feminist indignation. Later Burt implies the dangers in making one obvious didactic point of the Griselda story for the modern practice of "a good catch." She describes a "goody-goody" book that she once gave to a sixth-grade girl only to have it returned because the heroine—who dressed dolls for a church benefit to aid an army hospital and "was rewarded by getting a lame soldier for a husband" (*Jane Eyre* again)—was "too good." Burt's judgment is firm and strong: "All that writing which gives a husband as a 'Reward of Merit' is more or less lacking in balance, and resembles those problems in arithmetic whose answers are in the back of the book" (76).

The *Knight's Tale*, as table 1 at the back of this book indicates, was the most favored *Canterbury Tale*. Burt includes end-of-year essays that richly document how students read it. A seventh-grade girl's summary account of "Our Year's Work in Literature" describes a wide range of reading, including myths, Schiller, Bulfinch's *Age of Chivalry*, Cervantes— who "overthrew this kind of literature" and was "amusing" (47), a bit of Dante, and so on. In the midst: "Chaucer's The Knight's Tale was one of our favorite studies, and in connection with it we took Midsummer Night's Dream, which we found very similar to The Knight's Tale" (48). An eighth-grade girl accompanied her "Review of Our Year's Work in Literature" with a diagram of a huge river system to show connections; she records even more-extensive reading—Chaldean myths, Greek myths, Homer, comparative versions of Prometheus (Aeschylus, Goethe, Lowell, and Longfellow), Marcus Aurelius, twelve cantos of Dante's *Inferno*, *Ivanhoe*, a Chinese poem of Confucius, some Browning, and so on. Chaucer merits a full paragraph that explains how teachers were able to be so comprehensive and states the girl's critical understanding and preference:

> Our next lesson was a study from the Life of Chaucer, as he was one of the two great authors in the next age, after which we read The Knight's Tale in the Canterbury Tales. The teacher read the most of it in order to leave out some parts. Then we read some short criticisms of Chaucer by Walter Savage Landor, Elizabeth Barrett Browning, Tennyson, and Lowell. Of all the rivers in my diagram, I think Chaucer is the most sparkling yet peaceful river. We brought out that Chaucer played more on the emotions than those before him, and that he fixed the English language [54–55].

The list of authors suggests the significance of books of literary history for children, which is discussed in chapter 7, and that a pedagogy that combined it with reading of the text led to a depth of appreciation. Later the essay returns to Chaucer, when "we read from that great river—Shakespeare. We read Midsummer Night's Dream, and were delighted to find that Shakespeare used the same old woods which Chaucer used in The Knight's Tale as the scene, and that Shakespeare used the same form which Aeschylus used, but Shakespeare uses more characters" (56). This student's essay shows the success of a pedagogy that attempted to train students to connect and to delight them.

Not unexpectedly, publishers offered texts to achieve these ends. In addition to those already named, Burt lists the Riverside Edition of the British Poets: "A Complete collection of the Poems of the best English Poets, from Chaucer to Wordsworth, with Biographical, Historical, and Critical Notices by Prof. Francis J. Child, James Russell Lowell, Charles Eliot Norton, and Arthur Gilman." The contributors to the "eighty-eight volumes, printed on tinted paper, and tastefully bound" are familiar; the combination of a major poet and academics is cogent. Each volume sold for $1.50, and Chaucer was in three volumes, edited by Arthur Gilman. This is a sophisticated edition, undertaken before the publications of the Chaucer Society, and not expressly for children. The introductory material shows the consistency of nineteenth-century critical evaluations that praise Chaucer for "gentleness … hard work … the poet of his country" and much honored, not least by William Morris. More apt is Burt's additional listing—"Chaucer. (See British Poets)"—with costs of texts from Effingham Maynard & Co., "The Knight's Tale. 35 cents. The Squiere's Tale. 20 cents." Moreover, there is a description to promote each retelling by Charles Cowden Clarke: "The Knight's Tale is an exquisite study for eighth grade. The Squiere's Tale serves to show the influence of the Arabic on the English literature" (117–18).

An urging of these two stories is significant, since from the age of eight, the third grade, the child's outline could perhaps best be expanded by a new landmark, the "age of chivalry," because "so many tales appealing to childhood come in there" (64). Yet crucial in Burt's presentation of literary landmarks is that she avoids limitations, for she observed that the same story pleased and interested both second and sixth grade pupils: "indeed, age has little to do with the ability of children to receive classic thought and see its relation to modern thought. There is too much of a tendency to 'grade' everything. It is a pleasant sight to see a whole family from the aged grandparents to the wee bairnie enjoy the same story" (69). Reading stories like Chaucer's could, as the Newbolt Report urged for Britain, deeply affect the quality of life. Burt early cites a friend, Professor Hall of Clarkson University who asserted that "a tale of fiction may be the essential truth the growing soul needs." She explains, "The atheism, the materialism of the present day in our land, is largely due to the banishment of fiction and fairy tales by the Puritans. 'Facts,' Gradgrind, 'Facts,' drive beauty and holiness from the child's heart" (18). As seen repeatedly, those who thought, wrote, and spoke about children consistently believed that Chaucer stories, and other classics, foster adult ideals of high sentiment.

Equally concerned to lift the level of books read were librarians whose dedication to youthful readers was strong for nearly a century before children's literature entered English departments. *Children's Books and Reading* (1907) by Montrose J. Moses (1878–1934) is a history of children's books, a study of how libraries developed, recommendations for how they should be used, and lists of children's books.[20] His work centered in the New York Public Library, but he also consulted librarians at Columbia, and in Hartford, Pittsburgh, and Cleveland. Moses's premise is of the reading democracy created by the public library; his commitment is to providing the very best books, which leads to a strong advocacy of the classics, not least to replace the "pernicious" amount of "inane fiction" currently "concocted" for them: "Literature has been made cold to the child, yet there is nothing warmer than a classic, when properly handled" (171–72). Classics teach the mind and spirit to soar. He cites a modest author of boys' books who presents his work "to supplement and not to supplant the 'masterpiece'" (174).

Book lists make up a third of Moses's study, which offers selections suitable for both English and American children, after a few substitutions for local inclusions, since

> the American library shelves are stacked with the English make of book. And it must be acknowledged that, in point of scholarship, the English classics, given a library and literary format, surpass the school-book shape in every way [206].

A book's physical appearance is crucial to its attracting the child reader, and care should be taken against the look of supplementary readers that lack artistic merit. Classic masterpieces are listed in several categories like "Myths, Folk-lore, Legends, Fairy Tales, and Hero Tales," "Poetry and Verse," and "Historical Stories." "Classics" is a small section with only eleven names: Chaucer, Shakespeare, Spenser, five Greek, one Roman, Cervantes' *Don Quixote*, and Swift's *Gulliver's Travels*. A mark of Chaucer's popularity and significance for children is that three versions are listed for him: Percy MacKaye's *Canterbury Tales*, with W. Appleton Clark's illustrations, published by Duffield for $2.50; Frances Storr and Hawes Turner's *Canterbury Chimes*, from Kegan, Paul, 3s 6d; and Mrs. Haweis's *Chaucer for Children*, Scribner, $1.25. One reteller is American, two are English, with one available in an English edition. This is a richer resource than the one version for other authors (except two for Ulysses/Odysseus and Mary Cowden Clarke's *Girlhood of Shakespeare's Heroines* as well as Charles and Mary Lamb's *Tales from Shakespeare*).

Writing a few years later, another librarian Frances Jenkins Olcott (1872?–1963) also concluded her study, *The Children's Reading* (1912) with an extensive "Purchase List of Children's Books for Children and Young People from One to Sixteen Years of Age" that brings together and greatly adds to her short lists after each chapter. An introductory "Note to the Reader" identifies parents as the audience and sets out basic questions to be answered: the value of books in educating children, the danger of bad books, what books children like, what books should be given to a growing boy and girl, and where and how books can be procured. Educated parents, especially devoted mothers at home, play a crucial role, shown by examples of their early influence in the lives of great men. As the author of *Fairy Tales* (1898), *Arabian Nights* (1913), and *Story-telling Poems* (1913), Olcott favored imaginative stories.

Her criteria for recommending books are "standards based on Christian ethics, practical psychology, and the literary values of generally accepted good books."[21] Moving-picture shows, as well as dime and nickel novels are identified as "evil forces" that can undermine good reading when excessively indulged. Olcott accepts the appeal to children of books that are exciting or emotional, sensational adventures; but she believes that constructive influences can lead boys and girls to better choices: "the books that may forcibly impress on character ideas of justice, truth, honor, loyalty, and heroism, these must be introduced to the children through tactful and enjoyable methods, which will stimulate the imagination" (25). Given this list of admired qualities, a favoring of chivalry is inevitable. Olcott begins with Milton's emphasis upon

> the moral influence of romance [that] is to-day working upon the characters of thousands of modern boys and girls. Through the public libraries numberless copies of books of chivalry are widely circulated. Stories of chivalry and romance are recounted at the public story-hours, and an organization called the "Knights of King Arthur," is encouraged by religious and secular institutions [105–06].[22]

The high sentiment of chivalry, crucial in Victorian medievalism, is the context for planning a child's reading. Both girls and boys find the high realm of romance compelling, and girls especially gain from long following such romantic interests. Thus after initial pleasure in myth and wonder tales, Olcott describes the child's delight in stories from great literature. She charts a plan of reading from ballads to epic stories of Beowulf and Siegfried and *The Faerie Queene*.

After Spenser, Chaucer "may be read aloud or given to a child to read for himself. Unfortunately because of the archaic language of the 'Canterbury Tales,' they may not be fully enjoyed in their original form." Like Bates and Tappan, Olcott holds the view that Middle English is not to be attempted as earlier English retellers like Haweis had expected. She is, however, better placed to recommend two new adaptations, Darton and McSpadden, that "may be used to lead up to a good paraphrase of the tales. These two renditions preserve much of Chaucer's optimism, joyousness, and humor, and they render the stories with spirit." Chaucer is a splendid example of the case that children read classics because they combine excellence with the attractions of sensational fiction: "Stories from Chaucer are thoroughly enjoyed by children because of the adventure, rapid action, and thrilling plots, while the humane attitude, and genial humor, and wholesome thought of the poet are mentally salutary" (111–12). Olcott's next suggestions are stories from Carolingean and Arthurian romance, and such reading is expected to serve a child until the age of fourteen or fifteen years, after which Homer's poetry, or Shakespeare, poets, dramatists and novelists may be preferred.

Olcott's annotated book list for the chapter refers to a "Modern English paraphrase" without citing a specific one and expands her recommendations of the two favored adaptations. McSpadden's *Stories from Chaucer* is "One of the best prose renderings of Chaucer. Parts of the Original poems are woven into the narratives. Inexpensive." The Purchase List cites Crowell's "Children's Favorite Classics" for fifty cents. At $1.50 Darton's *Tales of the Canterbury Pilgrims*, with Thomson's illustrations, published by Stokes, is three times the price, for 125 pages instead of 123. But her description indicates value for money: "Retold from Chaucer, Lydgate, and others. English vigorous. Spirited illustrations by Hugh Thomson. Stories retain much of Chaucer's optimism, humor, and gentle courtesy" (124–25).

As is frequently said, the combination of text and visual image is crucial for children's literature. Although Olcott in "Picture Books and Illustrators," praises several illustrators of Chaucer, she singles out one: "Among the newer artists is Hugh Thomson, whose spirited illustrations of Darton's Canterbury Pilgrims are in keeping with the vigorous language of this rendition of Chaucer tales." In her list of "rising artists" who were doing successful work for juveniles is M.L. Kirk, who created memorable images of Chaucer described in chapter 4. As a librarian Olcott had immediate experience with how children select books to read, and she stresses the role of physical appearance:

> The placing on the shelf of the public library of a classic in textbook or other dull cover, and printed in small, close-set type, insures that the classic will carry out the saying: "Be good and you'll be lonesome." It is rarely stolen, and rarely worn; two proofs of unpopularity. But place on the shelf the same work in a gayly covered edition, illustrated in color, printed in a clear attractive type, and presto! the book disappears legitimately or otherwise. And often a child who reads this attractive volume will tell other children about the story, and behold, the formerly despised, homely volume becomes fashionable [148].

This pragmatic analysis of Edwardian extravagance in creating children's books clearly indicates the appeal of their beauty across economic and social classes in both the United States and Britain.

After her strong advocacy of high moral values, Olcott's conclusion is both confident and flexible. She faces the key "much-mooted" question, "whether great literature should be rewritten for children, and whether it should be expurgated," and answers with admirable flexibility. Great books are not all the same and children are not all the same, and the crucial issue is a proper match between the two specifics. She defends both excerpts and adaptations of full texts that may lead to subsequent reading of the full original, and she argues that expurgations more often express an adult anxiety than a child's cognizance. Her basic point is that children whose books have been carefully selected to make clear the difference between good and evil, weakness and strength, by the age of fifteen or sixteen will have a trained and independent "moral sense" and thus be able "to perceive for themselves when an author fails to uphold uniformly high standards of virtue, or confuses falsehood with truth" (117–19). Today's critics and theorists who question assumptions, or attribute to them motives of self-promotion and dominance for a special group, deconstruct and dismiss such arguments; but they are a strong reminder of the coherence and unanimity of judgments made at the start of the twentieth century that made English studies a significant discipline.

The long success of Chaucer's stories simply told at home, in school, and in libraries depended upon many retellings in attractive and serviceable books. As is the case with all children's literature, adults provided the impetus to read *The Canterbury Tales*, but skilled retellings, well illustrated, were sufficiently compelling to further adult concerns. However, as initially noted, national/racial interests were very influential, and a significant dynamic was the emerging dedication to English studies. Those who retell stories of Chaucer in modern English are sometimes flexible about whether the audience consists of children or adults; indeed the sophistication of many books makes them appropriate for the "educated reader" who is not a specialist in medieval language and literature. Librarians and teachers recommended versions of Chaucer and how they were to be used in books directed to adults, parents, teachers, and librarians. To recognize the strength of Edwardian advocacy of English studies we need to consider an ancillary of the Chaucer schoolbooks, literary history written explicitly for children.

❧ 7 ❧

Literary History for Children

The number, variety, and excellence of retellings of stories from Chaucer for children, and the beauty and skill of illustration, mark an Edwardian commitment to strengthen a literary tradition that begins with Chaucer as the Father of English Poetry. This study may aptly conclude with a review of the treatment of Chaucer in five histories of English literature for young people: H(enrietta) E. Marshall's *English Literature for Boys and Girls* (1909), Henry Gilbert's *Stories of Great Writers* (1914), Eva March Tappan's *A Brief History of English Literature* (1914), William J. Long's *Outlines of English and American Literature* (1917), and Amy Cruse's *English Literature through the Ages* (1914). Marshall, Gilbert, and Cruse are British, and Tappan and Long are American, a further example of a shared tradition. It is notable that three of the four histories appeared in 1914, which is the date of the enlarged edition of Storr and Turner's *Canterbury Chimes* that marked the success of establishing English studies in schools. That year also marks the start of World War I, whose conclusion in 1918 was followed by the start of English studies at Oxford and Cambridge. In many ways the Great War signed the end of the Edwardian Golden Age, a period of idealism and expectation, albeit also of tension and anxiety.[1] Nevertheless, as the Newport Report of 1921 made clear, a strong English literary tradition and universal study of it were deemed even more crucial than before the Great War, not least to sustain older readers.

Although several literary histories are examples of Edwardian extravagance, C. L. Thomson's *A First Book in English Literature* (1903), issued in seven parts by Horace Marshall and Son, is very much a schoolbook.[2]

Thus it serves as a transition from Chapter 6, which began with Thomson's retold *Tales from Chaucer.* Her Preface begins by conceding that "There has lately been a commendable and justifiable reaction against teaching the history of English Literature in schools." But she argues that the failure lies not in the subject but in the pedagogy—"mere lists of names and dates, with a few lines of borrowed criticism." Thomson's analysis comes from classroom experience:

> as an examiner in, and a teacher of English literature, I have felt the want of some book which shall provide a simple chronological framework into which later details may be fitted. I have found that pupils whose work in English has been confined to the study of two or three books are deficient in grasping their significance in the development of our literature, and in relation to the political history of the country. And as a teacher of English history, I have felt the need of some cheap and easily portable book which contains sufficiently long and interesting extracts from contemporary literature to illustrate the thought and social movements of the period studied [v].

A combination of literature and history is crucial to understanding, and her book aims to "meet both wants." She treats only "great authors of each age" with extracts that are sufficiently long to be interesting and illustrative. Thomson, like many others who retold Chaucer for children, acknowledges "the difficulties of language in the case of earlier literature … partially avoided by translation or paraphrase, and in some cases of Middle English and Scottish authors passages have been somewhat fully modernized." Her apology is practical: "For these liberties I beg the indulgence of scholarly critics, on the ground that the book is meant to interest children in general literature, rather than to provide an accurate text of medieval authors" (vi). Thus *A First Book in English Literature* has a modest objective, but remarkably broad coverage.

Two of the seven parts deal with earlier periods, Part I *To Wycliffe and Langland* and Part II *From Chaucer to Lyndsay.* The five other parts cover modern writers, ending with VII *From Tennyson to Stevenson.* There are many "great authors," but the attention given to each varies significantly. Part II has ten chapters—including Gower, James I of Scotland, Miracle and Mystery Plays, Malory, Caxton, Lord Berners, and later Scots poets—but Chaucer has seventy-two pages of the small book. Chaucer is first presented in the context of the Hundred Years' War, when national consciousness led to changes from French to English and King Edward III ransomed him for £16. Thomson notes Chaucer's role as scholar and courtier, the impact of his travel in Italy and his reading of

Italian (especially for the *Knight's Tale* and *Troilus and Criseyde*), the respect and love of his contemporaries, including Hoccleve's praise and portrait. She briefly summarizes most of Chaucer's works (with selective quoting) and evaluates, while linking poem to historical event; for example, *The Book of the Duchess* pleased John of Gaunt, and the *Parliament of Fowls* celebrated the betrothal of Anne of Bohemia to Richard II. Like Mrs. Haweis, Thomson stresses financial circumstances, sums received for his public service. Like H.E. Marshall, she finds a cogent appeal to children in *The Treatise on the Astrolabe*, written for his son Lewis. The role of father for the Father of English Poetry occasions Thomson's fullest moral characterization:

> From this tender preface we can gather that Chaucer had a kind of affectionate nature, as indeed we should have guessed from his other words. For they are full of genial feeling for mankind, and though, as we have seen with the description of the Canterbury pilgrims, the poet could be very severe on vice and hypocrisy, and laughed gently at the follies and whims of his fellow travelers, he had a genuine admiration and enthusiasm for virtue. He was fortunate in possessing a keen sense of humor, so that he could make a joke even of his misfortunes, as in the complaint to his purse; but he had his serious side too, ... [a Balade de bon Conseil], written in the time of his reverses, shows the courage with which he met his troubles [2:66].

Nevertheless, *The Canterbury Tales* is the key work for students. Thomson interlaces her discussion of it throughout the chapter to show connections between literature and history and to sustain interest.

Following this early biographical material is a paraphrase of the *General Prologue*, introduced by an illustration of the Tabard (41) and enlivened by pictures of ten Ellesmere pilgrims. Thomson then discusses the original plan and Chaucer's use of short conversations to link tales; she recognizes that the work is incomplete. She also ranks the quality of the tales; the *Knight's Tale* is best, followed by the *Tale of Constance*, *The Cock and the Fox*, and *Patient Griselda*. The frequency of their occurrence in books of Chaucer simply retold for children confirm these judgments. Next there are more financial details, the moral evaluation quoted above, and then texts of two of the favored tales, *The Knight's Tale of Palamon and Arcite* (68–88) and *The Story of the Cock and the Fox* (88–94). Chapter IV concludes with "Books for further study," both adult text and critical histories (Skeat, George Saintsbury, F.J. Snell, T.R. Lounsbury, A.W. Pollard) and three retellings suitable for children with their prices: Mrs. Haweis' *Chaucer for Children*, 10s 6d, F. Storr and H. Turner's *Canterbury Chimes*,

3s 6d and her own *Tales from Chaucer*, 2s. Obviously Thomson's retelling is the best value for money; the issue of cost parallels citings in several American surveys, as previously noted. Finally, ten "Questions and Exercises" provide various subjects to engage the interest of pupils: connections with John of Gaunt, the influence of Italian writers on Chaucer, a guild, a tournament in the reign of Edward III, and contemporary reception. About half of the suggestions require direct citing of Chaucer's texts to show: his life and character, humor and pathos, religious opinions, love of flowers, birds and animals, or pilgrims with agricultural pursuits.

Students answering these questions would become very aware of Chaucer's Englishness. Brief treatments of Chaucer without extensive retelling of stories are in Thomson's *A First Book in English History* (1901–09), also in seven parts, and in *Our Inheritance* (1910), an essay of thirty-nine pages published by Cambridge University Press.[3] Thomson's conclusion to the latter best explains why such schoolbooks presented literary history to Edwardians. It is a declaration of purpose and a challenge to her young audience—"We have tried in a little space to tell you of some of its glories. The inheritance is yours. Will you not enter in and possess it?" (39). A heading illustration of Stothard's *The Canterbury Pilgrims* on the first page signs both Chaucer's role as Father of English and the distinctive qualities of English characters; three pages offer a brief biography, prologue descriptions of the pilgrims, and a paragraph summary of the *Knight's Tale*, "the longest and best tale" (13–15). The book's final illustration, G.F. Watts' *Una and the Red Cross Knight*, a half-page in black and white, one of many Victorian and Edwardian paintings of chivalry, reiterates the appeal of adventure and nobility in literature. Other Edwardian literary histories for children suggest the attraction of such reading outside the schoolroom.

H.E. Marshall

H.E. Marshall's *English Literature for Boys and Girls* (1909) is intended to be read, "not as a task, but as a pleasure," or as she explains to adults, "The Olympians," her object is "to amuse and interest rather than to teach."[4] Marshall (b. 1876), one of the most prolific writers for children and a significant popularizer, insists that she is not writing a school text. She is best known for *Our Island Story* (1905), published in the United States as *An Island Story*, the most widely read history of England for children; and she extended the proud story of the race in *Our Empire Story Told to Boys and Girls* (1908), which chronicles the deeds of "such a breed of mighty men." In *Scotland's Story* (1906) she acknowledged indebtedness to Sir Walter Scott's *Tales of a Grandfather* (1828 and 1829), the archetype of history for children by the begetter of medievalism. All these are large octavo volumes, quite handsome, initially priced at seven shillings and sixpence. In the same style *English Literature for Boys and Girls* is white cloth with the title and five portraits in color (all are modern authors with Shakespeare at the center) stamped on the cover. The original publisher was T.C. and E.C. Jack, with E.P. Dutton in the United States; Thomas Nelson subsequently reprinted these volumes in a uniform format, navy blue with heraldic device to create the appearance of a book from a university press. As the titles of the history books indicate, Marshall's commitment is always to telling the story; she devoted much effort to literature, contributing several medieval titles to Jack's Stories Told to the Children Series (*Beowulf*, *Guy of Warwick*, and *Roland*) and later subjects to The Children's Heroes Series (*The Story of Oliver Cromwell* and *The Story of Napoleon*). She recapitulates some of these interests in *English Literature for Boys and Girls*, which gives special emphasis to early works and interlaces history with literature.

Marshall devotes three of her eighty-five chapters to Chaucer, and one of John R. Skelton's twenty colored illustrations is of the pilgrim company. Chapter XXII, "Bread and Milk for Children," discusses *A Treatise on the Astrolabe*, written by Chaucer for his son Lewis, and a way to introduce Chaucer as "a kindly father who saw the need of making simple books on difficult subjects for children" (131).[5] Marshall particularly notes Chaucer's Preface, in which he explains that he is writing in "easy English," since his ten-year-old son does not yet know Latin. Thus she makes the Father of English Poetry an accessible and caring father, as she fuses autobiography with traditional evaluation. Similarly, Edward Burne-Jones's woodcut in the Kelmscott *Chaucer* shows Chaucer with his son as they look at the star-filled sky and creates the same effect, a touching portrait of Chaucer as father. This context of parent and child perfectly fits a book seemingly gauged for the ten-year old. Chaucer asks tolerance of adults who may fault his "inditing and hard sentence," intended to help a child remember. Marshall wonders whether her audience would read the scientific treatise, but rejoices in its Preface. She explains that Chaucer's calling his King "Lord of the English" resonates in the everyday phrase "King's English" (131). This is an evocation of patriotism, but the English language was not, of course, limited to Britain. Thomas Cartwright, for example, dedicated the six little books in Every Child's Library, "To the Boys and Girls of English Speech. All the World Over." This series was published in 1907–08 in London by Heinemann and by

E.P. Dutton in New York. The argument for national identity, often reiterated by Marshall, a firm supporter of Empire, derives from the language.[6] Works like Marshall's, one among many, underlay the essential argument of the Newbolt Report that the study of English is fundamental, at the center of the curriculum, to teach both expression and meaning, but also to foster a common heritage of story, whose pedagogical usefulness is asserted in Katherine Dunlap Cather's *Educating by Story-Telling* (1919).[7]

While Marshall recognizes *The Canterbury Tales* as Chaucer's most important work, her chapter XXIII consists of a biography and social history, with three main points. Like Haweis, she uses Chaucer's changing fortune to epitomize his character: "But if he lost his money he did not lose his sunny temper, and in all his writings we find little that is bitter" (133). Chaucer's choice of subject matter is everyday people, for "although he was a soldier and courtier, he does not, in the book by which we know him best, write of battles and pomp, of kings and princes" (134). Thus the middle class of merchants and tradesmen is Chaucer's emphasis; "we have for the first time in the English language, pictures of real men, and what is more wonderful, of real women" (134). Skelton's illustration (136) shows the pilgrims riding on their way. Chaucer is at the center; the Knight rides on his left and on his right the Monk, who chats with Alison of Bath, who is just behind him, while other pilgrims follow in a line. The image evokes lively sounds with the bells on the harness of the Monk's horse and a tiny figure of the Miller with his bagpipe, stopped off the path by a tree. Other figures crowd together to indicate "a company." Marshall explains that pilgrimage was a common medieval experience used by Chaucer as a make-believe journey for tales that he meant to be read. Her final chapter "Chaucer—at the Tabard Inn" develops this literary history's point of view, an emphasis upon character and race; it is largely devoted to the *General Prologue*, which is "perhaps the most interesting part of the book" and "entirely Chaucer's own and it is truly English" (142). Nevertheless, Marshall's specific comments are highly selective. She ties medieval chivalry to contemporary ideals by identifying the Knight as not "of romance and fairy tale, but a good honest English gentleman who had fought for his King" (138); then she briefly notes the presence of the Squire and Yeoman.

Like Haweis, Tappan, and MacKaye, Marshall is aggressively Protestant, as in her account of pilgrims in religious orders: "All these, except the poor parson, Chaucer holds up to scorn because he had met many such in real life who, under the pretense of religion, lived bad lives" (139). This continues her argument in the preceding chapter about the Bible and

Wycliffe, who observed and protested corruption. Chaucer does not scorn the Church itself, since the lines about the Parson present an ideal. The two women pilgrims, the Prioress and Wife of Bath, are next. Chaucer is making fun of the Prioress "ever so gently" and describes "the vulgar, bouncing Wife" as gaudily dressed, somewhat deaf, married five times, and ready to marry again (140).

Finally Marshall quotes Chaucer's account of the Host, with his plan for telling tales. None is identified, but she observes their variety and, concerned about propriety, warns about choices: "Some of these stories you will like to read, but others are too coarse and rude to give you pleasure" (142). While acknowledging these as a way of understanding the age, Marshall rationalizes that Chaucer "himself perhaps did not care for them, indeed he explains in the tales why he tells them" (143). She quotes Chaucer's apologia for churls like the Miller; the reader can choose another tale, and men should "not make earnest of game." Her reading is unencumbered by ironic or dramatic possibilities.

Marshall's conclusion indicates that there is much to read in Chaucer, including many other books whose titles she does not give. Rather she returns to language: "He delights us not only with his stories, but with the beauty of the words he uses" (144). Thus the final pleasure she offers children is an introduction to the original poetry. Marshall quotes "The Complaynt of Chaucer to hys Purse" in Middle English with an interlinear modern translation. She makes a useful suggestion about sounding the final -e and indicates that reading will then go "easily and smoothly" (146), a confidence that recalls Haweis but is not commonly held. Like many retellings, this literary history expects subsequent sophisticated reading after a reassuring and enjoyable introduction.

Henry Gilbert

An alternative to the survey of literature is to concentrate on major authors, and Jack followed up Marshall's *English Literature for Boys and Girls* with Henry Gilbert's *Stories of Great Writers*.[8] The book was part of their In Days of Old Series, to which he also contributed *The Knights of the Round Table*, one of several versions of his extremely popular retelling, and *Robin Hood and His Merry Men*, a selection from his *Robin Hood and His Men of the Greenwood* (1912). Something of a devotee of medieval stories, Gilbert also retold *Northland Sagas* for Harrap's All-Time Tales Series. Books in the In Days of Old Series are smaller than Marshall's heavy volume, but Jack thriftily used the same illustrations (reduced) by

John R. Skelton. Thus there is a colored frontispiece of a monk copying a manuscript in a Welsh monastery, facing on the title page is a black-and-white drawing of a seated Shakespeare with a girl standing behind his shoulder, and "Chaucer rides with the pilgrims to Canterbury" (74). Where Marshall had eighty-five chapters and twenty full-color pages of illustration, Gilbert has eight chapters, each with one illustration. Marshall's preface for adults explained, "I have of set purpose treated the early portions of our literature at much greater length than is usual, it being my belief that what was attractive to a youthful nation will be most attractive to the young of that nation" (x). Gilbert shares this received wisdom of Victorian and Edwardian theories of racial identity and the childhood of nations, since half of his book is about medieval literature. But he begins with "A Bard of the Britons," Aneirin, which is not Marshall's emphasis. Next is *Beowulf*, followed by Langland, and then Chaucer. Something of Edwardian critical preference is evident in the selection of other great writers: Shakespeare, Addison and Steele, Johnson and Goldsmith, and Sir Walter Scott. This range is notable because it does not emphasize the Renaissance, not even Spenser, let alone Milton. As inclusion of Langland signs, Gilbert offers more for the common man. "The Wizard of the North," Scott, who is credited with inspiring enthusiasm in the Middle Ages, is the only nineteenth-century writer.

Gilbert enlarges Chaucer's claim by calling his chapter "The Father of English Writers" and beginning with an epigram, "Dan Chaucer, well of English undefiled, / On Fame's eternal beadroll worthy to be filed." Like retellers of Chaucer for children, Gilbert stresses biography and the state of the English language. What is most distinctive about his account is a comparison with Langland, "The Poet of Poor Men," from whom he was separated by "a great social gulf" (74). Chaucer lets us "into the minds of the comfortable middle classes and the courtiers" and Gilbert calls him "a man of the world":

> he saw the abuses which existed, he could scorn them and show up their faults, but he had not the earnest mind of Langland. He was fairly well satisfied with life and the world as he found it, and where Langland would pour scorn upon false pardoner and priest, Chaucer, equally aware of their shortcomings, would get them to talk, and so reveal their own weaknesses, while he would treat them with the easy forbearance of a man of the world [73].

Not surprisingly Chaucer's nature was more acceptable to his own and subsequent ages; Gilbert praises his "easy flowing style," keen observation and descriptive power, and his "kindly heart" (74). He summarizes briefly several portraits of pilgrims and concludes with praise for Chaucer's capacity to make his reader see "the people passing along the streets of any town in those years of the fourteenth century ... almost we know what they are thinking about, and at least we know well what are their tastes and ambitions" (77). Gilbert thus makes himself a "congenial soul." Although he is writing about the "great writers," his literary history remains largely concerned with social history. Nevertheless, it puts the view that a single author is the epitome of an age and early urges a limitation of the canon.

Eva March Tappan

Eva March Tappan, whose *The Chaucer Story Book* (1908) was discussed in chapter 5, is closer to Marshall's comprehensive coverage but like Gilbert in a commitment to major authors in *A Brief History of English Literature* (1914).[9] The publisher was Harrap, the house that issued the Told Through the Ages Series, which had included her *Heroes of the Middle Ages* (*Alaric to Columbus*) and *The Story of the Crusades* in 1911, and *In Feudal Times* in 1913. As earlier noted, Tappan epitomizes the successful writer for children; her books were usually published first in the United States, often with different titles, and then given wider circulation in Harrap's series. The chief distinction of *A Brief History* is that, unlike the literary histories by Marshall and Gilbert, two British authors, it includes American writers and thus demonstrates an early twentieth-century assumption that American literature is part of English literature. There are fourteen chapters, from the Early English period (beginning with *Beowulf*) through the nineteenth century. The last three chapters are: "The Victorian Era" (especially Tennyson and Browning), "The Poetry of America" (Bryant to Whitman), and "American Prose" (Irving to Twain). Perhaps the most interesting section is Tappan's preface, which offers her four convictions about the study of literature: (1) the prime object of studying literature is to develop the ability to enjoy it, (2) that in every work of literary merit there is something to enjoy, (3) that it is less important to know a list of an author's works than to feel the impulse to read one, and (4) that it is better to know a few authors well than to learn the names of many. These criteria of enjoyment and emphasis upon canonical authors made the developing study of English attractive and manageable.

For Tappan, then, the fourteenth century is Chaucer's, although she briefly refers to Mandeville, Langland, and Wycliffe. She characterizes Chaucer's time as the beginning of English thought and discontent with the Church, and she finds his most sympathetic portraits to be the Clerk and Parson. Tappan singles out Chaucer's love of nature, includes the Hoccleve miniature (61), and entices students with a reference to Chaucer's fascinating asides. Again the English language is an important element; the opening lines of the *Canterbury Tales* are compared to lines from *Beowulf.*

William J. Long

The very title—*Outlines of English and American Literature* (1917) by William J. Long (1867–1919)—declares the continuity affirmed by Tappan.[10] A single chapter, "The Age of Chaucer and the Revival of Learning," covers the fourteenth and fifteenth centuries. Langland, Malory, and Caxton are the principles, and Wycliffe is mentioned only as a reformer to contrast with Chaucer, who is the revered poet. Chaucer's role is signed by a line on the title page, "This is the wey to al good aventure," that announces the book's purpose "to introduce these writers not as dead worthies but as companionable men and women, and to present their living subject as a living thing, winsome as a smile on a human face" (v), an effort that was a great pleasure and followed from his advanced study, *English Literature and American Literature.* Since history and literature are "closely related," *Outlines* treats both, but Long stresses that "literature deals with life; and life, with its endlessly surprising variety in unity, has happily some suggestion of infinity" (vii). Chaucer, like a scop for an Old English chieftain, is true to a tradition of poetry with "local color," for which his varied professional activities were a solid resource, but his salient trait is universality: "His specialty was human nature, his strong point observation, his method essentially modern"—"modern," as Longfellow and Tennyson are not, because Chaucer's portrayal of men and women with humor and wisdom makes them recognizable and "welcome as friends or neighbors" (38).

After a brief biographical sketch, Long turns to "Reading Chaucer" and shows his bias to the pleasure of literature. He accepts that students will not get Middle English pronunciation accurately. Thus, while he offers a few general points, he suggests that time be spent on "more important matters, that is the poems themselves," which he succinctly summarizes. Again Urry's drawing of "Pilgrims setting out from the 'Tabard'" (45) marks the emphasis upon *The Canterbury Tales.* Long expresses his delight in the subtitle of his critical section, "The Charm of Chaucer"— an excellent storyteller, with an extraordinary power of observation and of description, and a "broad tolerance, his absolute disinterestedness" that makes him eschew reforms and present "a world in which the rain falleth alike upon the just and the unjust, and in which the latter seem to have a liberal share of umbrellas. He enjoys it all, and describes its inhabitants as they are, not as he thinks they ought to be" (49–50). The Canterbury pilgrims are "human types.... From century to century they change not, save in name or dress. The poet who described or created such enduring characters stands among the few who are called universal writers" (50). Long reiterates this judgment when he first quotes Dryden's estimate in *An Essay of Dramatic Poesy* (136) and then compares Chaucer with the limited Pope, who was "the poet of one period" (153). In a discussion of colonial American poetry, Chaucer and Langland are types of Cavalier and Puritan that represent two world views (348). Long's recommendations for reading include selections in Riverside Literature, King's Classics, Skeat's *The Student's Chaucer,* and "other school series." Again Tatlock and MacKaye's *Modern Reader's Chaucer* is judged "a good, but expensive, modernized version" (58). *Outlines* is readable, but essentially it is a school text that lacks the charm of Marshall and Gilbert, as does Tappan's literary history. Some differences between English and American approaches to literature are clear even in these early histories for children, written before a discipline of English studies became well developed.

Amy Cruse

Amy Cruse's *English Literature through the Ages* (1914) takes a more-advanced approach to Chaucer; undergraduates could profit from the information and quality of her analysis.[11] Like Marshall, Gilbert, and Tappan, Amy Cruse (b. 1870) wrote many books for children, including *The Book of Epic Heroes* (1926), an example of the popularity of traditional stories, many medieval, after the Edwardian period. The color frontispiece for *English Literature* is the Hoccleve "Authentic Portrait of Chaucer," and it signs Chaucer's place as Father in a story that begins with *Beowulf* and ends with Robert Louis Stevenson. Cruse's preface explains that she will tell it "through stories of individual books" (5) and titles a chapter *The Canterbury Tales.* However, it contains almost entirely biographical and bibliographical information, with a little about sources and influences. The student, it seems, is expected to know the tales; Edwardian stories from Chaucer for children at home and school were already an assumed base for the study of English literature.

A later book by Cruse illustrates continuity in the approach to

Chaucer for children. Harrap also published her *The Golden Road in English Literature: From Beowulf to Bernard Shaw* in 1931; here the Hoccleve miniature is on the cover, an icon of the Father of English Poetry. Cruse's enthusiasm is overt in the preface when she writes of the "wonderful possession that we call our literature ... a living thing, the product of the whole nation's growth, in which the humblest of our forefathers, working with the greatest, has had his small, unnoticed part." She offers a parable of English literature as "a fair and gracious garden" in which the soil is the people, the common grass is the everyday literature of use and necessity, the weeds are useless and harmful writing, some flowers last only a season, and perennials have a longer life but finally die. Then there are "the lovely, immortal flowers that grow and blossom, and for ever put forth new buds and are fresh and fragrant through all the ages."[12] This evocative metaphor for a canon infers a preference for certain works that transcend time and place because they touch human understanding in ways that are extraordinary. "Geoffrey Chaucer, The Great Teller of Tales" (chapter IX) is such a writer. Cruse concentrates on *The Canterbury Tales*, retelling the *Nun's Priest's Tale*, which signs its favored place in children's literature. Singling out the *General Prologue*, she maintains the stance of all those who retold Chaucer for the children, whom she urges: "When you are a little older, you must read it for yourselves, for no summary can give you more than just a bare idea of the fun and the kindliness, the insight and the zest, that Chaucer puts into his description of the pilgrims" (95).

Foundations for Appreciation and Comprehension

Reading a literary history may seem an unlikely activity for children, especially to many who read such books only as graduate students and then as a lesser device than close reading (strongest with New Criticism at mid-century) or theory (since the 1970s). These books are a mark of how well-read in canonical Western literature children were expected to be early in the twentieth century. The brief summaries of the treatment of Chaucer by Marshall, Gilbert, Tappan, Long, and Cruse indicate that their books emphasize history more than literature, that they were supplements to the reading of Chaucer's poetry itself—albeit in modern prose translation. There is a clear assumption that the child's knowledge of social and political traditions, here more stressed than genre or poetic form, is a foundation for extended appreciation and comprehension. Greater knowledge of the Middle Ages, a recognition of its difference

—albeit sometimes condescendingly noted—is thought to increase understanding and delight in the study of literature. The literary histories, like the retold stories, urge and expect ongoing, increasingly sophisticated reading of the canonical books read early by the child. It is worth remembering that Marshall, Gilbert, Tappan, Long, and Cruse all moved easily between literature and history; each wrote social history and retold stories for children.

Reading and study of Chaucer had no stronger advocate than Henry Newbolt, a popular poet and writer of criticism as well as a public servant. The trajectory of his personal experience of Chaucer reflects how expectations changed. His memoirs describe how as a Victorian child he had read Dante, Milton, William Morris, some lyric poets, and Shakespeare "through and through before I was fourteen"; but with Chaucer, "I was behindhand—at home we had nothing but Dryden's version, and in school we read only *The Knight's Tale*, and an expurgated edition of *Chanticleer and Partilote*."[13] In a literary history, written for the general public during World War I, Newbolt attempts to save others from this limitation. *A New Study of English Poetry* (1917) is both a discussion of the nature of poetry and a consideration of major authors (Chaucer, Shakespeare, Milton, British Ballads).[14] Newbolt praises Chaucer for the depth of his feeling, and posits a religious awareness that matches present needs: "He sees the life of the soul only in fitful and uncertain gleams, but they are gleams of a true inward light, of that indeed which is the master-light of all our seeing" (144). As a craftsman who "made a world, but does not inhabit it" (145), Chaucer is dramatic, not tragic: "He is often simply a reporter and always personally present with the audience. In short, his genius is essentially narrative ... the finest teller of stories who ever wrote in English verse" (146). Newbolt also names Chaucer the "first humorist of modern Europe ... the stroke of honorable laughter resounds on all sides" (147). In this context, and writing for adults, he identifies the tales of the Miller and Reeve as "of the kind now considered unrepeatable, but they are not unreadable, because, in spite of their coarseness, there is nothing in them tending either to sensuality or cruelty" (147–48). Furthermore, "as a character-study her [the Wife's] Prologue goes far beyond any drama ever written" (152). The case for *The Canterbury Tales* is less complex than Newbolt's analysis of *Troilus and Criseyde*, but it comes first to establish the place of Chaucer in literary history urged in children's books—the greatest storyteller and observer of English life.

There is little doubt that national, patriotic influences greatly influenced Edwardians and their American counterparts, not least educators who sought to make English studies a solid and respected discipline.

But there is also an element of commonsense, an acknowledgment of difference, to use a favored term from today's theory, albeit the difference is of era. As the redoubtable G.K. Chesterton put it in *Orthodoxy* (1908):

> Tradition may be defined as an extension of the franchise. Tradition means giving votes to the most obscure of all classes, our ancestors. It is the democracy of the dead. Tradition refuses to submit to the small and arrogant oligarchy of those who merely happen to be walking about. All democrats object to men being disqualified by the accident of birth; tradition objects to their being disqualified by the accident of death. Democracy tells us not to neglect a good man's opinion, even if he is our groom; tradition asks us not to neglect a good man's opinion, even if he is our father. I, at any rate, cannot separate the two ideas of democracy and tradition; it seems evident to me that they are the same idea. We will have the dead at our councils.[15]

Here tradition and populism are inseparable; Chaucer was one "father" not neglected by Chesterton, whose *Chaucer* (1932) was considered in chapter 1. This book came near the end both of his life—he died in 1936—and of the first phase of Chaucer criticism. Caroline Spurgeon published *Five Hundred Years of Chaucer Criticism and Allusion 1357–1900* in 1933, the date of the first appearance of F.N. Robinson's *Chaucer*, the major and most influential scholarly edition of the *Works* in the twentieth century. It is also the date that D.S. Brewer chose to conclude the second volume of *Chaucer: The Critical Heritage* because it precedes the twentieth-century's vast industry of Chaucer scholarship and theory. Spurgeon cogently observes the historical relativity of criticism when she notes the fluctuations of taste in different periods and concludes that the "measurement of judgment" is of the critics not of Chaucer himself. It is fitting to conclude with a brief look at today's Chaucer for children, where the comparison with the Edwardians amply justifies Spurgeon's dictum.

Epilogue

Just how far the end of the twentieth century was from its beginnings is obvious in a review of two 1980s versions of *The Canterbury Tales* for children by Selina Hastings and Barbara Cohen, both published in 1988. Francine Prose evaluates in a very non–Edwardian way, both in style and judgment:

> A version of Chaucer for children sounds, on the surface, only slightly less improbable than an I-Can-Read Henry Miller. Excise the bawdy sex, the aggression, the ribald humor, the flights of philosophy and metaphysics—and what's left? It's by no means an obvious or easy project....
>
> The problems involved in producing a PG-rated Chaucer are daunting. The first question, clearly, is one of language: how to translate eloquent Middle English poetry into contemporary prose without losing the beauty, grace and humor that depend so heavily on metaphor, word choice, subtle manipulations of tone? Beyond that, are the complex issues of content. Chaucer is very much a writer for adults, not so much because of his sexual humor ... as because his great themes—the workings of fate, the omnipresence of death, the often brutal power struggle between men and women—suggest harsh truths that we might actually wish to *spare* our children. Finally there are a myriad historical and social details: how to sustain a child's interest while pausing to explain what it meant to be a reeve, a franklin, or, for that matter, a pilgrim...?
>
> Their selection of tales ... demonstrates the breadth of Chaucer's vision from the fatalistic spookiness of the Pardoner's tale to the courtly romances of the Franklin and Knight to the low-down-and-dirty bawdiness of the Miller and the Wife of Bath.... Reading these, to ourselves and to our children, we keep thinking: what marvelous stories...!
>
> It may be that these editions will make lifelong Chaucer fans of their young readers, or, as Ms. Cohen hopes for her book, "lead some of [their] readers to the original." Somehow, however, I doubt it....

Ms. Hastings manages to offer a taste of the original—some notion of its magic, its wondrous sense of plot—but rarely have "The Canterbury Tales" seemed less modern and more medieval than in Ms. Cohen's version. To quote that old parental chestnut, some things are just not for children. And sadly, what both books seem to suggest is that Chaucer may be among them.[1]

The contrast with Edwardian enthusiasm not simply for Chaucer's poetry but also for the child's capacity to understand and to be inspired, tells us much about shifts in academic and social values. Sexy Chaucer has supplanted genial and pious Chaucer. Hastings includes a brief *Prologue* and the tales of the *Knight, Miller, Reeve, Nun's Priest, Pardoner, Wife,* and *Franklin.* In place of the two stories of high sentiment and noble women, the *Clerk's Tale* of Griselda and the *Man of Law's Tale* of Constance, are the *fabliaux* told by the churls, the Miller and the Reeve. Modest claims for translation have been replaced by insistence upon sophisticated nuances, and thus only adults can appreciate a poet like Chaucer. Where the Edwardian retellers and reviewers found a delightful and worthy teller of tales of value and interest to all ages in varying degrees of complexity, the New York reviewer despairs at the end of the twentieth century.

For different reasons, Judith Bronfman, a scholar who traced the Griselda story, judged another collection, Geraldine McCaughrean's *The Canterbury Tales,* a failure. She also expressed a longing for the Chaucer offered to children at the start of the twentieth century; the recent "version makes one very grateful for authors like Charles Cowden Clarke, who remained faithful to the original and dealt with uncomfortable material by glossing it for young readers."[2] In contrast, the *Clerk's Tale* of 1985 is so "trivialized and emasculated," as to be a "parody ... although an unintentional one" (79). The later reteller who could not present the idea of an ideal wife or spiritual example, produced a story about a "namby-pamby" girl who responds scarcely at all to Walter's testing that is identified as a "long joke" (80). The creation of new versions of Chaucer's stories for children suggests an ongoing recognition of the fourteenth-century poet, but the tales in a post-modern context have not been successful.

Another difference between the first two collections and the many Edwardian ones is that they are more obviously and primarily picture books. While Edwardian Chaucer books for children were greatly enhanced by illustrations, these were supports for the text, not rivals. Late-twentieth-century publishers seem to have decided that the picture book is the best approach to the child reader.[3] Books with one tale, by an illustrator-artist, show the same judgment. A prime example is Lee Lorenz's adaptations of *The Reeve's Tale* and the *Miller's Tale,* both also published

in the 1980s and further evidence of a favoring of the sexy, bawdy tales—
a reminder that children's literature is chosen and written by adults. There
is a paradox in the decision to combine a format now almost exclusively
associated with children's books and tales for which Chaucer felt compelled to offer an apologia and that were so long considered inappropri-
ate and excluded from selections for adults as well as children. Moreover,
the privileging of the illustrator over the reteller signs a decline of commitment to language and its power for storytelling in our visual age, which
itself is a reenactment of the role of images in the Middle Ages, a time
when many could not read.

Recent criticism and theory support F.J. Harvey Darton's claim that
children's literature makes astute social history. Table 1 at the end of this
book shows which tales were retold in each of twenty-eight collections
devoted exclusively to Chaucer; the *Knight's Tale* is in every book, and
the *Clerk's Tale* is in all but one. The *Man of Law's Tale* in twenty-four
and the *Nun's Priest's Tale* in twenty-three follow closely. Table 1a, showing eight quite different mixed collections, demonstrates the same first
preferences: five each for the *Knight's* and *Clerk's*. Victorian and Edwardian writers for children, publishers, and Chaucerian scholars delighted
in the Father of English Poetry, used him as a foundation for the study
of language and literature, and also fostered a moral tradition. The most-
favored stories are of high sentiment, generosity and courtesy, patience,
perseverance, and piety; or in the nostalgic words of Thomas Malory's
Morte Darthur, "than was love trouthe and faythefulness" (XVII. 25).
These virtues, albeit "adapted," are still evident in the ongoing success of
novels about medieval knights or in the heroes of today's analogous historical fantasies that exploit conventions of medieval romance.

Much of today's visual art and critical analysis lack such old-fash-
ioned virtues, which are frequently considered escapist. Children are
shown another "reality," the reality of a present-day urban world that is
not so optimistic; it is more harsh than noble, filled with violence and
selfishness, yet phrases such as "medieval barbarism" and "medieval savagery" are commonly used to contrast contemporary righteousness.[4] The
last decades of the twentieth century have forged an alternative view to
the initial assumption that in English literature was to be found a moral
strength to sustain the human spirit beaten down by the catastrophe of
World War I. To judge from the strength of English as an academic discipline following World War II, both British and American universities
confidently repeated this discernment at mid century.

Many Victorian and Edwardian retellers of Chaucer's tales for children are generally unrecognized, none is a "major author," and transla-

tion—even more simplified when the audience is children—is not a highly esteemed art. Most of the writers considered in this book may be called journeymen, or more often journeywomen (their gender not infrequently obscured by the use of initials). They were usually fairly prolific and often associated with a particular publisher at a time when the book trade of luxury items and schoolbooks was expanding rapidly. Some illustrators in the Golden Age, a period of great opportunity identified more broadly as 1880 to 1940, are major artists, notably Gordon Browne, Hugh Thomson, W. Heath Robinson, and Warwick Goble; but again "journeyman/woman" aptly describes many who pictured Chaucer's pilgrims and stories. Part of the intention in writing this book has been to present these writers and illustrators with sufficient detail to indicate the substantial nature of their accomplishment in creating books that were widely read and that remain a fascinating and revealing picture of social life at the start of the twentieth century. Chaucer's stories simply told for children are arguably a more cogent record of social life than the original "children's classics" that are a large part of current reading lists, assigned to undergraduates who sometimes have read a few of the titles as children. But they are very different in other ways. On the one hand, retellings of Chaucer for children, although they contributed to the development of the study of English and English studies as an academic discipline, often were not considered sufficiently important to become part of library collections for posterity so that they are not readily accessible. In this way, these children's books are repeating the history of their antecedents, the chapbooks. A current favoring of texts from popular culture marks both a lack of confidence in the appeal of canonical writers and student skills and a belief in the virtue of expanding the curriculum. Victorian and Edwardian retellings of Chaucer for children combine the appeal of the first author in the English canon with the cause of marginalized books, which is no mean achievement.

For several different reasons, the English major no longer enjoys great favor, and children's language skills are in decline. The best known formula of children's literature is "Once upon a time..."; stories can be retold yet again and again. At the start of the twenty-first century, writers for children, and Chaucerians, could do worse than to reconsider and perhaps recover something of the wisdom and idealism of their forebears in the Golden Age of children's literature when simply told stories from Chaucer delighted and taught the young in nursery, home, library and school throughout the English-speaking world in the opening decades of the twentieth century. Today, in spite of the demise of the British Empire, English is the common language for much of the world.

Tables

The following tables bring together data about collections that contain Chaucer's stories retold for children, both the occurrence of individual tales and kinds of illustrations. Table 1 is for 28 collections devoted exclusively to Chaucer; the retellers are indicated on the top line and pilgrim tellers for individual *Canterbury Tales* are listed in the first column, along with three additional tales sometimes included before the canon was firmly established, as well as the Prologue, Links, and Epilogue (or Retraction). If an author's collection was published as different books, these are numbered, as indicated in the list of "Victorian and Edwardian Books of Chaucer Simply Told to the Children," which contains bibliographical information. Table 1a offers similar information about tales in mixed collections, that is books not exclusively devoted to Chaucer. These tables are a quick guide to which tales are in each collection and which are repeated in different books by the same reteller. They also indicate popularity: for example, the *Knight's Tale* is most often retold, included in all collections devoted entirely to Chaucer, while next in frequency are the *Clerk's Tale* and the *Man of Law's Tale;* in contrast, the *Miller's Tale* and *Reeve's Tale* are found only in collections that include all of the tales.

Because illustration often shares importance with verbal text in children's books, Table 2 presents information about the extensive and varied use of figures—the total number, sizes, black-and-white and color, marginal decorations—and their subject matter—episodes in the story or pilgrim portraits, as well as reproductions of medieval art, especially the Ellesmere pilgrims, and of later art. The table shows a remarkable reliance upon medieval illuminations of pilgrims from the Ellesmere manuscript in five different collections; in two cases these are the only pictures. Mrs. Haweis, one of the earliest retellers, is the only writer who also illustrated her work. The list of illustrators includes several major artists—Anne Anderson, Warwick Goble, W. Heath Robinson, Hugh Thomson—and is a quick guide for the location of artist with author.

TABLE 1. TALES SELECTED FOR COLLECTIONS

	Bates	Bullard	Calder	Clarke		Darton			Hales	Haweis		Johnson	Kelman	MacCaulay	MacKaye	
				1	2	1	2	3		1	2		1		1	2
Prologue	X	X	X	X	X	X	X		X	X	X	X		X	X	X
Links	X plus		X		X	X	X		X	X				X	X	X
Knight	X	X	X	X		X	X		X	X	X	X	X	X	X	X
Miller			(X)			X	X									X
Reeve			(X)													X
Cook																X
Man of Law			X	X	X	X	X	X	X			X	X	X	X	X
Wife			X	X	X	X	X	X				X		X	X	X
Friar					X	X	X	X		X				X		X
Summoner																X
Clerk	X		X	X	X	X	X	X	X	X	X	X	X	X	X	X
Merchant																X
Squire	X		X	X	X	X	X		X					X	X	X
Franklin			X		X	X	X	X		X			X		X	X
Doctor						X	X								X	X
Pardoner	X		X	X	X	X	X	X	X	X		X		X	X	X
Shipman						X	X									X
Prioress	X		X	X	X	X	X	X	X					X		X
Thopas						X	X		X							X
Melibeus																X
Monk	X								X		X			X		X
Nun's Priest	X		X	X	X	X	X	X	X	X	X	X		X	X	X
Second Nun						X	X									X
C's Yeoman				X	X	X	X	X	X						X	X
Manciple			X			X	X	X						X	X	X
Parson						(X)	X							(X)	X	X
Epilogue			X			X	X							X	X	X
Beryn						X	X									
Gamelyn			(X)	X		X	X									
Lydgate						X	X									

	McSpadden 1	McSpadden 2	McSpadden 3	Seymour	Stead	Storr & Turner 1	Storr & Turner 2	Sturt & Oakden	Tappan	Thomson	Underdown 1	Underdown 2	Wilson
Prologue	X	X	X	X		X	X	X	X	X	X		X
Links	X	X				X		X	X		X		
Knight	X	X	X	X	X	X	X	X	X	X	X	X	X
Miller								X					
Reeve								X					
Cook								X					
Man of Law	X	X	X	X	X	X	X	X	X	X	X	X	X
Wife	X	X	X	X	X			X	X	X	X		
Friar	X	X	X	X				X	X		X		
Summnone													
Clerk	X	X	X	X	X		X	X	X	X	X	X	X
Merchant													
Squire	X			X	X	X	X	X	X				
Franklin	X	X		X	X	X	X	X	X		X		
Doctor				X				X	X				
Pardoner	X	X	X	X	X		X	X	X	X			
Shipman								X					
Prioress				X				X	X				
Thopas				X				X					
Melibeus				X				X					
Monk				X				X					
Nun's Priest	X	X	X	X	X	X	X	X	X	X	X		
Second Nun				X				X					
C's Yeoman				X				X	X				
Manciple				X				X					
Parson								X					
Epilogue	X	X	X					X			X		
Beryn													
Gamelyn	X	X	X			X	X	X					
Lydgate													

Key:

( ) = (Very brief) synopsis

1, 2, or 3 = Different titles by author/editor; see bibliography

TABLE 1A. TALES SELECTED FOR MIXED COLLECTIONS

	Atkinson	Bailey	Belgrave & Hart	Chaundler	Hope	In Golden Realms	Krapp	Richardson	Smith
Prologue	X					X			
Links									
Knight	X			X			X	X	X
Miller									
Reeve									
Cook									
Man of Law							X	X	
Wife								X	
Friar									
Summoner									
Clerk		X			X	X	X	X	X
Merchant									
Squire								X	
Franklin		X							
Doctor									
Pardoner							X		
Shipman									
Prioress									
Thopas									
Melibeus									
Monk									
Nun's Priest			X						
Second Nun									
C's Yeoman									
Manciple									
Parson									
Epilogue									
Beryn									
Gamelyn									
Lydgate									

TABLE 2. ILLUSTRATIONS IN CHAUCER COLLECTIONS   (*key to illustrators overleaf)

Illustrators*		Total Figs.	B&W Full P.	B&W Part P.	Marg., Cap.	Frame Pages	Color Full P.	Story	Pilgrim	Ellesmere	Art of M.A.	Later Art
Anderson	(1)	147			131		16	10	5			1
Anderson	(2)	8					8	6	2			
Clark		6					6	3	3			
Ellesmere	1	9	1	8					9	X	1	
Ellesmere	2	15	2	13					13	X		
Ellesmere	3	12	3	9		2			10	X	1	
Ellesmere	4	27	1	26					18	X	9	
Ellesmere	5	5	5				sepia		5	X		
Engravings		5	4		1				1			3
Ewen		29	16	13				29				
Goble		18					18	18				
Haweis	(1)	39	3	28			8	6	20			
Haweis	(2)	2	2								2	
Kirk	(1)	11					11	5	6			
Kirk	(2)	5				1	4	3	1			
MacDonald		57	5	49	3				23	X	25	3
Mott &	(1)	14	11	3				10	1		3	
Williams	(2)		12	1				11	1			1
Prout	(1)	30	16	14				12	18	X	1	2
Prout	(2)	8	6	1			1	6	1			
Robinson		8					8	8				
Scannell		11	11				sepia	10				
Seymour		171				171		[3]	1			
H. Thomson	(1)	53	26	2	25			10	[4]			
H. Thomson	(2)	7	3				4	7	10			
M. Thomson		53	10		31			10	11	X	1	2
Winter		4					4	4	4			

Key: *Marg, Cap.* = category for small figures that also includes headings and endings
  Ellesmere = category to indicate how these images were the major ones used repeatedly
  Art of MA = architecture, objects, ms. illuminations, etc.   *Sepia* = neither black and white nor color
  [ ] = the total number of designs, repeated for an entire book of bordered pages

Key to Illustrators of Books, Table 2

Anderson, Anne (1): Emily Underdown, *The Gateway to Chaucer*
Anderson, Anne (2): Emily Underdown, *Stories from Chaucer: Retold*
Clark, Walter Appleton: Percy MacKaye, *The Canterbury Tales of Geoffrey Chaucer*
Ellesmere ms 1: Francis Storr and Hawes Turner, *Canterbury Chimes* [1914 ed.]
Ellesmere ms 2: Eva March Tappan, *The Chaucer Story Book*
Ellesmere ms 3: M. Sturt & E.C. Oakden, *The Canterbury Pilgrims*
Ellesmere ms 4: Margaret C. MacCaulay, *Stories from Chaucer Re-told from the C T*
Ellesmere ms 5: Arthur Bullard, *The "Beeching" Chaucer Reader*
Engravings: William Calder, *Chaucer's Canterbury Pilgrimage*
Ewen, Edith: W.T. Stead, *Stories from Chaucer, being the CT...*, Books for the Bairns
Goble, Warwick: John S.P. Tatlock and Percy MacKaye, *The Modern Reader's Chaucer*
Haweis: *Chaucer for Children*
Kirk, M.L. (1): J. Walker McSpadden, *The Canterbury Pilgrims*
Kirk, M.L. (2): Darton, *The Story of the Canterbury Pilgrims*
MacDonall, Angus: Katherine Bates, *The Story of Chaucer's Canterbury Pilgrims*
Mott, W.H., and S. Williams (1): Charles Cowden Clarke, *Tales from Chaucer*
Mott, W.H., and S. Williams (2): Charles Cowden Clarke, *The Riches of Chaucer*
Prout, Victor (1): J. Walker McSpadden, *Stories from Chaucer*, Told Through the Ages Series
Prout, Victor (2): J. Walker McSpadden, *Tales from Chaucer*, All-Time Tales Series
Robinson, W. Heath: Janet Harvey Kelman, *Stories from Chaucer*, Told to the Children Series
Scannell, E.M.: Mary Seymour, *Chaucer's Stories Simply Told*
Seymour, Ralph Fletcher: Calvin Dill Wilson, *Canterbury Tales: Prologue and Selections*
Thomson, Hugh (1): F.J. Harvey Darton, *Tales of the Canterbury Pilgrims Retold*
Thomson, Hugh (2): F.J. Harvey Darton, *Pilgrims Tales from Chaucer*
Thomson, Marion: Clara L. Thomson, *Tales from Chaucer*
Winter, Milo: deluxe Katherine Bates, *The Story of Chaucer's Canterbury Pilgrims*

Notes

Chapter 1. Contexts and Criticisms

1. Typical is *British Children's Writers, 1880–1914*, ed. Laura M. Zaidman, *Dictionary of Literary Biography*, vol. 141 (Detroit, Washington, D.C., London: Gale Research, Inc., 1994); although it adds brief accounts of more illustrators, it is limited to seven major writers. "A Symposium on Children and Literature in the Middle Ages," for the MLA Seminar on Children's Literature, December 28, 1973, was published in *Children's Literature* 4 (1975): 36–63. Bennett A. Brockman identified Caxton's *Book of Curtesye* in 1477 as the earliest record of an adult's encouraging a child to read Chaucer, "Children and Literature in Late Medieval England," 59–60. This is a helpful introductory survey, albeit much concerned with how the child was represented. Even in a very helpful reference work remarkably rich in coverage, Chaucer rates a single paragraph, identifying him as the author of *The Canterbury Tales* and *A Treatise on the Astrolabe*, with no mention of the tradition of Chaucer's stories for children, Humphrey Carpenter and Mari Prichard, *The Oxford Companion to Children's Literature* (Oxford and New York: Oxford University Press, 1984), 108. Their entry for F.J.H. Darton, 142, does not include his version of *The Canterbury Tales*.

In contrast, the entry for Shakespeare names a few children's versions, 481, as does one for Spenser's *The Faerie Queene*, 173. Robin Hood and Arthur are more widely considered exceptions, and I have reviewed children's versions of the most popular medieval romance in *The Legend of Guy of Warwick*, Garland Studies in Medieval Literature, vol. 14, Garland Reference Library of the Humanities 1929 (New York & London: Garland, 1996), 313–67, 376–80.

2. Larry D. Benson, ed. *The Riverside Chaucer*, 3d ed. (Boston: Houghton Mifflin Co., 1987), 1195. Within this book, all quotations from Chaucer are from this edition.

3. David Matthews, *The Making of Middle English, 1765–1910*, Medieval Cultures, vol. 18 (Minneapolis and London: University of Minnesota Press, 1999). See also Matthews, ed., *The Invention of Middle English: An Anthology of Sources* (Turnhout, Belgium: Brepols Publishers, 2000).

4. Stephanie Trigg, *Congenial Souls: Reading Chaucer from Medieval to Postmodern*, Medieval Cultures, vol. 30 (Minneapolis and London: University of Minnesota Press, 2002), 234 and 144.

5. Steve Ellis, *Chaucer at Large: The Poet in the Modern Imagination*, Medieval Cultures vol. 24 (Minneapolis: University of Minnesota Press, 2000), 46–75. David Matthews followed Ellis's skeptical reading in "Infantilising the Father: The Edwardians,

Their Children, and Chaucer," *Studies in the Age of Chaucer*, ed. Larry Scanlon, 22 (Rutgers: The State University of New Jersey, XXXX): 93–114.

6. F.J. Furnivall, ed., *Caxton's Book of Curtesye*, EETS ES 3 (London: Trübner, 1868).

7. Seth Lerer, *Chaucer and His Readers: Imagining the Author in Late-Medieval England* (Princeton: Princeton University Press, 1993),117, 259 n. 1. On the claim of patriarchy, see Lee Patterson, *Chaucer and the Subject of History* (Madison: The University of Wisconsin Press, 1991), 16–17.

8. MS Princeton 100, Princeton University Library, and Huntington Library HM 140. On these two manuscripts Lerer bases his fine argument "Reading Like a Child: Advisory Aesthetics and Scribal Revision in the Canterbury Tales," 87–116.

9. John Foxe, *The Actes and Monumentes; or, Book of the Martyrs* (1570, repr. 1583); G. Townsend and S.R. Cattley, eds., *The Acts and Monuments of John Foxe* (London, 1837–41). The relevant passages from the 1570 edition (I:341 and II:965–66) are quoted in D.S. Brewer, ed., *Chaucer: The Critical Heritage, vol. I, 1385–1837* (London, Henley and Boston: Routledge & Kegan Paul, 1978), 107–09. John Fisher acknowledges Protestant expectations, "To teche hem letterure and curteisye," *Chaucer Newsletter* 10 (Fall 1988): 1–3.

10. Matthews, *The Invention of Middle English*, 14.

11. Lee Patterson, *Negotiating the Past: The Historical Understanding of Medieval Literature* (Madison: University of Wisconsin Press, 1987) has a helpful survey of issues in "Historical Criticism and the Development of Chaucer Studies," 3–39, and fully develops his alternative approach in *Chaucer and the Subject of History* (Madison: University of Wisconsin Press, 1991). An "Afterword" concludes that "the often smug naiveté of the pre theoretical past is well left behind" but acknowledges, as had the Introduction, that his "is very much a book of the 1980s," 425. After twenty years theoretical interpretations are being challenged. In short, the unresolvable oppositions in historical thinking that Patterson emphasizes persist, so that the issue remains one of interpreting and tolerance of others.

12. Katherine Lee Bates, ed., *The Story of Chaucer's Canterbury Pilgrims Retold for Children* (Chicago, New York, London: Rand McNally & Co., 1909). Bruce E. Graves, ed., *Translations of Chaucer and Virgil by William Wordsworth* (Ithaca, NY: Cornell University Press, 1998).

13. The first phrase is from "Essay, Supplement to the Preface," in *The Poetical Works of Wordsworth*, ed. Thomas Hutchinson, rev. Ernest de Selincourt (London, New York, Toronto: Oxford University Press, 1904, repr. 1946), 951. The second, cited by Matthews, *The Making of Middle English*, 217 n. 7, from the 1969 ed., 735 n. 1.

14. J.S. Bratton, *The Impact of Victorian Children's Fiction* (London: Croom Helm and Totowa, NJ: Barnes & Noble Books, 1981) argues that children's literature evolved from the early efforts of Sunday Schools, the Religious Tract Society (RTS), and the Society for the Propagation of Christian Knowledge (SPCK), which established principles of juvenile publishing, both Rewards and adaptation of popular romance models. Alec Ellis, *A History of Children's Reading and Literature* (Oxford: Pergamon Press, 1968), which traces the development of literacy for the working classes from the nineteenth century to the present, focuses on schools and libraries but also contains helpful information about publishing practices for children.

15. Frances Jenkins Olcott, *The Children's Reading* (Boston and New York: Houghton Mifflin Co., 1912), 112.

16. Horace E. Scudder, *Childhood in Literature and Art* (Boston and New York: Houghton, Mifflin & Co., 1894), 108–113, discusses pathos in tales told by the Prioress, Man of Law, and Clerk; he acknowledges that "childhood appears chiefly as an appeal to pity, rarely as an object of love and joy," 111. His survey of Shakespeare shows, in comparison, "how scantily ... [he] has made use of the figure and the image of childhood," 125.

17. Lee Patterson, "'What Man Artow?': Authorial Self-Definition in *The Tale of Sir Thopas* and *The Tale of Melibee*," *Studies in the Age of Chaucer*, ed. Larry Scanlon, 11 (1989): 160–75.

18. Lerer, 94–96.

19. Bates, "Introduction to the Series," 10.

20. Diana C. Archibald, "Beauty, Unity, and the Ideal: Wholeness and Heterogeneity in the Kelmscott *Chaucer*," *Studies in Medievalism* 7 (1995), ed. Leslie J. Workman and Kathleen Verduin (Cambridge: D.S. Brewer, 1996), 172–77, argues that Burne-Jones's "monolithic choice of chivalric subjects for the illustrations" limits Chaucer's variety. Actually Chaucer himself is present in thirty-one of the eighty-seven pictures, a sign of Victorian fascination with personality and the artist as hero. Children's books pose less difficulty because they emphasize stories of chivalry and noble women.

21. Quoted by Steve Ellis, 13, from *Signs of Change, Works*, 23: 52.

22. The sketch, now in the Bridwell Library, Southern Methodist University, Dallas, is reproduced in Stephen Wildman and John Christian, *Edward Burne-Jones: Victorian Artist Dreamer* (New York: The Metropolitan Museum of Art, Harry N. Abrams, 1998), 310.

23. Mark Girouard, *The Return to Camelot: Chivalry and the English Gentleman* (New Haven and London: Yale University Press, 1981).

24. Terry Eagleton, *Literary Theory: An Introduction* (Minneapolis: University of Minnesota Press, 1983), 27–30. A rich historical survey is provided by the documents in *The Nineteenth-Century History of English Studies*, ed. Alan Bacon (Aldershot, Brookfield, VT and Singapore: Ashgate, 1998). See also D.J. Palmer, *The Rise of English Studies: An Account of the Study of the English Language and Literature from Its Origins to the Making of the Oxford English School* (Oxford: Oxford University Press, 1965) and Chris Baldick, *The Social Mission of English Criticism, 1848–1932* (Oxford: Oxford University Press, 1983).

25. Baldick, 61.

26. Pamela Horn, *The Victorian and Edwardian Schoolchild* (Gloucester, UK, and Wolfeboro, NH: Alan Sutton Publishing, 1989); James Bishop, "*The Illustrated London News*" *Social History of Edwardian Britain* (London, Sydney, Melbourne, Singapore, Manila: Angus & Robertson Publishers, 1977), 118–35. Simplified adult classics were not a new phenomenon, as seventeenth- and eighteenth-century chapbooks bear witness. Children read shortened chivalric romances like *Guy of Warwick* and *Valentine and Orson*, and classics like *The Pilgrim's Progress, Gulliver's Travels, Robinson Crusoe*, and many other titles originally intended for the newly literate. See Mary F. Thwaite, *From Primer to Pleasure in Reading* (1963, Boston: The Horn Book, Inc., 1972), 39–42; Victor Neuburg, *The Penny Histories: A Study of Chapbooks for Young Readers over Two Centuries* (Oxford: Oxford University Press; 1968); Margaret Spufford, *Small Books and Pleasant Histories* (Athens: University of Georgia Press, 1981); Mary V. Jackson, *Engines of Instruction, Mischief, and Magic: Children's Literature in England from Its Beginnings to 1839* (Lincoln: University of Nebraska Press, 1989).

27. F.J. Harvey Darton, *Children's Books in England: Five Centuries of Social Life*. 3rd ed. rev. by Brian Alderson (1932, Cambridge: Cambridge University Press, 1982).

28. Paul Hazard, *Books, Children, & Men*, trans. Marguerite Mitchell (Boston: Horn Book, 1944), 128.

29. Humphrey Carpenter, *Secret Gardens: A Study of the Golden Age of Children's Literature* (London: George Allen & Unwin Ltd., 1985). This finely argued book centers on the same major authors (except Henty and Kipling, whose imperialism is not part of his thesis) selected by Laura M. Zaidman.

30. Alison Lurie, *Not in Front of the Grown-Ups: Subversive Children's Literature*. (London: Bloomsbury Publishing, 1990; Cardinal ed. Sphere Books, 1991); the American title is *Don't Tell the Grown-Ups: Subversive Children's Literature* (Little, Brown, & Co., 1990); Juliet Dusinberre, *Alice to the Lighthouse: Children's Books and Radical Experiments in Art* (New York: St. Martin's Press, 1987).

31. Bratton, 68–69, has a succinct statement about the archetypal Sunday School book's deployment of distinctive features of popular romance, and chapters "The Development of Juvenile Publishing and Children's Fiction, 1800–1850" and "The Flowering of the Evangelical Tradition."

32. Mary E. Burt, *Literary Landmarks:*

A Guide to Good Reading for Young People, and Teachers' Assistant with a Carefully Selected List of Seven Hundred Books, rev. ed. (Boston and New York: Houghton, Mifflin & Co., 1897, 9, 76). Page numbers for additional quoted phrases from this source are given in parentheses or brackets.

33. Steve Ellis, finding hope in the recent inclusion of more modern outlooks in Medieval Studies, makes an eloquent plea for connecting the academic and popular, 153–66. He singles out studies that stress "Chaucer's contemporary social relevance," which is a notable echo of a major dimension of children's literature and certainly a key impetus for Edwardian retellings. Trigg's *Congenial Souls* is less optimistic about the reception of several such studies, passim. Several essays in Jeffrey Jerome Cohen, ed. *The Post Colonial Middle Ages*, New Middle Ages Series (New York: St. Martin's Press, 2000), introduce this perspective to read Chaucer, most obviously to consider Orientalism, notably in the *Squire's Tale*.

34. For a brief evaluation of the role of the Early English Text Society in making available all of early English literature, as part of a patriotic and moral duty, see Matthews, *The Making of Middle English*, 147–51. William Benzie, *Dr. F.J. Furnivall: Victorian Scholar Adventurer* (Norman, OK: Pilgrim Books, 1983) is a helpful biography.

35. Four volumes suggest favored tales and combinations: *The Knight's Tale, or Palamon and Arcite*; *The Man of Law's Tale, The Nun's Priest's Tale, The Squire's Tale*; *The Prioress's Tale and Four Other Tales (Pardoner, Clerk, Second Nun, Canon's Yeoman)*; *The Prologue, Roman de la Rose, Minor Poems*. All were "Done into Modern English by Rev. W.W. Skeat" for the King's Classics (London), the first three in 1904 and the last in 1907. Skeat's *The Story of Patient Griselda: From the Clerk's Tale of Geoffrey Chaucer* (London: George Routledge & Sons and New York: E.P. Dutton & Co., 1906), illustrated by Gilbert James, is in The Photogravure Series and an elegant example of Edwardian book making. Its blue and gray cover is gold stamped "Patient Griselda by Geoffrey Chaucer with Photogravures after Gilbert James" and a

reduced image "Griselda goes home," one of eight illustrations. James illustrated several volumes in the series, including *Matthew Arnold's Poems* and Andrew Lang's *Aucassin and Nicolete. Dante's Vita Nuova*, translated and illustrated by D.G. Rossetti, is especially impressive.

36. Alderson, "Some Additional Notes on Victorian and Edwardian Times," in Darton, *Children's Books*, 316–31; John Feather, *A History of British Publishing* (London and New York: Routledge, 1988); George G. Harrap, *Some Memories 1901–1935: A Publisher's Contribution to the History of Publishing* (London, Bombay, Sydney: George G. Harrap, 1935); J.D. Newth, *Adam & Charles Black 1807–1957: Some Chapters in the History of a Publishing House* (London: Adam & Charles Black, 1957); Agnes A.C. Blackie, *Blackie & Son 1809–1959: A Short History of the Firm* (London and Glasgow: Blackie & Son Ltd., 1959).

37. Renee Swanson, "The Living Dead: What the Dickens Are College Students Reading?" *Policy Review* 67 (1994), 72–73; quoted by Trigg, 240 n. In 1994 *The Canterbury Tales* was sixth in the top ten; but it dropped to the next most popular grouping in the Cliff Notes Catalog for 1998. Matthews races the shift "From the Chaucer Society to the Universities" 1900–1910, in *The Making of Middle English*, 162–86. Derek Brewer's *Chaucer: The Critical Heritage*, stops at 1933, a date after which academic interpretations dominate.

38. Matthews, *The Making of Middle English*, 183.

39. Arthur Burrell, ed. and trans., *Chaucer's Canterbury Tales for the Modern Reader* (London: J.M. Dent and E.P. Dutton, 1908), vii–viii. Steve Ellis, 106, sees limitations in a translation that leaves much unchanged to keep the "quaintness" of the original and avoids issues by retaining the language of tales deemed not "suitable." The New York Grolier Club exhibition catalog indicates respect for rich resources.

40. The title of Newbolt's autobiographical reflections can be read as a conscious apology or defense, *My World as in My Time: Memoirs of Sir Henry Newbolt 1862–1932* (London: Faber & Faber Limited, 1932). Susan Chitty, *Playing the Game: A Biography of Sir Henry Newbolt* (London:

Quartet Books, 1997) is a sympathetic re-assessment.

41. Henry Newbolt, *The Teaching of English in England: Being the Report of the Departmental Committee Appointed by the President of the Board of Education to Inquire into the Position of English in the Educational System of England* (London: His Majesty's Stationery Office, 1921). Henry Newbolt was chairman; the other members were John Bailey, K.M. Baines, Frederick S. Boas, H.M. Davies, D. Enright, S.H. Firth, J.H. Fowler, L.A. Lowe, Arthur Quiller-Couch, George Sampson, Caroline F.E. Spurgeon, G. Perrie Williams, and J. Dover Wilson. J.E. Hales, secretary, signed the date 23rd April 1921—appropriately St. George's Day and Shakespeare's birthday. Page numbers for additional quoted phrases are given in parentheses. On the context of the report and its authors, see Baldick, 93–105.

42. See Matthews, *The Making of Middle English*, 188–90 and Baldick, 93–98.

43. G.K. Chesterton, *Chaucer*, new ed. (London: Faber & Faber, 1948), 213, 214.

44. Miriam Youngerman Miller, "Illustrations of *The Canterbury Tales* for Children: A Mirror of Chaucer's World?" *The Chaucer Review* 27 (1993), 293–304.

45. This extract is from the Skeat archive of King's College, London (Skeat Papers 3/5), first printed in Matthews, *The Invention of Middle English*, 231. The lecture was a popular one, for a nonacademic audience, and "shows Skeat in informal, proselytising mode," 227.

46. Matthews, *The Invention of Middle English*, 234.

47. Matthews, *The Invention of Middle English*, 238.

48. Robert Kilburn Root, *The Poetry of Chaucer: A Guide to its Study and Appreciation* (Boston and New York: Houghton Mifflin Co., Riverside Press Cambridge, 1906) and George Lyman Kittredge, *Chaucer and His Poetry* (Cambridge: Harvard University Press, 1915; repr. 55th anniversary ed., with introduction by B.J. Whiting, Cambridge: Harvard University Press, 1970). It is often not easy to identify whether a modernization was for children or adults. Sometimes the title, preface, or illustrations make this explicit, but pub-lishers also presented the same prose versions with different accompanying materials. Eleanor P. Hammond's *Chaucer: A Bibliographical Manual* (1908, repr. New York: Peter Smith, 1933) has a section "Versions for Children," 234–35, but lists F.J. Harvey Darton's *Tales of the Canterbury Pilgrims* in the general section of "Modernizations and Imitations" for adults, that has the full entry for Charles Cowden Clarke, who is cross-referenced from "Children's Versions."

49. Girouard's *The Return to Camelot: Chivalry and the English Gentleman* is a beautifully illustrated and richly varied popular account, but his being an "enthusiast" has influenced reception. Debra Mancoff's review considers the strengths and weaknesses of a work that "does not pretend to be a scholarly investigation," has a strong thesis about the relation of chivalry to World War I, and recreates the spirit that inspired chivalry, "Mark Girouard, An Enthusiast for Chivalry," *History and Community: Essays in Victorian Medievalism*, ed. Florence S. Boos (New York and London: Garland Publishing, Inc., 1992). 209–20.

50. Jeffrey Richards, *Happiest Days: The Public Schools in English Fiction* (Manchester: Manchester University Press, 1988), 18.

51. J.K. Rowling, *Harry Potter and the Sorcerer's Stone* (New York: Scholastic Press, 1998), 118. This first book in Britain was more cogently titled *Harry Potter and the Philosopher's Stone* (London: Bloomsbury, 1997). Other books of a projected seven are: *Harry Potter and the Chamber of Secrets* (1999), *Harry Potter and the Prisoner of Azkaban* (1999), *Harry Potter and the Goblet of Fire* (2000). The American edition added pictorial headings for chapters by Mary Grand Pré. The release of film versions, *Harry Potter and the Sorcerer's Stone* in autumn 2001 and *Harry Potter and the Chamber of Secrets* in autumn 2002 as well as a sizable range of related items has meant another kind of success that will continue with subsequent offerings.

52. Paul Fussell, *The Great War and Modern Memory* (London, Oxford, New York: Oxford University Press, 1975), 21–22. He attributes the literary quality of World War I to Victorian pseudoromances, such as William Morris's *The Well at the*

World's End (1896), and to John Bunyan's *Pilgrim's Progress* (1678); he does not recognize children's literature.

53. Richards, 50

54. Fussell, 26, puts the counterargument about Newbolt, a friend since schooldays of Douglas Haig, the general whose character he praised for its acceptance and faith. Fussell cites Patrick Howarth's term "homo *newboltiencis*, or 'Newbolt Man': honorable, stoic, brave, loyal, courteous— and unaesthetic, unironic, unintellectual and devoid of wit." The definition points discrepancies between Edwardian ideals for youth and late twentieth-century revisions and favors a taste for sophisticated literary critics.

CHAPTER 2.
VICTORIAN BEGINNINGS

1. Virginia Surtees, ed., *The Diary of Ford Madox Brown* (New Haven and London: Paul Mellon Centre for Studies in British Art Yale University Press, 1981), 2. The triptych is now in the Ashmolean Museum, Oxford; there are two versions of *Chaucer at the Court of Edward III*, the largest in the Art Gallery of New South Wales, Sydney, and a smaller version in the Tate Gallery, London.

2. Kenneth Bendimer, *The Art of Ford Madox Brown* (University Park, PA: Pennsylvania State University Press, 1998) includes Brown's text of *Exhibition of WORK and Other Paintings 1865* as Appendix 3.

3. Charles Cowden Clarke, *Tales from Chaucer in Prose, Designed Chiefly for the Use of Young Persons* (London: Effingham Wilson, 1833). Illustrations are at the start of the book, each facing a blank page. Pages cited for the following Clarke quotations are from a reprint, *Tales from Chaucer: The Canterbury Tales by Geoffrey Chaucer: Selected Tales Told for Young People* (New York: The Heritage Press, 1947).

4. Betsy Bowden, ed., *Eighteenth-Century Modernizations from* The Canterbury Tales, Chaucer Studies, vol. 16 (Woodbridge, Suffolk: D.S. Brewer, 1991), xix–xx. Bowden includes four versions of the *Shipman's Tale*, three each of the *Miller's Tale* and *Reeve's Tale*, with reference to at least

eleven reprintings of the former and thirteen of the latter, usually in miscellanies. Enthusiasm and new versions of the *Squire's Tale*, two at the end of the century, mark an interest in Oriental romance, x, and affinity with nineteenth-century taste. Thus although Bowden emphasizes diversity and rejects intentions of modernizing "to express the era's Zeitgeist," a broad shift in views of propriety is clear, x–xi.

5. Charles Dickens, "The Spirit of Chivalry," *Douglas Jerrold's Shilling Magazine* (August 1845) Victoria and Albert Museum, London, Miscellaneous Papers 1:20–25, quoted in Debra N. Mancoff, *The Arthurian Revival in Victorian Art*, Garland Reference Library of the Humanities, vol. 1034 (New York and London: Garland Publishing, 1990), 95.

6. Steve Ellis, *Chaucer at Large: The Poet in the Modern Imagination* Medieval Cultures, vol. 24 (Minneapolis and London: University of Minnesota Press, 2000), 47.

7. Marchette Chute, *Geoffrey Chaucer of England*, Everyman paperback edition (New York: E.P. Dutton & Co., 1958), 7.

8. The novel had at least a seventh impression, in The Laurel and Gold Series (Glasgow: Collins Clear-Type Press, 1958). In addition to a picture of Chaucer's domestic life and process of writing and interacting at court, there is historical material about the Peasants' Revolt, the Duke of Lancaster, court intrigue including the characters of Richard II and Queen Anne, and life at a blacksmith's with two lively foster brothers.

9. See Velma Bourgeois Richmond, *The Legend of Guy of Warwick*, Garland Studies in Medieval Literature, vol. 14, Garland Reference Library of the Humanities, vol. 1929 (New York and London: Garland Publishing, 1996), 313–67. Guy is the most popular romance hero for centuries.

10. A facing two-page frontispiece shows the Host standing in the doorway of the Tabard Inn toward which a large company of pilgrims ride. Of the six large figures four are developed later as full pages: the Host to illustrate the Prologue and the Knight, Squire, and Wife their tales, while the other two, the Monk and Miller, do not

recur. Each pilgrim teller reappears as a standing figure, in which Szyk repeats and develops his elaborately designed costumes with details like long pointed shoes, fur trimming, belts, purses, weapons, and distinctive hats. These show boldly against a white background and suggest stage costumes. While there is no image of Chaucer inside the book, he dominates the cloth cover, which has a pattern of medieval tiles with two larger alternating designs, a flower and an equestrian Chaucer, superimposed on the larger floor tiles.

11. Charles Crowden Clarke, *The Riches of Chaucer*, vol. 1 (London: Effingham Wilson, Royal Exchange, 1835). Page numbers for additional quoted phrases from this volume are given in parentheses or brackets.

12. D. Beale, ed., *Reports Issued by the Schools Inquiry Commission on the Education of Girls* (1869), 145, cited by Baldick, *The Social Mission of English Criticism 1848–1932* (Oxford: Clarendon Press, 1983), 68.

13. The full title is a comprehensive description: *Life of Geoffrey Chaucer, The Early English Poet: Including Memoirs of His Near Friend and Kinsman, John of Gaunt, Duke of Lancaster: With Sketches of the Manners, Opinions, Arts and Literature of England in the Fourteenth Century*, 2 vols. (London: Richard Phillips, 1803).

14. Seth Lerer, *Chaucer and His Readers: Imagining the Author in Late-Medieval England* (Princeton: Princeton University Press, 1993), 102–03.

15. Eleanor P. Hammond, *Chaucer: A Bibliographical Manual* (1908. repr. New York: Octagon Books, 1965), 230, from Thomas Wright's *Life of Walter Pater* (London, 1907), 2: 268.

16. Mrs. H.R. Haweis, *Chaucer for Children: A Golden Key*, new ed. (London: Chatto & Windus, 1900). The author's personal copy was given as a prize for English at St. Margaret's School, Bushey, December 13, 1904. Page numbers for additional quoted phrases from this source are given in parentheses or brackets.

17. Birthday books were one ancillary to children's literature. Harriet Waechter followed Mrs. Haweis with a less complex *Chaucer Birthday Book* (London: 1884).

18. This is a commonplace of early criticism, noted by John H. Fisher, "To teche hem letterure and curteisye," *Chaucer Newsletter* 10 (Fall 1988), 1–3, who acknowledges how much his early study of Chaucer was informed by the Protestant interpretation, a view that bore subsequent revision.

19. Miriam Youngerman Miller identifies Mrs. Haweis as "the most explicitly historical and didactic" and finds her notes "unparalleled in the world of juvenile Chaucer illustrations," in "Illustrations of *The Canterbury Tales* for Children: A Mirror of Chaucer's World?" *The Chaucer Review* 27 (1993): 296.

20. Roy Strong, *And When Did You Last See Your Father?: The Victorian Painter and British History* (London: Thames & Hudson, 1978), 49–64, usefully surveys "Historic Dress."

21. The naming of the heroine of the *Man of Law's Tale* by a great historical painter is a curious detail of her appeal to Victorians. Item 380 for 1851 in the dictionary of exhibitors of art in London is: "Ford Madox Brown, *Geoffrey Chaucer reading the 'Leading of Custance' to Edward III and his court, at the palace of Sheen, on the anniversary of the Black Prince's forty-fifth birthday, etc.*" Cited from Algeron Graves, *The Royal Academy of Arts* (London, 1905–06) in Strong, 158.

22. Many such review comments were printed in subsequent editions.

23. Haweis's influence was wide. Routledge's World Library Series, *Tales from Chaucer* (1887), for adults, has a bowdlerized prose paraphrase of the *Miller's Tale*.

24. Mary Seymour, *Chaucer's Stories Simply Told* (London: T. Nelson & Sons, 1902), vi. Page numbers for additional quotations from this source are given in parentheses or brackets. There were many printings, but there are no changes in the text or the illustrations by E.M. Scannell, from the 1884 or 1888 issues. Hammond, 234, refers to an edition for Germany by F. Klopper.

25. Mary E. Burt *Literary Landmarks: A Guide to Good Reading for Young People, and Teachers' Assistant* (Boston and New York: Houghton Mifflin & Co., 1889; repr. 1897), 118.

26. This and succeeding quotations are from Francis Storr and Hawes Turner, *Canterbury Chimes of Chaucer Tales Retold for*

Children (London: C. Kegan Paul & Co., 1878). Preceding quotations are from the Preface.

27. Children have always read adult books, as the enormous popularity of chapbook medieval romances such as *Guy of Warwick, Bevis of Southampton,* and *The Seven Champions of Christendom,* and Bunyan's *Pilgrim's Progress,* Defoe's *Robinson Crusoe,* and Swift's *Gulliver's Travels* reveals. The inspiration for John Newbery's first chapbooks for children was his recognition that they were reading those intended for adults. Many were simplified versions of canonical adult books, intended for the increasing numbers of literate people in the seventeenth and eighteenth centuries; this market continued through the nineteenth century. A useful introduction is Victor E. Neuburg, *The Penny Histories: A Study of Chapbooks for Young Readers over Two Centuries,* The Juvenile Library (London: Oxford University Press, 1968).

28. See, e.g., "Chivalry for the People" in Mark Girouard, *The Return to Camelot: Chivalry and the English Gentleman* (New Haven and London, 1981), 249–58.

29. William Calder, *Chaucer's Canterbury Pilgrimage* (Edinburgh and London: William Blackwood & Sons, 1892), 3–5. Page numbers for additional quotations from this source are given in parentheses or brackets.

30. David Murray Smith, *Tales of Chivalry and Romance* (London: Virtue & Co., 1869), Preface.

31. The choices give some insight to Victorian interests. Shakespeare stories are *The Enchanted Isle* [*The Tempest*] and *Shylock's Revenge* [*The Merchant of Venice*], while Froissart's *Death of Sir John Chandos* and *Eustace de St. Pierre* both involve the Black Prince. Malory stories are *King Arthur and the Round Table, The Blameless Sir Galahad,* and *Sir Lancelot of the Lake*—edited to stress his feats of knighthood and the death of Arthur.

32. Quotations are from a slightly later edition, Abby Sage Richardson, *Stories from Old English Poetry* (Boston: Houghton Mifflin & Co., 1891).

33. It included A.R. Hope-Moncrieff's *Heroes of European History* (London: Gresham, 1906) and *Heroines of European History* (London: Blackie and Son, New York:

Dodge, 1913), E.S. Brooks's *Historic Boys: Their Endeavours, Their Achievements and Their Times* (London: Blackie, 1886, new ed. 1905). Page numbers given in parentheses for the following quotations refer to *Stories of Old Renown* (London: Gresham, 1883).

34. From Felix Summerly's prospectus for *The Home Treasury,* quoted in F.J. Harvey Darton, *Children's Books in England: Five Centuries of Social Life,* 3rd ed. rev. Brian Alderson (Cambridge: Cambridge University Press, 1982), 233–34. Helpful bibliographical information about Cole's planning and work to achieve his goal is in Geoffrey Summerfield, "The Making of The Home Treasury," *Children's Literature* 8 (1979): 35–52. Humphrey Carpenter and Mari Prichard, *The Oxford Companion to Children's Literature* (Oxford: Oxford University Press, 1984) is a good starting point; on Goodrich and Peter Parley, 212–13, 407–08; on Thoms, 523. See also Joyce Irene Whalley and Tessa Rose Chester, *A History of Children's Book Illustration* (London: John Murray with the Victoria and Albert Museum, 1988), 55–56, 60–61.

35. John Ashton, who included the Aldermary Church Yard version, *The History of the Noble Marquis of Salus and Patient Grissel,* in *Chap-Books of the Eighteenth Century* (1882; reissued New York: Benjamin Blom, 1982), 171–83, quotes a stanza from Chaucer and corrects his attribution from Petrarch to Boccaccio; he also cites *The Pleasant Comedie of Patient Grissill,* played by the Lord High Admiral's men and printed in 1603. Samuel Pepys owned a twenty-four page quarto, a double-book that sold for 3d., printed in the 1680s, *Vulgaria,* IV.20, according to Margaret Spufford, *Small Books and Pleasant Histories: Popular Fiction and Its Readership in Seventeenth-Century England* (Athens: University of Georgia Press, 1981), 156. Much of Griselda's history is in Judith Bronfman, *Chaucer's Clerk's Tale: The Griselda Story Received, Rewritten, Illustrated,* Garland Studies in Medieval Literature, vol. 11, Garland Reference Library of the Humanities, vol. 1831 (New York and London: Garland Publishing, 1994); but there is little about Griselda's place in children's literature.

36. The illustrations described are from a personal copy of *The Home Treasury of Old Story Books* (London: Sampson Low, Son, and Co., 1859), 179. It is one of "Fifty Engravings by Eminent Artists," identified in a "List of Illustrations," and hand colored. Editions vary.

37. *Nursery Stories & Pictures for the Young* (London: Ward, Locke, & Co., 1878). Descriptions are from a personal copy in which the pagination is 225–315; in such a small book, this suggests sheets intended for a larger collection. Certainly other copies are different. The frontispiece shows "Robin Hood and Little John" hunting, but that story is not included; of the eleven illustrations, six are for Peter, two each for Guy and Bevis, one for Tom.

38. *Old English Ballads: A Collection of Favourite Ballads of the Olden Times* (London: T. Nelson & Sons, 1888), 269. Although headnotes precede ballads, no editor is named. Page numbers for additional quoted phrases are given in parentheses or brackets.

39. Quotations are from a later edition in a series *Home Stories for Young and Old* (New York: John B. Alden, Publisher, 1885), which includes two other books *History of My Pets* (1850) and *Recollections of My Childhood and Other Stories* (1851).

40. Quoted in Wylie Sypher, *Rococo to Cubism in Art and Literature* (New York: Vintage Books, 1960), 164.

CHAPTER 3. CHAUCER IN THE NURSERY

1. Sally Wood, *W.T. Stead and His "Books for the Bairns"* (Edinburgh: Salvia Books, 1987) lists numbers and titles for the First Series, 23–41. There are also twenty-eight titles in the New Series, from January 30–July 31, 1923; while Ernest Benn's edition, September–October 1926, has twenty-five titles, 45. Wood also has incomplete checklists for the Edition Français: the First Series in 1907 has thirteen, and a Second Series, 1910–1918 goes to 191, 47–52. Like Stead's Books for the Bairns, Wood's pamphlet, albeit a bit larger in format, is paper-covered in pink and in many openings an illustration faces a page

of text. The summary of Stead's career comes from this study.

2. The "dainty volumes" often include a list of the Told to the Children Series, edited by Louey Chisholm. The longest list includes thirty-six titles; one unlisted item is in this author's collection, so there may have been others. Among these thirty-seven, the national distribution is eighteen British (*Robin Hood, King Arthur, Beowulf,* Chaucer, *Faerie Queene,* Shakespeare, *Ballads, Guy of Warwick, Celtic Tales, Pilgrim's Progress, Robinson Crusoe, Gulliver's Travels,* Maria Edgeworth's *Simple Susan,* Thackeray's *The Rose and The Ring,* and Kingsley's *The Heroes* and *The Water Babies*), *Nursery Rhymes, Little Plays* [three English subjects, one American, and one Andersen tale]); three religious (*Old Testament, Life of Christ,* and *Three Saints* [Francis, Columba, and Cuthbert]); three classical (*Iliad, Odyssey,* and *Aesop*); *Arabian Nights*; six European (*Don Quixote, William Tell, Roland, Siegfried, Wagner,* and *Dante*); four fairy stories (*Nursery Tales,* Grimm, Andersen, and La Motte Fouquet's *Undine*), two American (Hawthorne's *Tanglewood Tales* and Harriet Beecher Stowe's *Uncle Tom's Cabin*). This is the most impressive series for very young children, but somewhat comparable are Blackie's Stories Old and New: A Juvenile Library for the Eight to Ten Year-Old, Dent's Tales for Children from Many Lands, and Nelson's Golden River Series in the same small format that sold for one shilling. Subsequent page references for quoted phrases from Janet Harvey Kelman, *Stories from Chaucer* (London: T.C. and E.C. Jack, February 1906) are given in parentheses.

3. Miriam Youngerman Miller, "Illustrations of The Canterbury Tales for Children: A Mirror of Chaucer's World?" *The Chaucer Review* 27 (1993), 297, stresses Pre-Raphaelite influence.

4. Eds., Hamilton Wright Mabie, Edward Everett Hale, and William Byron Forbush, *Classic Tales and Everyday Stories,* vol. 3 (New York: University Society, 1919), 171–202.

5. The University Society first published *Young Folks' Treasury* in 1900–01 in twelve volumes, and followed it with *Boys and Girls Bookshelf* in 1912, 1915, and 1920. Hamilton Wright Mabie (1879–1917) was a prolific

essayist, who also edited a series called *What Every Child Should Know* for The Parents' Institute, published by Doubleday, Page and Company, 1906. That title proclaims a canon, and an ongoing commitment to canonical texts is evident in a 1948 edition of *The Bookshelf for Boys and Girls*, vol. 6, *Famous Stories and Verse*, where ten sections are arranged by topics. It begins with The *Arabian Nights* (32 pages), and the longest part is "Some Good Stories Retold" (251 pages), including *Canterbury Tales* (150–164). The Robinson color illustration is one of only seven; the others are: "The Magic Carpet" (as frontispiece), "Peter Pan and Wendy in the Treetop House" paired with "Gulliver" who is eating (at 70), "Bob Cratchit and Tiny Tim" on the reverse of Dorigen (at 164), and a third pair—oriental figures riding through the city and "The Knight Goes Forth on his First Quest," a standing figure in plate armor with shield and sword, and a female allegorical figure rising behind him (at 272). The latter is especially appropriate since among the stories retold are *King Arthur and His Knights* and *Prince Gareth*. Chaucer, then, is here a part of the chivalric tradition of medievalism. The remaining eighty-three pages are entirely verse (much of it American), arranged in eight sections: Fancy, Magic and Mystery, Love of Country, Poems about Holidays, Nature Verses, The Best Things in Life, Tales of Joy and Sorrow, Funny Verses, and Story Poems. Even when an encyclopedia did not include stories from Chaucer, his chivalric presence was crucial. In *My Book House* (1920), ed. Olive Beaupré Miller, volume 10 is *From the Tower Window*, "primarily the book of romantic as well as heroic adventure" with "stories from all the great national epics" repr. (Lake Bluff, IL: Book House for Children, 1963), 3. Geoffrey Chaucer's description of "A Perfect Knight" introduces the collection and establishes the chivalric ideal. Lines from the *General Prologue* (I. 43–50, 69–72) are printed on a bold page, a blue frame with a heading of a white knight in armor, red cross on shield and lance in hand, 7.

6. *The Delphian Course* (Hammond, IN: W.B. Conkey Co. for Delphian Society, 1913), 9 vols. Page numbers for additional

quoted phrases from this source are given in parentheses or brackets.

7. Carolyn Sherwin Bailey, *Stories of Great Adventures* (Springfield, MA: Milton Bradley Co., 1919). Page references for quoted phrases from this source are given in parentheses.

8. Bailey is probably evoking the current popularity of Pan, best known in J.M. Barrie's *Peter Pan* (1904), especially through the performance of the American actress Maude Adams. The other notable Pan figures are "The Piper at the Gates of Dawn" in Kenneth Grahame's *The Wind in the Willows* (1908) and Dickon in Frances Hodgson Burnett's *The Secret Garden* (1911). The popularity of Pan continues in the key image in Anna Curtis Chandler's *Pan the Piper and Other Marvelous Tales* (New York and London: Harper & Brothers Publishers, 1923).

CHAPTER 4. EDWARDIAN EXTRAVAGANCE FOR YOUTH

1. The numbered copy in the Huntington Library has signed certification in the front. The quotation is printed entirely in capital letters opposite page 38.

2. Ambrose Dudley, *The Prologue to the Canterbury Tales of Geoffrey Chaucer* (London: Chatto & Windus, 1909). The colophon is "Printed by Campfield Press." Page numbers for subsequent descriptions of this source are given in parentheses.

3. Katherine Dunlap Cather, *Educating by Story Telling* (London: George G. Harrap & Co., 1919) gave a notable exposition, based on the work of the Demonstration Play School of the University of California, Berkeley, first used in the summer of 1914. The basic theory is that story is a natural form for revealing life, and its functions are to mold ideals and illuminate facts, 14. Cather identified eight to twelve years as the "Heroic Period," when boys and girls share a "ravenous appetite" for adventure stories—well served by national epics in which the Middle Ages abounds—with physical bravery, 58. The next stage is the "Romantic Period" that favors greater idealism found in romantic tales, 67–68. Eva March Tappan, whose work is discussed in

Chapters 4 and 7, eschewed grouping stories by their difficulty but showed similar conceptual ideas when arranging stories in the ten-volume encyclopedia, *The Children's Hour* (Boston: Houghton Mifflin, 1907), which she edited. Volume four is *Stories of Legendary Heroes*, all from medieval literature. Tappan's *The Chaucer Story Book* (Boston: Houghton Mifflin, 1908) is listed as supplementary reading in Robert Newton Linscott, *A Guide to Good Reading* (Boston: Houghton Mifflin Co., 1912), 29, that offered practical directions for the use of the encyclopedia. Somewhat analogous is the point made by Alison Lurie, who identifies the years from six to twelve as "the final stage of childhood" that "corresponds to early civilization" when myth and ritual develop, *Not in Front of the Grown-ups: Subversive Children's Literature* (London: Bloomsbury Publishing, 1990), 218.

4. See Velma Bourgeois Richmond, *Geoffrey Chaucer* (New York: Continuum, 1992), 96–102, and "Pacience in Adversitee: Chaucer's Presentation of Marriage," *Viator* 10 (1979), 323–54.

5. The title "Edwardian Extravagance" is from Joyce Irene Whalley and Tessa Rose Chester, *A History of Children's Book Illustration* (London: John Murray with the Victoria & Albert Museum, 1988), 151. Other useful works are Percy Muir, *Victorian Illustrated Books* (New York: Praeger, 1971, rev. ed. 1985) and Richard Dalby, *The Golden Age of Children's Book Illustration* (New York: Gallery Books, 1991).

6. F.J. Harvey Darton, *Tales of the Canterbury Pilgrims Retold from Chaucer and Others* (London: Wells Gardner, Darton, 1904). Page numbers for quoted phrases from this source are given in parentheses.

7. Miriam Youngerman Miller, "Illustrations for *The Canterbury Tales*: A Mirror for Chaucer's World," *The Chaucer Review* 27 (1993), 296–97, citing Muir, 199, describes Thomson's engravings as "'nostalgic' ... satisfied the Victorian need to escape the effects of the Industrial Revolution by retreating into a mythical time when England was a 'pastoral paradise' ... peopled by benevolent squires, served by a retinue of loyal and picturesque rustics.'"

8. "When Shakespeare Was a Boy," in E(dith) Nesbit, *Children's Stories from*

Shakespeare (London, Paris, New York: Raphael Tuck & Sons, [1912]), an expanded edition of one of her several early books, *The Children's Shakespeare* (1897). This beautiful volume, in The Raphael House Library of Gift Books, ed. Edric Vredenburg, was published after Furnivall's death.

9. Stephanie Trigg, *Congenial Souls: Reading Chaucer from Medieval to Postmodern*, Medieval Cultures, vol. 30 (Minneapolis and London: University of Minnesota Press, 2002), 166–73, reviews ambivalent evaluations of Furnivall by Chaucerians. William Benzie, *Dr. F.J. Furnivall: A Victorian Scholar Adventurer* (Norman: Pilgrim Books, 1983) is a standard biography.

10. John W. Hales, introduction to *Stories from the Faerie Queene*, by Mary Macleod (London: Gardner, Darton & Co., 3rd ed. 1903), vii.

11. Hales, xvi–xvii.

12. John M. Bowers, ed., *The Canterbury Tales: Fifteenth-Century Continuations and Additions* (TEAMS, Kalamazoo, Michigan: Medieval Institute Publications, 1992) and Seth Lerer, *Chaucer and His Readers: Imagining the Author in Late-Medieval England* (Princeton: Princeton, NJ: Princeton University Press, 1993).

13. The copy, in The Beinecke Manuscript and Rare Book Room, Yale University, is reproduced in Trigg, 169.

14. A standing youth in shining armor, holding a shield and a banner with the title, looks down upon a dragon in a cage with bars inscribed with virtues and maxims for scouts. Mark Girouard, *The Return to Camelot: Chivalry and the English Gentleman* (London and New Haven: Yale Univeristy Press, 1981), Plate XXIV, opposite 240, is a color reproduction.

15. F.J. Harvey Darton, *Children's Books in England: Five Centuries of Social Life*, 3rd ed. rev. Brian Alderson (Cambridge: Cambridge University Press, 1982), 92.

16. F.J. Harvey Darton, *Pilgrims Tales from Chaucer* (London: Wells Gardner, Darton & Co., 1908), 74.

17. F.J. Harvey Darton, ed., *A Wonder Book of Beasts*, with illustrations by Margaret Clayton (London: Wells, Gardner, Darton & Co., 1909). Page numbers for quoted phrases from this source are given in parentheses. The book includes *Reynard*

the Fox, adapted from Caxton by E.L. Darton, which is the largest item. A cheap abridgment was issued in the Children's Bookshelf Series as *Three Bears and Other Wonder Tales of Beasts* (1915) and an elegant *Reynard the Fox* (1928), adapted from Caxton by E.L. and F.J. Harvey Darton, with Clayton's illustrations.

18. Frances Jenkins Olcott, *The Children's Reading* (Boston and New York: Houghton Mifflin Co., 1912), 125.

19. F.J. Harvey Darton, *The Story of the Canterbury Pilgrims Retold from Chaucer and Others,* illus. by M.L. Kirk (New York: J.P. Lippincott & Co., 1914). Page numbers for descriptions from this source are given in parentheses.

20. Many of the same titles are included in both series, with a similar emphasis upon medieval narratives. Thus Told Through the Ages also has Robin Hood, King Arthur, Roland, Guy of Warwick, Dante, Welsh and Celtic tales. Harrap favored Northernness (the Edwardian racial/ national preference), and the series includes Hereward, several volumes of tales of the Northmen from sagas and eddas. Many books are of major authors: Spenser, Shakespeare, Cervantes, along with classical writers Homer and Virgil, and modern British authors Dickens, George Eliot, William Morris. "Stories from History" are part of the same series: Britain Long Ago, English, Scottish, French, Spanish, and so on. Harrap continued to reprint the earliest titles and to add new ones long after the Edwardian period. Newer copies include publishing history that usually indicates numerous reprintings.

21. Olcott, 124.

22. J. Walker McSpadden, *Stories from Chaucer: Retold from the Canterbury Tales* (London: George G. Harrap, 1917). Page numbers for descriptions from this source are given in parentheses.

23. J. Walker McSpadden, *The Canterbury Pilgrims: Retold from Chaucer* (London: George G. Harrap, 1907). Page numbers for descriptions from this source are given in parentheses.

24. Inez N. McFee, *The Story of Idylls of the King: Adapted from Tennyson with the Original Poem* (New York: Frederick A. Stokes Company, 1912), 26.

25. This episode is in F.J. Harvey Dar-

ton's expansion in *The Chequer of the Hoop,* when the Wife is "so weary that she had no wish for further wanderings," so that she invites the Prioress simply to walk in the garden, 287. This amusing way of putting together Chaucer's memorable women dates from the fifteenth-century *Tale of Beryn,* first included by John Urry in *The Canterbury Tales* in 1721. Percy MacKaye's play *The Canterbury Pilgrims* develops it fully as comedy, discussed in Chapter 5.

26. Ann Douglas, *The Feminization of American Culture* (New York: Avon Books, 1977). Gender issues in children's fiction are not always predictable, as two recent studies demonstrate. Claudia Nelson, *Boys Will Be Girls: The Feminine Ethic and British Children's Fiction, 1857–1917* (New Brunswick and London: Rutgers University Press, 1991) considers children's books that advocate a feminine ethic and ideal for both boys and girls, while Beverly Lyon Clark, *Regendering the School Story: Sassy Sissies and Tattling Tomboys* (New York and London: Garland Publishing, 1996) discusses the implications of "crossgendering—women writing about boys and men writing about girls—that gave play to the contradictions of the genre," vii.

27. Miller suggests that images of the pilgrims and of figures in the illustration for the *Nun's Priest's Tale,* which are the nonaristocratic elements, show that Anderson "used her art to make some sort of a statement about social class and hierarchy to her youthful audience," 301. This seems counter to the emphasis and advocacy of chivalry in children's literature, especially prior to World War I. Underdown published *War Songs* in 1914.

28. Emily Underdown, *The Gateway to Chaucer: Stories Retold* (London, Edinburgh, Dublin, New York: Thomas Nelson and Sons, 1912). Page numbers for quotations from this source are given in parentheses or brackets.

29. The Golden River Series included small selections from The Gateway Series, and as its title (taken from John Ruskin's *The King of the Golden River and Other Stories*) suggests, emphasizes fairy tales and stories by nineteenth-century authors, both English and American: Lewis Carroll, Charles Dickens, Charles Kingsley, Walter

Scott, Thackeray, Nathaniel Hawthorne, Henry Wadsworth Longfellow, Joel Chandler Harris. However, the chivalric Middle Ages is well represented with *Knights of the Grail, The Linden Leaf, The Arabian Knights,* and *Don Quixote.*

30. M. Dorothy Belgrave and Hilda Hart, *Children's Stories from the Poets,* Raphael House Library of Gift Books (London, Paris, New York: Raphael Tuck & Sons, 1915). Page numbers for quotations from this source are given in parentheses or brackets.

31. Christine Chandler, *My Book of Stories from the Poets Told in Prose* (London, New York, Toronto and Melbourne, Cassell & Co., 1919).

32. R. Brimley Johnson, *Tales from Chaucer* (London & Glasgow: Gowans & Gray, 1909). Page numbers for quotations from this source are given in parentheses.

CHAPTER 5.
AMERICAN RETELLINGS

1. Percy MacKaye and John S.P. Tatlock, *The Modern Reader's Chaucer. The Complete Poetical Works of Geoffrey Chaucer: Now First Put into Modern English* (New York: Macmillan, 1912), vii. Page numbers for additional quotations from this source are given in parentheses or brackets. Not all editions include the color illustrations of Warwick Goble.

2. Olena S. Bunn rated it "most interesting and professional" in "A Bibliography of Chaucer in English and American Belles-Lettres since 1900," in Anne Sutherland, ed. , *Bulletin of Bibliography and Dramatic Index,* 19 (September 1946–December 1949), 205–06.

3. Percy MacKaye, *The Canterbury Pilgrims: A Comedy* (New York and London: Macmillan Company, 1903); the musical score, *The Canterbury Pilgrims* (Cincinnati, New York, London: John Church Company, 1906); *The Canterbury Pilgrims: An Opera,* text by Percy MacKaye and music by Reginald de Koven (New York: Macmillan Company, 1916).

4. MacKaye's *St. Louis: A Civic Pageant* had a cast of 7,500 and attracted an audience of at least 500,000 for its five performances in 1914.

5. Percy MacKaye, *The Canterbury Tales of Geoffrey Chaucer: A Modern Rendering into Prose of the Prologue and Nine Tales* (New York: Fox, Duffield, 1904). Facsimile with introduction by Kenneth H. Brown (New York: Avenel Books, 1987), xxi. Subsequent quotations and descriptions are to the facsimile edition, with page numbers given in parentheses.

6. Zaidee Brown, *Standard Catalog for High School Libraries: A Selected Lit of 2600 Books* (repr. New York: H.W. Wilson Co., 1929), 1:128.

7. This illustration, in black-and-white, marks the end of the *Knight's Tale* in the reprint.

8. Kenneth H. Brown's Foreword to the facsimile, dated 1987, is a revealing gloss on changing values, which are startling in late-twentieth-century retellings. Brown finds in the fourteenth century "the mysteries and visions of medieval people steeped in superstition and an early Christianity that predates Shakespeare by three hundred years" (xi). While arguing for universal human "feelings and states of being" expressed in *The Canterbury Tales,* he finds "a major difference in our modern life ... missing today: the miracles. There are no more miracles. At first, this is the saddest of all realizations, and then a corresponding fact softens the blow. As there are no miracles, neither are there inquisitions, burning at the stake, trials of witches, or devils in the moonlight. Religious persecution, where it exists—and it still does—is considered evil by rational people everywhere. It would be wonderful to witness a miracle, but if such a phenomenon is not possible without the corresponding horror, we are, no doubt, better off without it" (xii). Like Edwardians, critics today present a simplified and, in their own way, overly optimistic interpretation that misses the complexity of Chaucer's vision.

9. The author's copy, *The Canterbury Pilgrims: A Comedy* (New York and London: Macmillan Co., 1909), has the production notes and cast lists for a school performance using ten boys and eleven girls. The cover resembles those of Edwardian Reward books; Chaucer, the Ellesmere equestrian pilgrim, points to the title stamped in gold in a frame of decorated manuscript that also

encloses the author's name at the bottom. Page numbers for subsequent quotations or descriptions from this source are given in parentheses.

10. Archives of Doe Library, University of California, Berkeley.

11. Julian Wasserman, "Chaucer for the Masses: Geoffrey Goes to Mardi Gras," New Chaucer Society Conference in London, July 17, 2000.

12. Calvin Dill Wilson, *Canterbury Tales: Prologue and Selections* (Chicago: A.C. McClurg & Co., 1906). Page numbers for additional quoted phrases or descriptions from this source are given in parentheses.

13. Robert Newton Linscott, *A Guide to Good Reading: With Practical Directions for the Use of* The Children's Hour *in the Home* (Boston, New York: Houghton Mifflin Co., 1912), ix–x.

14. The others are Bunyan's *Pilgrim's Progress*, Defoe's *Robinson Crusoe*, Swift's *Gulliver's Travels*, *Don Quixote*, *Arabian Nights Entertainments*, some *Adventures of Baron Munchausen*.

15. Eva March Tappan, *The Chaucer Story Book* (Boston and New York: Houghton Mifflin Co., 1908), v. Page numbers for additional quoted phrases from this source are given in parentheses or brackets.

16. George Philip Krapp, *Tales of True Knights* (New York: Century Co., 1921). Page numbers for additional quoted phrases from this source are given in parentheses.

17. Ascott R. Hope is one of the names used by A.R. Hope-Moncrieff. *Stories of Old Renown* was widely available in an inexpensive series (London: Gresham Publishing Co., 1915).

CHAPTER 6. CHAUCER IN SCHOOLBOOKS

1. Clara L. Thomson, *Tales from Chaucer*, illustrated by Marion Thomson (London: Horace Marshall & Son, 1903). Page numbers for quoted phrases from this source are given in parentheses.

2. F.J. Harvey Darton, *Children's Books in England: Five Centuries of Social Life*, 1932, 3rd ed., rev. by Brian Alderson (Cambridge, U.K.: Cambridge University Press, 1982), 92.

3. Margaret C. MacCaulay, *Stories from Chaucer Re-told from* The Canterbury Tales (Cambridge: Cambridge University Press, 1911). Page numbers for quoted phrases are given in parentheses.

4. Katherine Lee Bates, ed., *The Story of Chaucer's Canterbury Pilgrims Retold for Children*, illustrated by Angus MacDonall (Chicago, New York, London: Rand McNally & Co., 1909). Cited is the school edition, 9–10. Page numbers for additional quotations from the school edition are given in parentheses.

5. Agnes Repplier (1858–1950), American essayist, begins her wide-ranging critical study *In Pursuit of Laughter* (Boston and New York: Houghton Mifflin, 1936) with an eloquent statement that contrasts the medieval and modern ethos: "No man pursues what he has at hand. No man recognizes the need of pursuit until that which he desires has escaped him. Those who listen to the Middle Ages instead of writing about them at monstrous length and with undue horror and commiseration, can hear the echo of laughter ringing from every side, from every hole and corner where human life existed. Through the welter of wars and famine and pestilence, through every conceivable disaster, through an atmosphere darkened with ignorance and cruelty and needless pain there emerges, clear and unmistakable, that will to live which man shares with the beast, and which means that consciously, he finds life worth the living. Henry James, in whom the disease of thinking had reached an acute stage, expressed his wistful envy of 'the stoutness of the human composition in medieval days, and the tranquillity of nerve of people to whom the groaning captive and the blackness of the living tomb were familiar ideas, which did not at all interfere with their happiness or their sanity,'" 3.

6. See Stephanie Trigg, *Congenial Souls: Reading Chaucer from Medieval to Postmodern*, Medieval Cultures, vol. 30 (Minneapolis and London: University of Minnesota Press, 2002). As a professor of English literature in Wellesley College, Bates is an apparent exception to the dominance of male academics that Trigg presents, albeit she is a poet and publishing children's literature, then a noncanonical area.

7. Ada Hales, *Stories from Chaucer,* Stories from the Great Writers Series (London: Methuen & Co., 1911). Page numbers for quotations from this source are given in parentheses or brackets.

8. E.M. Wilmot-Buxton, *Stories from Old French Romance* (1910); Joyce Pollard, *Stories from Old English Romance* (1912); and Susan Cunningham, *Stories from Old Italian Romance* (1910). In the United States the publisher was Frederick A. Stokes Company in New York.

9. For useful general discussions of late Victorian and Edwardian childhood and schools, see Joanna Smith, *Edwardian Children* (London: Hutchinson, 1983); Jane Pettigrew, *An Edwardian Childhood* (London: Little, Brown & Co. [UK], 1991); Pamela Horn, *The Victorian and Edwardian Schoolchild* (Gloucester, UK: Alan Sutton, 1989).

10. M. Sturt and E.C. Oakden, *The Canterbury Pilgrims: Being Chaucer's Canterbury Tales Retold for Children,* The King's Treasuries of Literature, ed. Sir A.T. Quiller Couch, #94 (London and Toronto: J.M. Dent & Sons and New York: E.P. Dutton & Co., 1923, repr. 1925, 1927). Page numbers for quotations from this source are given in parentheses or brackets.

11. Arthur Bullard, *The "Beeching" Chaucer Reader: An Introduction to Chaucer* (Norwich: W.J. Pack & Co., 1925?). Page numbers for quotations from this source are given in parentheses.

12. The edition read, in the Harry Ransome Library, University of Texas, Austin, is marked "Third Thousand."

13. Rossiter Johnson, ed., *Works of the British Poets from Chaucer to Morris, with Biographical Sketches,* 3 vols. (New York: D. Appleton & Co., 1876), I: 1.

14. This refers to a later edition (Chicago: Scott, Foresman, & Co., 1908). Page numbers for additional quotations from this source are given in parentheses.

15. Zaidee Brown, ed. *Standard Catalog for High School Libraries: A Selected List of 2600 Books* (repr., New York: H.W. Wilson Co., 1929), 1:128.

16. On a list of about two hundred titles that include poetry, drama, essays, novels, and a few histories, writers with the highest numbers are seven for Scott; six for Macaulay and Hawthorne; five for Long-

fellow and Irving; four for Tennyson and Stevenson; and three for Fenimore Cooper, Dickens, and Pope. Two versions of both the *Iliad* and *Odyssey,* the prose translations for children by A.J. Church and Pope's verse translations, most specifically indicate alternate levels for assignment of a text.

17. Alice M. Atkinson, *The European Beginnings of American History: An Introduction to the History of the United States, Designed for Grammar Schools* (Boston, New York, Chicago, London: Ginn & Co., 1912). Page numbers for quotations from this source are given in parentheses or brackets.

18. Alec Ellis, *A History of Children's Reading and Literature* (Oxford: Pergamon Press, 1968) is a detailed analysis written by a librarian who worked with young people.

19. Mary E. Burt, *Literary Landmarks: A Guide to Good Reading for Young People, and Teachers' Assistant with a Carefully Selected List of Seven Hundred Books,* rev. ed. (Boston and New York: Houghton, Mifflin & Co., 1897), 65. Page numbers for additional quotations from this source are given in parentheses or brackets.

20. Montrose J. Moses, *Children's Books and Reading* (New York: Mitchell Kennerley, 1907). Page numbers for additional quotations from this source are given in parentheses or brackets.

21. Frances Jenkins Olcott, *The Children's Reading* (Boston and New York: Houghton Mifflin Co., The Riverside Press, Cambridge, 1912), vii–viii. Page numbers for additional quotations from this source are given in parentheses or brackets.

22. This was William Forbush's organization, one inspiration to Robert Baden-Powell, who founded the Boy Scouts.

CHAPTER 7. LITERARY HISTORY FOR CHILDREN

1. J.B. Priestly, *The Edwardians* (New York and Evanston: Harper & Row Publishers, 1970) and Rebecca West, *1900,* a Studio Book (New York: Viking Press, 1982) are reflections of two who lived Edwardian childhoods and attempt a balanced account of the period's strengths and inadequacies.

2. C.L. Thomson, *A First Book in*

English Literature 7 vols. (London: Horace Marshall & Son, 1903). Page numbers for quotations are given in parentheses or brackets.

3. C.L. Thomson, *A First History of England* 7 vols. (London: Horace Marshall & Son, 1904–09); there was a revision in 1930. C.L. Thomson, *Our Inheritance* (Cambridge: Cambridge University Press, 1910) was paper-covered and cost 6d. Page numbers for quotations are given in parentheses.

4. H.E. Marshall, *English Literature for Boys and Girls*, illustrated by John R. Skelton (London and Edinburgh: E.C. & T.C. Jack, 1909), vii, x. The distinction between task and pleasure is not always sharp. The author's personal copy was a Prize "For Honours in English Language, Algebra, French, Nature Study" awarded December 1914. Page numbers for additional quotations from this source are given in parentheses.

5. "Brede and milke for children" is the title in three fifteenth-century manuscripts—Bodley 619, Bodley 68, E. Museo 54—of *A Treatise on the Astrolabe, The Riverside Chaucer*, ed. Larry D. Benson, 3rd ed. (Boston: Houghton Mifflin Co., 1987), 1195. Two points are notable: the designation indicates a specific recognition of children's literature in the fifteenth century; Marshall's Preface is signed "Oxford, 1909," so that she may well have been aware of the manuscripts in the Bodleian Library.

6. A helpful gloss is Henry Cecil Wyld, *The Place of the Mother Tongue in National Education* (London: John Murray, 1906), which deplores the fact that the study of English language is not introduced until the last two years of school life, ages 15–17 and 16–18 years. Wyld argues for a living language, one that is spoken and changes, and he opposes "the present system of teaching the classics [that] may enable a few boys and girls in each class to write fairly good Latin prose, but it produces a terribly unintelligent and reactionary view of language," 15. Thus he proposes a method for the study of the history of the language that moves toward comparative philology. Chaucer is "the most suitable example to take of earlier English ... undoubtedly the best author for our purposes, because he is a great poet,

whose writings the young can be taught to love for their beauty, and because he forms a convenient halfway house between Present-day and Old English," 20.

7. Katherine Dunlap Cather, *Educating by Story-Telling: Showing the Value of Story-Telling as an Educational Tool for the Use of All Workers with Children* (London: George G. Harrap & Co., 1919). Based on the work of the Demonstration Play School of the University of California, Berkeley, this first volume in a new series of a British publisher marks close relations between England and the United States. The pedagogical emphasis is upon pleasure in learning, and many recommended books are canonical texts adapted for children in Harrap's Told Through the Ages Series. Part One is "Story-telling and the Arts of Expression—Establishing Standards."

8. Henry Gilbert, *Stories of Great Writers* (London, Edinburgh, New York: T.C. & E.C. Jack, 1914). Page numbers for quotations from this source are given in parentheses or brackets.

9. E.M. Tappan, *A Brief History of English Literature* (London: George G. Harrap & Co., 1914). The use of her initials on the title page possibly reflects uneasiness about gender. Page numbers for quotations from this source are given in parentheses.

10. The full title is *Outlines of English and American Literature: An Introduction to the Chief Writers of England and America, to the Books They Wrote, and to the Times in which They Lived* (Boston: Ginn & Co., 1917). Page numbers for quotations from this source are given in parentheses.

11. Amy Cruse, *English Literature Through the Ages: Beowulf to Stevenson* (London, Calcutta, Sydney: George G. Harrap & Co., 1914). The author's personal copy shows that the book was reprinted in 1919, 1922, and 1925. Page numbers for quotations are from the author's personal copy and are given in parentheses.

12. Amy Cruse, *The Golden Road in English Literature: From Beowulf to Bernard Shaw* (London: George G. Harrap & Co., 1931), 5. Page numbers for additional quotations from this source are given in parentheses.

13. Henry Newbolt, *My World as in My Time: Memoirs of Sir Henry Newbolt 1862–*

1932 (London: Faber & Faber, 1932), 75. T.S. Eliot worked at Faber and Faber and published two of Newbolt's poems in Faber's Ariel Series. Newbolt admired Eliot's early poems but found *The Waste Land* "excessively depressing." See Susan Chitty, *Playing the Game: A Biography of Sir Henry Newbolt* (London: Quartet Books, 1997), 264–65. Another positive encounter between Victorian/Edwardian and Modern was with John Betjeman, later Poet Laureate, who was delighted to be accepted by John Murray, publisher of Newbolt's poems which he admired. Betjeman shared Newbolt's efforts to preserve England from ugly development. Chitty, 273.

14. Henry Newbolt, *A New Study of English Poetry* (London: Constable & Co., 1917). Page numbers for quotations from this source are given in parentheses.

15. Gilbert K. Chesterton, *Orthodoxy* (repr. London and New York: John Lane, 1919), 83.

EPILOGUE

1. Francine Prose, "Other Worlds," *The New York Times*, Sunday, 11 December 1988, 20–21.

2. Judith Bronfman, *Chaucer's Clerk's Tale: The Griselda Story Received, Rewritten, Illustrated*, Garland Studies in Medieval Literature, vol. 11, Garland Reference Library of the Humanities, vol. 1831 (New York and London: Garland Publishing, Inc., 1994), 80, commenting on "The Scholar is persuaded to tell us The Test of a Good Wife," in Geraldine McCaughrean, *The Canterbury Tales* (Chicago: Rand McNally & Co., 1985). Page numbers for additional quotations from the Bronfman source are given in parentheses.

3. Three additional retellings should be mentioned as examples of transition. Eleanor Farjeon, *Tales from Chaucer: Done into Prose* (Great Britain: The Medici Society and New York: Jonathan Cape & Harrison Smith, 1930) with color illustrations by W. Russell Flint in a lingering Art Nouveau style, still closely resembles Edwardian collections. Farjeon includes all of the prologues and tales, albeit abstracts of *Melibeus* and the *Parson's Tale*. The knight in

the *Wife of Bath's Tale* "insulted a maiden he found walking alone," and the *fabliaux* are quite respectable: in the *Miller's Tale* Nicholas and Alison "made merry" and the misdirected kiss is to Nicholas's head, put out the window; Alain and John simply try to sneak away in the *Reeve's Tale*; "naughty" May in the *Merchant's Tale* accepts a green pear from Damian in the tree; the Cook again tells *Gamelyn*. In short, this very comprehensive collection (that follows Richard Morris's order in the Aldine edition and relies upon Alfred Pollard's notes in the Globe edition) of prose translations with twelve beautiful color plates is a late example of Edwardian extravagance, also available in cheaper editions. Thirty years later, A. Kent Hieatt and Constance Hieatt, both professors of English, selected and adapted *The Canterbury Tales of Geoffrey Chaucer* as a De Luxe Golden Book, with illustrations by Gustaf Tenggren (New York, 1962). The pictures are boldly modern and numerous, one on almost every page. But, no doubt reflecting the date that is pre-revolutions of the 1960s, the selection of tales is still largely conventional (no *fabliaux*): the General Prologue and eleven tales are each present with a prologue (*Knight, Wife of Bath, Friar, Clerk, Franklin*, Chaucer's *Sir Thopas* (in doggerel verse), *Nun's Priest, Pardoner, Canon's Yeoman, Manciple*, and *Man of Law*). There is much cutting and rearranging, especially in prologues, and the order is a bit unusual. Mark Van Doren's introduction praises the "rapid, witty and sensible prose" translation and comments most fully on the *Knight's Tale*. Ian Serraillier's *The Road to Canterbury* with wood engravings by John Lawrence (Harmondsworth, Middlesex, England: Penguin Books, 1979; New Windmill Series ed. Oxford et al: Heinemann Educational Books, 1981) includes a biographical survey with exact details of Chaucer's life and times. Where earlier retellers stress a genial man, religious, and steadfast, Serraillier concludes: "His last poems tell of the sadness of growing old, of the loss of poetic powers, of illness and disillusionment, though he seems to have met these blows with courage and acceptance" (11). Chaucer's lines about the wild daisy give a hint of the nature poet, and an introductory note for *The Canter-*

bury Tales identifies the *Prologue* as "a reflection of the nation as it was in his day" (13). The tales omit "the rhetoric and digressions that a medieval audience expected but most people find tedious today" (15). The *Prologue* is in verse, using Chaucer's meter; it is divided into pilgrim portraits to introduce the nine tales, several before each. The tales have modern titles and names of some pilgrims are also updated: "Prisoners of War" (*Knight's*), "The Cock and the Fox" (*Nun's Priest's*), "Patient Griselda" (*Scholar's*), "A Hundred-Franc Loan" (*Sea Captain's*), "The Wild Waves" (*Judge's*), "The Black rocks of Brittany" (*Franklin's*), "The Queen's Riddle" (*Wife of Bath's*), "The White Crow" (*Steward's*), "In Search of Death" (*Pardoner's*). The knight in the *Wife's Tale* "seduced" the young lady, Walter treats Griselda "cruelly" and is "astonished" and "amazed" by her patience; and spending money on clothes is the emphasis in the *Shipman's Tale*, not sex as in the *fabliaux*. Such detail sustains decorum, and the wood engravings also suggest older children's literature, specifically chapbook illustration. The reordering of tales partially mirrors Serrailler's emphasis in the biographical sketch, and the three-sentence conclusion "The Poet Geoffrey Chaucer Says Good-bye" is from the *Retraction*.

4. A.N. Wilson, "The Middle Ages Pale by Comparison," *The Sunday Telegraph*, 17 January 2002, p. 27, responds to the casual way in which phrases like "medieval savagery," "medieval brutality," and "barbarism" are commonly used, especially by politicians, as terms of abuse to make a contrast with contemporary righteousness. He offers details to show that recent events are "totally modern" not "almost medieval," and like Chesterton, urges older traditions, by making favorable comparisons for the Middle Ages, such as the books read by Chaucer's Clerk, with the intellectual limitations of modern curriculum.

Bibliography

Victorian and Edwardian Books of Chaucer for Children

Bates, Katherine Lee, ed. (1) *The Story of Chaucer's Canterbury Pilgrims: Retold for Children.* Illustrated by Angus MacDonall. Chicago, New York, London: Rand McNally & Co., 1909.
_____. (2) deluxe ed. Color illustrations by Milo Winter.

Bullard, Arthur. *The "Beeching" Chaucer Reader: An Introduction to Chaucer.* Norwich: W.J. Pack & Co., [1921].

Calder, William. *Chaucer's Canterbury Pilgrimage.* Illustrated. Edinburgh and London: William Blackwood & Son, 1892.

Clarke, Charles Cowden. (1) *Tales from Chaucer in Prose: Designed Chiefly for the Use of Young Persons.* Illustrated with wood engravings by W.H. Mott and S. Williams. London: Effingham Wilson, 1833.
_____. repr. Illustrated by Arthur Szyk. The Heritage Illustrated Bookshelf. New York: Heritage Press, 1947.
_____. (2) *The Riches of Chaucer.* Illustrated with wood engravings by W.H. Mott and S. Williams. London: Effinghman Wilson, Royal Exchange, 1835.

Darton, F.J. Harvey. (1) *Tales of the Canterbury Pilgrims Retold from Chaucer and Others.* Introduction by F.J. Furnivall. Illustrated by Hugh Thomson. London: Wells Gardner, Darton & Co., 1904.
_____. (2) *The Story of the Canterbury Pilgrims Retold from Chaucer and Others.* Illustrations by M.L. Kirk. Philadelphia & New York: J.B. Lippincott Co., 1914.
_____. (3) *Pilgrims Tales from Chaucer.* Children's Bookshelf Series. Illustrated by Hugh Thomson. London: Wells Gardner, Darton & Co., 1908

Hales, Ada. *Stories from Chaucer.* Stories from the Great Writers Series. London: Methuen & Co., 1911.

Haweis, Mrs. (1) *Chaucer for Children: A Golden Key.* Illustrated with colored pictures and numerous woodcuts. 1876. new ed. London: Chatto & Windus, 1900.

_____. (2) *Chaucer for Schools.* new ed. 1899. London: Chatto and Windus, 1881.

Johnson, R. Brimley. *Tales from Chaucer.* London & Glasgow: Gowans and Gray, 1909.

Kelman, Janet Harvey. *Stories from Chaucer.* Told to the Children Series. Illustrated by W. Heath Robinson. London: T.C. and E.C. Jack and New York: E.P. Dutton, 1906.

MacCaulay, Magaret C. *Stories from Chaucer Re-told from the Canterbury Tales.* Cambridge: Cambridge University Press, 1911.

MacKaye, Percy. (1) *The Canterbury Tales of Geoffrey Chaucer: A Modern Rendering into Prose of the Prologue and Nine Tales.* 1904. Illustrated by Walter Appleton Clark. Facsimile New York: Avenel Books, 1987.

_____, and John S.P. Tatlock. (2) *The Modern Reader's Chaucer. The Complete Poetical Works of Geoffrey Chaucer: Now First Put into Modern English.* New York: Macmillan, 1912; repr. 1940.

McSpadden, J. Walker. (1) *The Canterbury Pilgrims: Retold from Chaucer.* Illustrated by M.L. Kirk. London: George G. Harrap, 1917.

_____. (2) *Stories from Chaucer: Retold from the Canterbury Tales.* Illustrated by Victor Prout and others. Told through the Ages Series. London: George G. Harrap, 1907.

_____. (3) *Tales from Chaucer.* All-Time Tales Series. Illustrated by Victor Prout. London: George G. Harrap, 1909.

Seymour, Mary. *Chaucer's Stories Simply Told.* Classic Stories Simply Told Series. Illustrations by E.M. Scannell. 1884. London: T. Nelson & Sons, 1902.

Stead, W.T., ed. *Stories from Chaucer, Being the Canterbury Tales in Simple Language for Children.* Books for the Bairns, no. 83. Illustrated by Edith Ewen. London: Books for the Bairns Office, 1902.

Storr, Francis, and Howes Turner. (1) *Canterbury Chimes, or Chaucer Tales Retold for Children.* London: C. Kegan Paul & Co., 1878.

_____. (2) *Canterbury Chimes, or Chaucer Tales Retold for Children.* new ed. London: Kegan Paul, Trench, Trübner & Co. and New York: E.P. Dutton, 1914.

Sturt, M., and E.C. Oakden. *The Canterbury Pilgrims Being Chaucer's Canterbury Tales Retold for Children.* The Kings Treasuries of Literature, ed. A.T. Quiller Couch, #94. London and Toronto: J.M. Dent & Sons and New York: E.P. Dutton and Co., 1923.

Tappan, Eva March. *The Chaucer Story Book.* Illustrated with Ellesmere pilgrims. Boston and New York: Houghton Mifflin Company, 1907.

Thomson, Clara L. *Tales from Chaucer.* Illustrated by Marion Thomson. London: Horace Marshall and Son, 1903.

Underdown, Emily. (1) *The Gateway to Chaucer: Stories Retold.* Illustrated by Anne Anderson. London, Edinburgh, Dublin, New York: Thomas Nelson and Sons, 1912.

_____. (2) *Stories from Chaucer: Retold.* Golden River Series. Illustrated by Anne Anderson. London, Edinburgh, Dublin, New York: Thomas Nelson and Sons, 1913.

Wilson, Calvin Dill. *Canterbury Tales: Prologue and Selections.* Decorated by Ralph Fletcher Seymour. Old Tales Retold for Young Readers Series. Chicago: McClurg & Co., 1906.

In Mixed Collections

Atkinson, Alice M. *The European Beginnings of American History.* Boston, New York, Chicago, London: Ginn & Co., 1912.

Bailey, Carolyn Sherwin. *Stories of Great Adventures*. For the Children's Hour Series. Illustrated by Clara M. Burd. Springfield, MA: Milton Bradley Co., 1919.

Belgrave, M. Dorothy and Hilda Hart. *Children's Stories from the Poets*. Raphael House Library of Gift Books for Boys and Girls, ed. Capt. Edric Vredenburg. London: Raphael Tuck & Sons, 1915.

Chaundler, Christine. *My Book of Stories from the Poets: Told in Prose*. Illustrations by A.C. Michael. London, New York, Toronto, Melbourne: Cassell & Co., 1919.

Hope, Ascott R. (A.R. Hope-Moncrieff). *Stories of Old Renown*. Illustrated by Gordon Browne. London: Gresham Publishing Co., 1883.

In Golden Realms: An English Reading Book for Junior Forms. Illustrated by famous paintings. Arnold's School Series. London: Edward Arnold, c.1902.

Krapp, George Philip. *Tales of True Knights*. Illustrated by Henry C. Pitz. New York: Century Co., 1920/21.

Richardson, Abby Sage. *Stories from Old English Poetry*. Boston: Houghton, Mifflin & Co., The Riverside Press, Cambridge, 1891.

Smith, David Murray. *Tales of Chivalry and Romance*. London: Virtue & Co., 1869.

Index